Whole Therapist,

Integrating the work of Reich, Masterson, and Jung, *Whole Therapist, Whole Patient* is a step-by-step guidebook for professionals to learn about the psychology of their patients and conduct treatment in a dynamic way. This text combines Reich's character analyses, Masterson's work on personality disorders, and Jung's dream analyses to create a clear typology of character types that therapists can use to understand themselves and their patients. Also included are case management techniques and guidance for working with difficult patients. In addition, readers can turn to the book's online resources to access a downloadable patient package, case presentation guide, and psychological history form.

Patricia R. Frisch, PhD, MFT, is a licensed psychologist, as well as founder and executive director of the Orgonomic Institute of Northern California (OINC), where she mentors, supervises, and trains professionals in character analysis, somatic interventions, and diagnostic typologies. She authored a chapter in *Encyclopedia of Theory in Counseling and Psychotherapy* (SAGE Publications, 2015). Dr. Frisch also maintains an active private practice in Mill Valley, California.

"In bringing together three of the most significant theorists of modern psychology—Wilhelm Reich, James Masterson, and Carl Jung—Patricia Frisch has developed distinct ways of championing the revitalization of Reichian theory and practice toward a masterful blend in which the body remains at the center of the work. *Whole Therapist, Whole Patient* is a must read, both for senior practitioners who will be guided to develop their own work to the next level of sophistication as well as for graduate students who will learn grounded theory and practice toward the integration of soma and psyche."

—**Melissa Schwartz, PhD**, *vice president of academic affairs, Meridian University*

Whole Therapist, Whole Patient

Integrating Reich, Masterson, and Jung in Modern Psychotherapy

Patricia R. Frisch

Routledge
Taylor & Francis Group

NEW YORK AND LONDON

First published 2018
by Routledge
711 Third Avenue, New York, NY 10017

and by Routledge
2 Park Square, Milton Park, Abingdon, Oxon, OX14 4RN

Routledge is an imprint of the Taylor & Francis Group, an informa business

Library of Congress Cataloging-in-Publication Data
Names: Frisch, Patricia R., author.
Title: Whole therapist, whole patient: integrating Reich, Masterson,
    and Jung in modern psychotherapy/Patricia R. Frisch.
Description: New York: Routledge, 2018. | Includes bibliographical
    references and index.
Identifiers: LCCN 2017039092| ISBN 9781138562356 (hbk.: alk.
    paper) | ISBN 9781138562363 (pbk.: alk. paper) |
    ISBN 9780203702888 (ebk.)
Subjects: | MESH: Reich, Wilhelm, 1897–1957. | Masterson,
    James F. | Jung, C. G. (Carl Gustav), 1875–1961. | Psychotherapeutic
    Processes | Psychological Theory | Professional-Patient Relations |
    Personality Disorders—therapy
Classification: LCC RC480 | NLM WM 420 |
    DDC 616.89/14—dc23
LC record available at https://lccn.loc.gov/2017039092

ISBN: 978-1-138-56235-6 (hbk)
ISBN: 978-1-138-56236-3 (pbk)
ISBN: 978-0-203-70288-8 (ebk)

Typeset in Goudy
by Apex CoVantage, LLC

Visit the eResources: www.routledge.com/9781138562363

Contents

The following chapters and appendices can be found at the Online Resource Guide for this book

Acknowledgments

First and foremost, I want to thank all my patients who have invited me into their lives and hearts and who have inspired and sustained my devotion and passion for clinical work. Their integrity, discipline, and commitment to their growth and transformation heightened my appreciation of the tenacity of the human spirit. I have witnessed the profound will to live and surmount suffering and learned to admire and respect the endurance and resilience of the human psyche. My patients have tolerated my foibles and given me countless opportunities to learn and grow as a clinician and writer. Over the course of 40 years of practice, I have fine-tuned my sensitivity and deepened my compassion as my own inner qualities developed in their presence.

I thank my students who have worked so hard to learn my method and have shared their struggles as they progressed into excellent clinicians. By having the opportunity to teach, I gained clarity and wisdom as I created my method. Our training groups have been a model for therapists willing to become "whole therapists" through facing their strengths and weaknesses, and doing their inner work with honesty and integrity. Their discipline, commitment, and sacrifice allowed them to become incredibly skilled therapists.

I am grateful for my editor, Barbara Moulton, whose guidance and precision editing facilitated the evolution of this book. She guided me to create a lively book that did not bog down in academic detail. Her encouragement and knowledge of the process was essential for my first foray into writing and publishing.

I am thankful and grateful for all my dear friends, writers and nonwriters alike, who backed me and listened to my process as I doggedly kept at it. Your support and encouragement have meant so much to me.

My executive assistant, Lisa Nichols, has been essential to the development of the Orgonomic Institute. For over 10 years, she has managed my classes, the website, and any and all projects that could have consumed me. She has always jumped in to rescue me from details and projects in a way that facilitated the progress of my work.

Doreen Patrick, my marketing consultant, has been a steadying hand and expert in managing the book rollout and is a fountain of new ideas.

Heather Rhine, my web master and graphic designer, has been an incredible creative force and helped me actualize my creative flow through imagery, color, and her excellence in design. She steps into my fray and provides a solution.

My tech, Allen Klein, has been by my side and kept me up and running so computer glitches did not occur and all systems were go. This allowed me to work uninterrupted and enhanced my productivity.

My two kids have always been lovingly supportive, and their existence in my life challenges me to be at my best. They provide frequent alerts when I falter. I am inspired by their unique choices as their lives unfold with boundless creativity. They teach me how to be a decent mom and a better person.

Many thanks to my life partner, Allan, who has been with me every step of the way. He has helped by providing input at critical moments, suggestions along the way that assisted and supported my discipline and writing obsession that dominated weekends and retreats. His wonderful cooking at Sea Ranch made my time there cozy, sumptuous, and conducive to hours of writing without distractions.

You are all blessings.

Foreword

When Patricia Frisch told me of the work she was doing as director of the Orgonomic Institute, she informed me that her institute's teachings relied not only on the theories of Wilhelm Reich but also on those of James Masterson, founder of the International Masterson Institute, of which I am now director. I was pleased to let Dr. Frisch know that those of us who adhere to the Masterson Approach have continued to explore and expand our knowledge with regard to the personality disorders (once known as character disorders), key elements of Reich's work, particularly those that relate to character types, character resistances, and defense analysis, which have always been taught in our institute as part of the historical foundations upon which the Masterson Approach rests.

As I learned more about Dr. Frisch's organization and her work, I was increasingly pleased to have our connection. I am honored to write a foreword to what I, to my great pleasure, discovered to be a remarkable and aptly titled book. As I delved into *Whole Therapist, Whole Patient*, I knew I had encountered an eminently sane, organized, and thoughtful primer on the proper approach to the practice of psychotherapy. At the same time I also realized that a book of this breadth and depth could only have been written by a seasoned therapist who was herself an intelligent, compassionate, and fully integrated human being.

And this impression only strengthened as I reviewed Dr. Frisch's curriculum vitae. For as I read it through, it became increasingly clear that it was the range of her own work in the field, as well as the continuous expansion of her arenas of self-actualization, that stood as the linchpins underlying Dr. Frisch's knowledge of and commitment to the sound, clearly stated therapeutic principles permeating every page of her work. Therefore, before journeying into the contents of her book, I'd like first to share with you a glimpse of what I learned about Dr. Frisch's work and experience. There is, of course, the prominent fact that she is currently Director of the Orgonomic Institute of Northern California, which she herself founded and where she teaches and supervises in conjunction with having her own practice of individual, group, marital, and family therapy. For most of us, this level of achievement would be enough to establish our bona fides. But equally notable in Dr. Frisch's case is the fact that she has engaged in extensive therapeutic work with disenfranchised populations, including prison inmates, AIDS patients and their families, and troubled adolescents. Further, she has participated in many community-based projects, conducting workshops designed to relieve stress and facilitate good mental health. All this and the study of dance and philosophy, too! In short, all of Dr. Frisch's far-reaching professional activities, as well as the emphasis she has placed on the expansion of her own mind, body, and spirit, provides testimony to the fact that she practices what she preaches—working constantly to attain the virtues characteristics of the Whole Therapist she describes in her book. In life, then, as in her work, Dr. Frisch shows herself to be fully cognizant of the fact that in order to help patients attain their highest potential, therapists must strive to reach theirs. A truism, I know, but one that is far easier to advocate than to follow.

In my own training with Dr. Masterson, he as well focused on the need for therapists to know and expand themselves, as he reiterated innumerable times that there exist but two major impediments to doing good clinical work, these being lack of knowledge and counter-transference. And the most pernicious of these is counter-transference.

Whole Therapist, Whole Patient deals with both these problems, demonstrating the difficulties occasioned by each, as well as the ways in which they reinforce each other. For, without a clear set of principles guiding the process of therapy, counter-transferential issues are much more likely to govern the process. Conversely, where counter-transferential pulls are powerful, they often act as barriers to effective learning. But Dr. Frisch does more than just send out a warning, alerting clinicians to these twin dangers. Rather, she makes sure to provide her readers with clear, succinct, and specific guidelines for recognizing and addressing them, taking time to develop what she calls "reference points"—a series of progressive, interlocking guideposts, each of which is designed to define and explicate the steps needed to be taken in order to ensure a good therapeutic outcome.

She begins by describing in detail the procedures the therapist must employ to determine the nature of the patient's dynamics, including core issues, character type, and character defenses. An essential step in this process, familiar to most of us, is the taking of a careful history. But Dr. Frisch goes deeper, reminding us that oftentimes the most significant knowledge we can obtain about our patient comes not only from what he or she tells us, but even more saliently, from the manner in which this information is related. So, for example, does the patient always wait for the therapist to start the session? Does he or she rarely make eye contact? Does his or her posture signify being weighed down, or haughty, or rigid? Is his or her voice too loud, or barely audible? These and myriad other behavioral, facial, vocal, and bodily forms of expression can all be used to alert the therapist to the character type being dealt with, as well as the defenses and resistances that will need to be addressed throughout the therapy.

Having given us the tools required to arrive at a diagnostic picture of the patient, Dr. Frisch then turns her attention to the central tenets governing the therapeutic process itself. She begins where therapy should begin, detailing the steps involved in the formulation and communication of a clear, consistent frame that serves to inform the patient of all the therapist's policies with regard to such administrative matters as fees, payment schedules, absences, vacations, and rules governing the means and frequency of between-session communications. Dr. Frisch's emphasis on the need to establish the frame resonated strongly with me, for in my training I learned that setting up the frame not only helps to organize the therapy but also sets limits on the potential for acting out for both the patient and the therapist. As Masterson put it, the frame stands for reality, and a significant task of therapy is to aid the patient in coming to grips with the dictates of reality, rather than be governed by impulse or the fantasy elements intrinsic to his or her internal world. So for me, Dr. Frisch's inclusion of this often-neglected aspect of the process of psychotherapy served as an essential reminder. And as is her wont throughout her book, Dr. Frisch does not just tell us the "whys" of the frame; she also provides us with the "hows," offering specific examples and clinical vignettes designed to clarify the nature of the frame, and the pitfalls a therapist is likely to encounter in adhering to it.

The vicissitudes of the patient-therapist relationship is the next reference point Dr. Frisch discusses, as she highlights that therapy must not be viewed as a circumstance where one person operates on the other. Rather, she rightly describes it as an interactive process during which both parties significantly affect each other. Which is why Dr. Frisch stresses that it is as important for the therapist to monitor his or her own internal states during a session as it is to keep track of the patient's. For not only can our reactions be a source of information with regard to our patient's state of mind; they can also serve as warning signal, letting us know that our counter-transference has been activated.

Having laid out these general principles, Dr. Frisch turns her attention to the ways in which we can and should implement them in each and every session, as she delineates the ways in which the therapist can best track the material being presented and utilize appropriate interventions designed to keep the focus on the patient's core issues, and thereby avoid getting bogged down in his or her defensive diversions.

Expanding further on the best-practice use of interventions in psychotherapy, Dr. Frisch combines her own acute sensibility with the work of Carl Jung, providing the reader with a comprehensive guide to understanding and interpreting dreams. For me, this section of her work proved to be particularly illuminating, for although we therapists have all at one time or another been made aware of the fact that dreams are, as Freud indicated, "the royal road to the unconscious," the art of analyzing them can ofttimes seem a mystifying bit of business.

Speaking of business, it was heartening for me to read Dr. Frisch's words enjoining therapists not to shy away from the fact that our work, as humanely significant and satisfying as it might be, is also a business. We are not, by and large, hobbyists, and for the great majority of us, running a practice is the way we earn our living. Much as we love it, we all know that doing therapy is challenging work that we have learned to do at the emotional and financial cost of years of education, training, and supervision. Dr. Frisch's firm insistence that both the patients' interests and our own are best served by not neglecting the monetary side of our work is a very helpful and, I might add, rarely seen, addition to a book designed to offer useful advice to clinicians.

The penultimate chapter of Dr. Frisch's work concerns itself with the use of bodywork in therapy. In explicating her views on this topic, Dr. Frisch provides us with a detailed overview of Reich's theories, as he describes the ways in which the patient's pathology becomes manifest in the body, and the techniques that can be employed to heal the mind through healing the body. In emphasizing the need for bodywork as an adjunct to verbal therapy, Dr. Frisch echoes the adjurations of trauma specialists such as Bessel van der Kolk, who clearly asserts that in cases of trauma, "the body takes the hit." In this same vein, Dr. Frisch emphasizes the importance of bodywork for all patients, but also makes sure to pay special attention to techniques that can be used to address the pathology held in the bodies of patients suffering the residual effects of trauma.

Dr. Frisch concludes her book with an inspiring clarion call to all therapists, encouraging them to expand their personal and professional horizons by engaging fully in their lives and work. She informs us of the necessity to continue to study and train, noting that academic work will keep us in touch with and connected to the ethos and ongoing developments of our chosen profession. But she also reminds us that the most significant aid to our learning often appears in the form of a wise, knowledgeable, and supportive mentor, who, preferably, has a passion for the work. I was fortunate enough to find such a mentor in James Masterson, who trained and supervised me at the start of my career, and for many years thereafter. Having read her book, I am sure that Dr. Frisch's students and supervisees have also been privileged to enjoy the experience of being taught by someone who knows and loves the work, and who thoroughly enjoys passing on the hard-won fruits of her experience to those coming into the field. How fortunate, then, that the exemplary quality of Dr. Frisch's mentorship is now available to every therapist. For in setting forth her wisdom and knowledge in *Whole Therapist, Whole Patient*, Dr. Frisch has given us nothing less than a whole book.

—Judith Pearson, PhD

Part I
Reich's Influence

Introduction

Purpose of My Guidebook

As a psychologist in private practice for over 40 years, I have the honor of being with people through their tumultuous conflicts, the steady ebb and flow of their feelings, memories, and experiences as they examine their lives and try to guide their own ship. There are intervals of accomplishment, satisfaction, resolution, and creativity in the therapeutic process. As well as times when my office is filled with jagged emotions of conflict, pain, fear, and grief for what was and what is. Psychotherapy is heartfelt and soulful work.

It can be extremely challenging when patients come in with their built-in, tried-and-true character styles that are no longer working for them. They haven't had the opportunity or they haven't been ready to look honestly at how they relate and behave. They do not know another way to be. Sometimes they lack an intention to actually change, although they do demand to feel better. As psychotherapists, we do our best to be the clearinghouse for their mind's roiling perceptions and try to help make order out of chaotic thoughts, fears, and concerns.

We can feel a myriad of reactions to the process—anything from complacency about our skill level to disappointment that we can't do more to insecurity when patients stop therapy on a dime after a few sessions or longer and we wonder what we did wrong that this patient ran out the door. We can experience boredom, impatience, and restlessness; we can feel strain if we feel devalued, insulted, or attacked. We may be kept up at night with fear for a patient in crisis, or unable to clear our *own* roiling mix up of images that bang around in the middle of the night.

It is a profession fraught with shadowy times as well as sweet successes that feel warmly satisfying. It is also a profession that grows us up from within as we hold the impossible while trying to metabolize unthinkable situations— the contorted distortions of human life. Relationships are created that dig as deep as the old, dank, gnarled roots of a tree. Our patients know us as they learn how to know themselves more and more. These therapeutic relationships develop over time and have their fair share of conflicts, disappointments, and potential ruptures that may bring the existence of the relationship to the edge of the abyss. Who knew, when the therapy began, where it would wind its way? Therapeutic relationships have a life of their own. The therapist, in the process of learning to be effective, matures, settles, and becomes whole in the process of good work. The patient also is demanded to grow, to stretch far beyond what he thought was possible—entering dark terrain and coming out the other side, he too becomes whole. Therapy moves beyond personal history and pathology to become an opportunity for transformation and individuation. Thus, therapy engenders the archetype of the mandala as both therapist and patient achieve wholeness through the rigors of the process.

The therapist needs a capacity for fierceness. Patients will trample us as they do others, and we are the ones who have to be clear, neutral, and intolerant of abusive attitudes and behaviors. We draw the line in the sand and patients learn not to cross it. Support is one aspect of treatment; fierceness and courage are other necessary qualities to be developed in the therapist.

I decided to write this guidebook as a way to speak directly to therapists and impart definitive trail posts to the unwieldy path of psychotherapy. I have supervised psychotherapists for many years in many contexts. I have taught interns to work with inmates and correctional officers at San Quentin State Prison. I have guided students at their practicum and intern placement sites. In 2000 I formed the Orgonomic Institute of Northern California (OINC) with Richard Blasband, MD, an original founding member of the College of Orgonomy (ACO) founded by Elsworth Baker, MD, at the request of Wilhelm Reich. OINC was established to teach the theories and mind/body approach of Wilhelm Reich, MD. As the training program evolved, I acquired the institute and expanded the model, integrating other theorists, which led to the creation of my own particular approach and method. Through the institute, I teach character analysis and biophysical interventions (Reich's verbal and somatic therapy model), while expanding on specific elements that update the theory. I accredit therapists in this modality called Orgonomy. My live training program and independent study modules provide a comprehensive method of doing therapy that is applicable to psychotherapists whether they are beginning students or mature professionals.

Why Wilhelm Reich

Why Wilhelm Reich? I came to psychology through the avenue of dance and philosophy. I was always interested in the realm of ideas, European and Asian philosophy, and religion. While inhabiting my philosophical head, I also lived in my body through dance. I danced early in my life in Los Angeles, learning jazz dance with some of the great master choreographers of Hollywood musicals. In college in San Francisco, I continued to dance in the plentiful modern dance venues, as well as African and jazz classes offered in the city. After I graduated from San Francisco State University, I returned to Hollywood and danced with a modern ballet troupe for more than five years, performing locally and in New York City. I lived and breathed physical/emotional expression through dance. Later I taught a variety of movement and dance classes and became interested in how we can live more in our bodies. That track, mixed with important spiritual seeking at that time, led me back to college to get my master's degree in psychology. I later completed my PhD and sat for my psychologist license.

My experience as a dancer immersed me in an exquisite form of expression that merged body and mind into one. Then I took those skills to become a trainer in the holistic mind/body/spirit program of Arica. Conducting movement exercises with participants to introduce them to their bodies and psychic makeup was the beginning of my trajectory in psychology. Although the path of psychology captured me, I never lost my connection to the importance of physical expression. This deeply felt understanding of mind-body experience soon guided me to the founder of classical somatic therapy, Wilhelm Reich.

Reich's contribution to the field of psychiatry, medicine, and science is panoramic. Trained as a psychoanalyst in the Freudian community in Austria in the late 19th century, he later formulated his own unique form of therapy. He rejected the analytic passive approach as ineffective when defenses are left intact. He engaged the patient's defensive structure in a radically different way. This method was known as character analysis and is still a highly respected theory. As Reich's thinking evolved, his investigations in science and medicine led him to include a biophysical aspect to his treatment protocol. He discovered an energetic component that he applied to psychotherapy years before the current acceptance of energetic concepts. He understood that mind and body are indivisible, one functional unit, and it was imperative to treat the whole person. He created a theoretical platform that resulted in an efficient, effective therapeutic approach that included direct biophysical interventions and expressive exercises.

Reich was a controversial figure in his time. He challenged the orthodoxy with his radical ideas in many areas beyond psychotherapy. Yet it was his rambunctious personality that infused his approach with a fearlessness that allowed for creativity and spontaneity in the room with patients. Out-of-the-box interventions that are methodical in relation to the system, yet inspire a freedom to speak honestly to the patient, come from Reich's profound understanding of defensive structures and how they block aliveness and authentic access.

My Method—Additional Character Types

Wilhelm Reich's theories have an overarching influence on my approach. Of course, as a mature therapist, I utilize many colors on my palette. As I worked with Reich's character typology that developed within the Freudian analytic period in the history of psychiatry and psychoanalysis, Oedipal issues held central sway. Later, object relations theorists researched important earlier developmental passages and attachment issues were integrated into the developmental paradigm of health and psychopathy. I felt Reich's typology of character types was incomplete as it relied almost exclusively on the Oedipal pathway. So I incorporated, with the help of the brilliant work of James Masterson, MD, and the Masterson Institute theorists, additional character types or personality disorders originating from earlier stages of developmental arrest. That filled out, updated, and made complete the system of character types.

As psychodynamic therapists we also need tools to investigate the unconscious. Orgonomy includes dream analysis. Carl Jung, MD, was a master of that sphere and his dream theory is invaluable to the therapist. Dreams are a way we can enter the deepest world of the patient's unconscious and hear the guidance the dream offers. Jung and his concept of the individuated self guide us in treating the final years of life; therapy makes possible a metamorphosis from small ego to spirit. Jung's theories and specific instructions in dream analysis are discussed in the online resource section "Dream Analysis and Individuation."

So the spectrum of my method spans in utero to death in the sense that there is a full tool chest within my method to handle the entire scope of a life.

One of the most important tenets of this guidebook is know and understand your patient. That does not mean know her story nor does it mean know her problematic symptoms. It means delineate the basic structure of *how* the patient is. Then you have a road map that can address that particular structure in a systematic way. You are not walking in the dark, but rather have clear light to see and effect change. That excites me and I want to impart this systematic approach to you.

Understanding the patient goes beyond the structure of the psyche to include understanding how the patient manifests that structure in his physical body. Reich called this body armor, the way energy moves or is held back in the physical structure. How that very immobility or stasis creates the personality or character armor. How blockage in the eyes, the ocular segment, affects the contact the patient makes in the world. How the longing in the mouth, the oral segment, creates habits of overeating, substance abuse, or overtalking and therefore driving potentially debilitating habits.

The system I teach gives you tools to see character and body armor, and gives you schematics to treat your patient. Then you have a map of the terrain and your interventions make sense. Ultimately, if you choose to add biophysical interventions to your tool kit you can learn that modality directly from my institute. That modality takes specific skill development. Understanding the biophysical segmental armoring patterns as defined here will allow biophysical interventions that are feasible within the context of verbal analysis.

This book is full of nuts-and-bolts suggestions, with clear, concise instructions and protocols to inspire therapists and challenge their style. I will give step-by-step guidelines from the first patient phone call, to stages of treatment, to the business of therapy. Most importantly I will teach you how to dismantle the patient's defensive structure that is preliminarily in the way of deepening to the innermost feelings that need to be understood and released. I will utilize camouflaged patient examples as well as training vignettes to help illuminate our discussion. Working with trauma, abandonment depression, and termination are thoroughly covered in the online resource section "Progression into Trauma."

After graduate school and internships and licensure, there is not, necessarily, a clear-cut path of how to actually do therapy and locate the effective strategies or dangerous pitfalls. There are treacherous inclines on this path. With this book you can come away with tools to help you begin.

1 History of Wilhelm Reich

The Approach in Practice

In my 36 years of practice as a psychologist, I have seen hundreds of patients transform their lives through mind-body therapy. Patients enter my practice sometimes at the end of the line, after trying multiple clinical approaches yet still feeling frustrated that their symptoms and difficulties remain. Involving the body alongside the verbal therapy makes the difference. We can understand our life stories, we can discuss events that led to our difficulties, we can explain our current challenges, but cognitive recognition and verbalization is not sufficient to effect change.

The body has an expression; it may want to cry deeply with abandon, kick vigorously as it expresses pent-up frustration, anger, and rage or weep and reach out with tender feelings. Nothing is more relieving than to thoroughly express what you actually feel in a safe setting. But we learn, depending on our personal history and culture, to stymie emotional expression, hold it back with gritted teeth, a rigid jaw, a squeezed throat, and a compressed chest resulting in a loss of capacity to breathe fully. Our habitual repression creates chronic pain, physical stress, and disease in our body and we can become physically ill as a form of unconscious expression. Authentic emotional expression with fluidity of movement is impossible due to our taut and tensely woven bodies. I fortunately found a system of therapeutic interventions that soften the body and the mind, making it pliable, healthy, and responsive—with the goal of teaching patients their lost art of self-expression and authentic living.

Wilhelm Reich, MD, defined health as the capacity to be flexible and non-defensive with ease of expression of authentic feeling both emotionally and sexually. His innovative thinking, still cutting edge in our time, offered me an approach that engendered a complete and whole pathway to mental health with a mind-body orientation.

I have worked with multitudes of men who were never allowed to cry, had constricted voices, stiff chests, and rigid personalities. Through our therapy, they learned to express long-held pain and grief that had been bound-up throughout their lifetimes. This allowed them to be emotionally vulnerable and available within their family relationships. I have worked with many women with traumatic histories, burdened with physical symptoms: irritable bowel, chronic headaches, and tight painful muscles. They became comfortable expressing pent-up feelings of anger and fear as they unlocked painful memories and relieved their sore bodies of its chronic pain.

Most psychotherapists are not trained to work with the body. Reich taught a comprehensive method that addressed the personality structure and how it manifests in body type. With an organized and systematic approach, the clinician can treat the body along with the character problems that result in serious challenges. I had found my niche and have been developing Reich's platform into my own method since graduate school.

In this book I will invite you into my method and my therapy practice and help you discover my Whole Therapist/Whole Patient process. This process incorporates the work of Wilhelm Reich, James Masterson, Carl Jung, and my own unique experience as a therapist, teacher, mother, wife, and human.

History of Reich and Development of His Theories

Wilhelm Reich's clinical approach laid critical groundwork for my method. Throughout his life he pursued a broad spectrum of scientific inquiry and wrote on a wealth of topics, including biology, family practices, weather patterns, politics, and society, but we will address only his relevant clinical ideas. I will explain his history and how his life and theoretical development progressed.

The vast majority of Reich's lines of inquiry, research results, and contributions are quite relevant and applicable to today's scientific conversations and therapeutic formulations. Here I will bring aspects of Reich's clinical theoretical conceptualization into contemporary psychological application. And I will simplify Reich's vast clinical theoretical bounty so that specific aspects are accessible and useful to the contemporary therapist.

Reich was a product of his times. It is the context of the times, and the initial influence of his mentor Sigmund Freud, that oriented his view and defined for him the driving forces and critical phases of human development. I have altered that orientation to be compatible with my clinical experience. In my opinion, Reich overemphasized the Oedipal complex and childhood development seen solely through the lens of sexual development. This emphasis, with its strict gender roles and binary gender assumptions, precluded an understanding of flexible family models that include shifts in gender identity and expression. I have added this viewpoint to the conversation. I have eliminated some assumptions from his model, kept others, and added the earliest attachment developmental phases that are clinically and pragmatically relevant to my understanding of our patients. In other words, I picked and chose elements of Reich's theories that make sense to me while keeping the integrity of his contribution.

In-depth research has continued into the causes of psychological difficulties. The complex interplay of forces that influence our psychological condition include genetic contributions, family systems, and external circumstances.

There is also extensive research on attachment theory, which is a strong factor. I have expanded on Reich's character types by utilizing attachment theory to delineate *earlier* developmental passages that mark specific additional character types. These earlier development phases are critical and expand on Reich's emphasis that was singularly focused on Oedipal phases and development of sexuality. I give these details so you can understand the historical context and the etiology of Reich's thinking and to shed light on why I expanded on that paradigm to include significant additions to his character typology, an expanded perspective on nontraditional family systems including gender fluidity, and added Carl Jung's quintessential contribution to dream analysis.

I will explain Reich's mind-body formulation without much change in the basics although I add my own twist. The model of adding bodywork to analysis is as applicable and innovative today as it was when he created it. To this day, and to our detriment, the mind is separated from the body in the vast majority of psychiatric and psychological therapeutic approaches (excepting the use of drugs). The medical establishment's emphasis on psychogenic drugs is the standard traditional approach to mental illness. I have been consistently able to titrate patients off medications using the biophysical work along with character analysis. The whole modality has strong ameliorative impacts on patients' physiological symptoms.

Wilhelm Reich developed Orgonomy in the 1930s. He was born in 1897, in Galicia, now the Ukraine, then included in the Austro-Hungarian empire. He was the eldest son of a wealthy Jewish landowner and grew up in a rural area on a farm. The farm setting stimulated his early interest in natural science and biology. Reich set up his first laboratory at age eight and studied butterflies and insects. He had a private teacher who guided his education. Reich's fascination with natural life functions determined his later interest in the biological foundations of mankind's emotional life. Throughout his life, his research pursuits in biology and natural sciences gave him scientific reference points that he applied as a bio-psychiatrist in the development of his theoretical approach with patients.

Following graduation, he entered the Austro-Hungarian army, and served as a lieutenant in World War I (1916–1918). With the end of the war, in the fall of 1918, Reich was accepted into medical school at University of Vienna and completed his university studies with an MD degree in 1922. During medical school, Reich was interested in the question of psychic drives, particularly sexuality. His scientific predisposition led him to hypothesize and research bioenergetic problems including the biological basis of instincts, the nature of pleasure and tension, the role of genitality, the function of the orgasm, and the sources of neurotic anxiety.

Psychoanalysis to Character Analysis

His psychiatric career was launched within the psychoanalytic movement. He was one of Sigmund Freud's (1856–1939) stellar pupils, becoming a member of the Vienna Psychoanalytic Association in 1920 while still a medical student. Reich, as a faculty member of the Psychoanalytic Institute and chairman of the Vienna seminar in 1924, gave lectures and wrote papers on clinical subjects and bio-psychiatric theory. In his 20s he had already made many important discoveries in the understanding and treatment of neuroses.

The psychoanalytic approach with patients frustrated Reich. He found the nonengaged blank screen stance—as well as the exclusive reliance on free association, interpretation, and dream analysis—ineffective. He felt the process to be chaotic in that the patient led with her free association and the analyst's interpretations followed. There was no order to what the analysts interpreted as they analyzed whatever the patient offered up. Also there was insufficient application of analytic principles regarding patient resistance, and so it was avoided. Reich saw the limitations of interpretation as he felt it inevitably reinforced intellectualization and therefore detachment from the patient's inner material and it ignored the patient's resistance and negative feelings toward the therapist. The interventions were not grounded in the patient's emotions but actually facilitated a covering up of important material (Reich, *The Function of the Orgasm*, 1973, 117–121).

Reich was further frustrated by the lack of guidance from his mentors regarding silent patients who produced few associations or dream material. Analysts would typically maintain silence and wait. Reich, in *The Function of the Orgasm*, described the quintessential technique of the analysts— "waiting . . . which was supposed to have a meaning"; Reich described this waiting as "sheer helplessness" (Reich, *The Function of the Orgasm*, 1973, 119). He found the seminars uninspired as they lacked a systematic technique and practical guidelines for problems analysts were facing. At that time there were few requirements to become an analyst. Reich addressed these concerns by forming clinical seminars with fellow students and began developing what he described as an organized method. He tried to bring order to analytic chaos. He designed an appropriate format for case presentations that shifted the prior practice of presentations that were ramblings of patient history without noting the therapeutic problem and suggestions for analytic direction. Reich encouraged discussions regarding patient criticisms and developed a method that addressed practical aspects of treatment heretofore ignored. He later described his method in his seminal book, *Character Analysis* (1972).

In my 30 years of supervising I have come across a similar problem in the present state of clinical training. You try a little of this and a little of that without a game plan or an orderly systematic way to organize the case and treat the patient; both students and professionals feel desperate and helpless too much of the time. The overarching principle of my approach is to delineate an applicable, clinically relevant, systematic set of guidelines such as a definitive case presentation format to make case consultation seminars efficient, instructions on precise summaries given to the patient at various intervals in treatment (and in the case seminar) that include the essence of the patient's problems and why, and a precise therapeutic approach based on character.

Reich's character analytic and biophysical method laid groundwork elements for a structured approach within the psychoanalytic maze; he provided an orderly method through his diagnostic typology and clearly defined treatment concepts. This book will outline specific protocols to follow so your clinical work can be effective.

Reich learned, through hours of psychoanalytic patient sessions, how patients blocked the analytic process by their chronic patterns of thought and behavior. Essentially, Reich understood that patients develop a character style early in life to protect against difficult feelings and experiences that need to be avoided or forgotten by the conscious mind. The character structure becomes a defensive mode that is maintained throughout life, unless challenged. The character defenses are not conscious, as they fit like a second skin. Yet, character defenses act as a psychic barrier in the way of accessing deeper layers of feeling, memory, and insight necessary for mental health. Reich, in developing his systematic approach, realized that from the outset of treatment, defenses need to be dismantled by engaging them directly in an organized fashion starting with surface defenses and moving gradually into the deeper defensive structures (Reich, *The Function of the Orgasm*, 1973, 141–150)

In reading *Character Analysis* in graduate school, I was impressed with Reich's precise method of engagement with the patient about *how* the patient is in the room rather than focusing on the story relayed. In order to help the patient see his defensive patterns, the therapist must point them out in a direct fashion. Noting the style, the attitudes, and the facade of the patient, through dialoguing about how a patient is, allows awareness and ultimately a falling away of those defensive layers. As we work through the defensive layers, the barriers drop away and deeper feelings, memories, and insights emerge. Reich created a systematic way of working that dismantles the character style starting from the outside layers and moving inward. This was a radical approach and differed greatly from the passive style of psychoanalysis of the time. This approach to the client hour is still experienced as radical to many therapists I have supervised.

Here is an example that illuminates character analysis: A male patient who has suffered isolation from intimate relationships for most of his adult life is employed in a managerial position and is successful at his job—but not in relationships. What is he like in the therapist's office? He presents as reasonable, friendly, and open, yet right under the pleasing surface he is emotionally distant and underneath that is a tinge of anger and resentment two layers down from the pleasant presentation.

The therapist was busy discussing content with his reasonable facade even though she noticed his detachment and irritability bordering on slight hostility when she made an intervention. I suggested she comment on both the detachment and the hint of hostility underneath the seemingly friendly facade. She was quite taken a back with my suggestion as it felt threatening to mention those negative feelings. I guided her to comment on the obvious character traits in the room and bring them to his attention for exploration.

This is how character analysis is accomplished, noting the exact style and emotional process in the room.

Another aspect differentiating Wilhelm Reich and the analysts of his time was the typical analyst's reliance on an assumed context of positive feelings between patient and psychotherapist. Reich notes how the analyst was reluctant to bring out patients' negative feelings toward the therapist. He commented that analysts were personally insecure and therefore avoided their patients' negativity. These negative feelings, then, went underground and were not dealt with in the treatment room but contributed to active resistance to therapy and the therapist. Reich wrote extensively on the topics of patient resistance, latent negative transference (hidden patient ambivalence, hatred, or anger at the therapist) as he defined his systematic techniques that would become the basis of his own theoretical and clinical approach.

Reich's personality comes through in his writings. He used out-of-the-box interventions, meaning he was willing to apply many different types of creative interventions to "shake" patients out of their habits. He would imitate the patient at times, take actions that shocked the patient, and give provocative messages to stimulate awareness and change. I have compared his approach to that of a Zen master who uses his stick on the back to stimulate immediate awakening. Reich was fearless in his style, unique with a creative approach that emanated from his free expressive personality and his intense, contactful way of being.

The concept of libido and how libidinal instincts and societal restrictions interplay became divisive points of contention between Reich and Freud. Freud initially viewed neurosis as a conflict between sexual instincts and society's repudiation of sexuality. Originally, Freud hypothesized libido, a term he coined, as a biological sexual energy. But as time went on Freud settled on libido as exclusively a psychic concept. Reich, on the other hand, was convinced that frustration of sexual instincts was the cause of most neurotic symptoms and suffering. He believed that if sexual energy is not released, the organism will be plagued with energetic imbalances. According to Reich, built-up energy needs to be discharged, and if not released, it creates stagnation and neurotic/physical symptoms. Reich's orgasm theory affirmed the real physical, measurable, energetic quality of libido, therefore separating him from his colleagues. He concluded that social institutions needed to be changed to reflect a more open attitude regarding the essential role of sexuality (Reich, *The Function of the Orgasm*, 1973, 96)

Freud felt that people should accommodate to the norms of the culture and social structure. Freud believed that individuals have destructive instincts as well, that need to be curbed by societal limitations. Reich believed we are born without destructive drives but that societal repression creates irrational and neurotic behaviors. And repression of libido results in a buildup of tension causing destructive drives. These differences led to the break between Freud and Reich. Reich, during the postwar period, devoted his resources to social issues: educating the working class and setting up clinics to provide medical and educational help in the areas of sex education, divorce rights, birth control, and other assistance (www.wilhelmreichtrust.org).

The larger historical context is critical to our understanding of Reich and Freud, as there were tidal waves of change in Europe at the time. The First World War (1914–1918), or Great War, had ended, having impacted most of the nations of Europe, along with Russia, the United States, the Middle East, and other regions. There was immense carnage, destruction, and death from the war resulting in massive political, cultural, and social change across Europe. Empires collapsed and new ones were formed along with new boundaries and development of new ideologies.

Reich had been forced to flee his home, never to return, in 1914. He fought with the Austrian Army from 1915 to 1918. Germany and Austria were defeated and the Austro-Hungarian Empire was divided up. Reich entered medical school in Vienna, after years of fighting in the war. He had lost his homeland and all his possessions. Freud and Reich had been swept up in the upheaval and bore witness to the trauma of war neurosis. The chief psychoanalytic institutes of the time in Berlin, Vienna, and London were also caught up in the massive tumult of the Great War and the rise of the Nazi party in Germany in 1930s.

Reich's interest in developing new social structures led to his exploration of the Socialist and Communist parties in Vienna and later in Berlin. Reich was an outspoken man who criticized ideologies when they failed to support what he felt was right, leading to his expulsion from the Communist Party. Reich was forced to flee Germany in 1933 when Hitler came to power due to his opposition to Nazism. Freud, too, was forced to flee to London in 1938, at the end of his life, to escape Nazism.

Within this context of change and turbulence between World War I and World War II, Freud and Reich were revolutionaries, willing to investigate, discuss, and promote sexuality as part of their search to unlock the mysteries of the psyche, the unconscious, and penetrate the source of human problems. In a historical period of sexual repression in Europe, Reich became the true radical, promoting a non-repressive society that fosters children to be raised with freedom of emotional and physical expression, in a climate of sexual openness and acceptance.

Discovery of Orgone Energy

Reich's theories and research that affirmed energy as real and measurable was also revolutionary for his time. Reich understood the deleterious effects of repression and how blocking our free-flowing energy creates patterns of disease and psychic pain. Reich traveled to Oslo, where he continued his research to verify the existence of a physical biological energy expressed in emotions with laboratory experiments (1934–1939). He demonstrated a changing level of charge at the skin surface directly related to feelings of pleasure and anxiety. He found that pleasure created a movement of energy from the core to the periphery and conversely that anxiety moved the energy toward the center of the body. He assumed that biological excitation might be electrical, but his scientific experiments did not support that assumption. He continued to study energy functions through the study of basic life forms using time-lapse motion picture equipment, microscopes, and over 3,000x magnification to record the functions of protozoa. Under specific conditions, organic substances like grass, sand, and blood disintegrate into pulsating vesicles with internal motility and radiate a bluish color illustrating an energetic effect. These vesicles, which he called *bions*, exhibited the effects of energetic movement in its most primitive form. His research demonstrated that bions emit a potent radiation that could kill bacteria as well as charge organic materials. The radiation did not obey any known laws of electricity or magnetism. Reich discovered and named the energy *orgone* because of the original impetus to investigate the orgasm function. He defined orgone energy as a primordial cosmic energy universally present and in the living organism, a biological energy (www.wilhelmreichtrust.org). The terms *Orgonomy* and *medical orgone therapy* include broad scientific research to study and verify the physical biological energy expressed throughout all life forms. With the natural science of orgone energy and its functions (Baker, 1967, xxix), Reich was developing a unique paradigm that radically altered the landscape of psychoanalysis.

Healthy Sexuality

Reich's attention and research focused on the unitary functioning of mind and body, finding that they function together in an interwoven, inseparable relationship. The function of the orgasm is to maintain an energetic balance within by releasing excess energy, defined in his theory of *energy economy*. Reich stated that in psychic disturbances, this biological energy is bound up not only in physical symptoms, but more importantly, in the individual's personality style and muscular patterns—what he called *character and body armor*. Armoring against the free flow of life energy blocks aliveness and stunts creativity, authenticity, and open expression in life. Reich developed new therapeutic techniques, including biophysical interventions to eliminate bound musculature, tension, and stasis, permitting *streaming*, pleasant, wave-like currents of energy. The expressive exercises encourage vocal emotional expression and release of the entire spectrum of feelings, allowing the patient deep access to long-suppressed experiences and sensations and the unwinding of traumatic material.[1]

Reich's interest in sexuality went beyond the energy economic perspective to emphasize the importance of a loving sexual relationship that encouraged surrender to one's partner. The capacity for surrender to the involuntary contractions of the orgasm and complete discharge of sexual excitation in the sexual act he called *orgastic potency*. The vegetative streaming sensations and natural pulsation results in a sense of satisfaction, sweet feelings, and complete release and relaxation. Healthy sexual functioning was an integral part of his theory and methods.

Wilhelm Reich left Europe due to the tumult of the war years and moved to New York in 1939. He trained American physicians in his therapeutic techniques and continued his research. In 1942 he purchased a large plot of land and a farmhouse in Rangley, Maine. That became his research laboratory and teaching center called Orgonon and is now the Wilhelm Reich Museum. There he studied single-celled organisms, human blood composition, and the origins of life, and he experimented with the basic energy he found in all living things. He built what he called an orgone accumulator (1940) made up of organic and metal layers that attracted and contained atmospheric energy. Reich was informed by his experimental study of the amoeba, which illustrated the principles of expansion, contraction, and pulsation important to his work with patients. Reinstating movement, expansion and contraction, and pulsation are goals of the treatment approach (www.wilhelmreichtrust.org).

Reich's Controversial End

Reich was an iconic and controversial figure who was singled out during the McCarthy era of the 1950s and eventually imprisoned for contempt of court. In 1947, an article by a freelance writer entitled "The Strange Case of Wilhelm Reich" implied that Reich was a danger to the public. The author insisted the medical authorities take action against Reich through the Food and Drug Administration (FDA). This evolved into a 10-year campaign by the FDA to discredit his work. The FDA was preoccupied with discrediting the orgone energy accumulator and the experiments Reich was doing with patients. In 1954, the FDA filed a serious complaint against Reich in Maine. It declared the nonexistence of orgone energy and asked the court to stop any shipments of accumulators in interstate commerce. The injunction further banned Reich's published books and articles. Reich responded with a letter to the judge that stated he would not appear in court as it would, by nature of appearance, validate a court of law to judge his scientific research and validate a complaint not founded on scientific research and science. The judge did not accept his letter and escalated the injunction. One of Reich's students, without Reich's permission, moved some accumulators and books from Maine to New York. The FDA then charged Reich with contempt of court. Reich was convicted and sentenced to two years in federal prison. Reich appealed but meanwhile the government destroyed his orgone accumulators and his literature was burned in Maine. In New York in 1956, the FDA burned several tons of Reich's publications including major works, such as *Character Analysis* and *The Function of the Orgasm*. With his appeals denied, he was taken to a federal penitentiary in Pennsylvania in 1957 and soon after died of heart failure. Throughout Reich's life, and continuing today, many of those who have studied his contributions realize the applicability of his visionary ideas to clinical modalities (www.wilhelmreichtrust.org).

Note

1 Reich's orgasm theory theoretically separated him from his peers. Building from this platform, he created a comprehensive paradigm that described the characterological and biophysical ramifications of stasis or blockages of energy within our whole system. Reich developed new techniques, *character analysis* and later *vegetotherapy*, that went beyond the limits of psychoanalysis. Vegetotherapy later became Orgnonomy to include the biophysical interventions as well as character analysis. He coined the terms *character* and *body armor*, which supported his mind-body approach to health.

2 Why Reich's Model Makes Sense

Wilhelm Reich's theories and mode of practice are the bones of my style of therapy and central to my method. Reich's therapeutic paradigm makes so much sense. This chapter will give you an overview of some of his concepts, their development, and application so that Reichian therapy/Orgonomy can begin to make sense to you, too. Patients and trainees who experience the breadth of the approach are incredulous as to why more therapists aren't exposed to this method. Many graduate programs touch briefly on Reich as part of the history of psychoanalysis and he is referenced in universities with a somatic psychology program, but his comprehensive theory and systematic mode of mind-body therapy is not covered. His treatment model attends to every part of the client's life, including creating a direct relationship between the therapist and the patient's body. Psychologists rarely, if ever, touch the patient's body and certainly that touch is not part of the treatment approach. There are many other "somatic approaches" that, I believe, do not organize and treat character problems as well as Reich. Wilhelm Reich is considered by most as the originator of mind-body and somatic psychotherapy.

Why is he not more familiar to students and professionals, accepted and incorporated into traditional psychology and psychiatric training programs? Certainly the limited views of the 1950s and McCarthy era in the United States influenced academic acceptance of his theories. His legal problems and conviction, stemming from the government's campaign, marginalized him in conventional academic settings and analytic circles. His early death cut short his influence, which might have continued beyond this historic period. Clinical applications of mind-body approaches remain in stone-age conceptual storage. Although we recognize how good health habits affect the body and therefore the mental state, we still have not defined a therapeutic approach beyond words to help patients manage their stress and biophysical aliments. Body tensions, nervous system disorders, and a multitude of diseases can be psychologically and emotionally based and live in the patient's body. These physical repercussions need to be directly addressed as part of psychotherapy. Psychology and psychiatry rely on talk therapy and medications. Orgonomy directly attends to the relationship between the mind and its expression in the body. Although Reich addressed this missing connection in a systematic way, he was not influential.

Yet, there has always been a small and loyal band of interested individuals and academics in Europe and the United States that has sustained focus on his work and kept Reich alive in the university and public setting. I believe there is a growing renewed interest in Wilhelm Reich with a film documentary in the works and isolated colleges now offering courses on his work.

The goals of Reich's treatment approach are to reinstate energetic movement, natural expression, release, and relief. And to change the defensive nature of long-term character patterns that result in repetitive psychological and relational problems as well as physical ailments. I have practiced for over 30 years and have sat with patients as they break through to insights and the rich feeling states and expressions that have long been inhibited. They learn how to access relevant historic experiences and push through a myriad of attitudinal, emotional, and physical inhibitions, learning to yell, scream, kick their legs, pound their fists, and sob, as well as soften into their vulnerability. These expressions were not available to them when they started. Or, if emotional outbursts are over the top, then patients learn containment and tolerance of anxiety so they are not flooded with feeling and suffocating others with excessive emotions. In the therapeutic process, tension is released and patients experience pleasurable streamings of energy from head to toe. Their body-mind becomes agile and able to experience and tolerate natural energy flow. They experience feeling alive. I wish more therapists could both find that aliveness in themselves and help others to achieve that end in whatever degree possible for each individual.

Natural Self-Regulation

Reich's paradigm of human potential is a positive one. He believes when we are healthy, we naturally self-regulate. That means healthy choices will emanate from a flexible character and an open, unrestricted body. With health, we are connected to sensations within that guide us to treat our minds and bodies well. We desire movement and as we move, we feel energetic. We want to be emotionally expressive so we are free to say what we think, feel, want, and don't want. We need to have access to all of our feelings: anxiety, anger, sadness, longing, disappointment, grief, and love. When we have access we can listen carefully to those feelings, understand their meaning at a given time, express them if need be, and invite responsiveness from others. If others are not able to respond, we can readjust as we see the other realistically. We can move toward and away from environments that don't contribute to our well-being. As we dismantle our defensive armoring we become less harsh and more flexible in all situations. We are honest and sincere in our dealings. As we maintain our vitality, we have resources for creativity. We can access our core intentions and manifest our purpose. We can feel for others and act lovingly. We can also set clear limits when needed in all circumstances. Health gives us the ability to self-regulate and regulate our larger environment, promoting healthy habits, lifestyle choices, and conducive relationships. Health increases our capacity to negotiate our needs so our life can flow reasonably well, with a sense of meaning and satisfaction.

A Unified Approach

Reich's model is comprehensive of mind and body so we don't have to chase after health, mixing and matching a multitude of approaches. Some of us become experts in all the various offerings, as we compulsively seek a sense of well-being by running from practitioner to practitioner, always with the hope of feeling better. We get massages and acupuncture, visit coaches and psychics, go on retreats, sign up for transformational workshops, take Chinese herbs and multiple medications—the list goes on and on. Many of these treatments are excellent, helpful, high-quality modalities, but we can end up with conflicting and chaotic treatments as we lack a central plan and understanding of our problems. Those that can afford them can keep up a busy schedule getting cured. Orgonomy puts many of these efforts under one umbrella. A patient can work his psychological issues and understand how they are playing out in physical symptoms. Our symptoms are understood as part and parcel of our character style and its mirror image in the body. Reich's approach weaves together problems into an understandable configuration thereby reducing the need for multiple interventions that can cause confusion.

Others simply seek traditional medical attention and are often medicated when they shouldn't be. Increasingly, the medical system is advocating healthy lifestyle habits and that is good. Yet there is a need for a greater understanding of the psychological roots of mental and physical problems so the treatment approach can be inclusive. Many medications, including psychotropic drugs, are part of the problem. Patients suffer from a cocktail approach of multiple medications and lose contact with their baseline experience without medication as they are jockeyed about with various medication side effects. Addiction to pain medications is increasingly a problem as access to them is easy, although cultural and medical compliance with overprescribed opioids is shifting.

My hope is that *Whole Therapist, Whole Patient* introduces you to a sophisticated and well-organized method of treatment that addresses our suffering in an integrated, efficient, and effective way. I believe Orgonomy and my method could provide a prototype of treatment sorely needed in the psychological and medical community.

Overview of Basic Concepts

This section introduces you to a few of Reich's concepts that explain his premises and are foundational to this model: energetic concepts of aliveness, stasis, mobility, expansion and contraction, charge and discharge, and pulsation; the importance of breathing, contact, and frankness in the therapeutic relationship.

Reich postulated and proved in his research that Orgone energy exists as a primary, universally present force that flows infinitely and pervasively. This energy flows within our bodies, and the more easily it flows, the more we feel alive. Reich used the term *motility* to describe the natural movement necessary to health and consistent energy flow. Reich's analysis of patient problems over time led to his understanding that psychological problems are created by stasis within our psyche and corresponding stagnation within the body. What do we mean by *stasis*? Think of a dank pond of water verses a flowing, fresh water stream. The stream moves, reflecting the shimmering light of the sun, and looks and tastes fresh, clean, and inviting. In a stagnant pond, the water putrefies and is filled with pond scum and decomposed materials, as the rush of cleansing water is stymied.

Stasis in our bodies is created in a myriad of ways. With shallow breathing we diminish our respiratory functions, resulting in reduced capacity to oxygenate and release toxins. With lack of movement and exercise, our blood flow slows, diminishing necessary blood flow to our brain and other organs. Our intestines become sluggish, leading to constipation and toxic build up, which can affect the quality of our gut flora. Intestinal stasis can lead to an experience of chronic bloating, gas, and pain in our gut plus problems of elimination. Our muscles are underutilized, lose tone and elasticity, and become flaccid, affecting the health of our joints. Our spine lacks flexibility, resulting in chronic immobility and pain. We carry excess fat that insulates us from sensation and inhibits our movement by weighing down our joints. Our self-image suffers from obesity. These are examples of physical stasis. Our energy becomes trapped inside our bodies without an outlet. We become numb to sexual sensation and likely have limited sexual contact and release. We may feel weak, lethargic, or fraught with tension, tightness, and rigidity. Our bodies become like the dank pond: our movement is stymied, we feel ill frequently, and there is visible pain seen in the despair and suffering exhibited on our faces. We become robots who are in survival mode. In this state we do not feel alive, we do not feel healthy, and we lack energy.

We develop static ways of thinking, feeling, and reacting that create a repetitive pattern that lacks flexibility and attunement to current situations. We live inside habitual ways of being that cause us chronic problems yet we lack the awareness that we are limited. A static mind is circular and less open to input. We describe the person as defensive, warding off self-awareness, insight, lacking an ability to change and develop. We must remove stasis within our body-mind so as to discover our natural state of motility and healthy adaptation. If the primary orgone energy can move easily through us, we can feel our aliveness through our capacity to be responsive, to feel joy and tenderness, and to feel aligned with our deepest sense of self.

Expansion and Contraction, Pulsation

Reich's model of treatment developed from his experience with patients and his ongoing experiments on basic functional aspects of life. When I did my master's thesis on Reich, I focused on the foundational stones of his method of practice; one being the innate biological principal of *expansion and contraction*. I was fascinated by his studies of the amoeba, a single-celled organism that occurs in protozoa, fungi, algae, and animals. The amoeba consists of a core or nucleus, protoplasm, a membrane, and an energy field. It can extend its shape by extending and retracting its pseudopods. The energetic center is the nucleus and contains the highest energetic charge. The charge comes from energy drawn from the protoplasm that ingests food. From the nucleus, waves of excitation flow intermittently through the organism. There is a *charging and discharging* of excitation, another one of Reich's basic principles. The result is a pulsatory effect with alternating expansion and contraction, building charge and discharging charge. This process of energy metabolism Reich extended to his orgasm formula: tension—charge—discharge—relaxation. Without appropriate discharge, energy is built up within the organism and causes tension and disequilibrium. Reich suggested that energy needs to be discharged on a regular basis so the organism feels balanced, otherwise surplus energy can build up and lead to unhealthy symptoms. Orgasm is one of the ways we, as humans, maintain healthy energetic balance.

Energy cannot be seen under the microscope, only its manifestations. The amoeba continually moves as waves of excitation flow through the protoplasm. If you look carefully you can see a pulsating energy field that surrounds the organism.[1] Reich researched how amoebas respond to attack. He analyzed the dual functioning under the microscope and found that the amoeba would contract when pricked with a pin and expand with excitation toward the membrane when reaching for food. After repeated pricks the amoeba would contract and stay in a state of shrinking. Studying these organisms illuminates basic biological, functional principles applicable to us. Organisms expand and contract in pulsatory waves. If the organism is attacked once or twice, it rebounds normally. If attacked more often, it becomes cautious and expands furtively and minimally. If there are too many attacks, the amoeba reduces its size, diminishes its movement, and the inner pressure increases as it is not discharged with elongation and cell division. We can say the amoeba is *armored* in response to continued threats. If the attacks continue it will cease building up energy and the energy level will decline. As it loses its shape, the membrane withers and it shrinks and dies.

We can see the parallels in our human condition. We are sophisticated extensions of the amoeba. As humans on this lumbering phylogenetic spectrum, we respond similarly in our organism. The core is our vegetative nervous system; the protoplasm is our blood, lymph, and tissue fluids; the membrane is our skin; and we have an energy field as well. Our autonomic nervous system has two opposing systems, the sympathetic and parasympathetic, that create the contraction and expansion, respectively. Our automatic nervous system pulsates between the sympathetic and the parasympathetic. Simply stated our sympathetic system activates our fight-or-flight stance. Our parasympathetic modulates our relaxation responses. Our circulatory, respiratory, and nervous systems allow us to respond to stimuli from outside with excitation flowing to the surface of our muscles and skin in response. This is the sympathetic system in action, charging our muscles to respond. Or we can move energy toward our core to our digestive tract in order to digest food. The parasympathetic system expands us into a relaxation mode. If we have intense stimuli from outside, like a confrontation with another, our sufficient energetic supplies become available and support a strong charge or push to respond, even physically, if necessary. We are in fight mode with our sympathetic system at the helm. The energy flow can be felt both physically in our taught muscles and in our emotions. If our nervous system is balanced we feel good, as we are not overly stressed in fight and flight patterns. I will say more on this topic in further chapters, as resetting the nervous system is a basic goal of Orgonomic treatment, meaning we reinstate a balance of expansion and contraction.

Like the amoeba, we contract away from adverse experiences and expand toward positive ones like warmth and pleasurable stimuli. We armor if repeatedly wounded, first reacting with anxiety and caution but continuing to move. If we are wounded further, we will amplify our retreat, becoming more permanently contracted with increased inner pressure and anxiety. If there is too much trauma, we may end up in a chronic state of shrinkage, seen in intractable depressions. Mobility, building, and releasing excitation (charge) and natural, pulsating contraction and expansion are necessary functions of healthy living. We can move toward and move away in a natural rhythm. We build a charge with food, sleep, and sunlight, and we dissipate the charge through work, activities, exercise, and sexual discharge. Reich's biological basics describe critical elements of our human condition and give us a road map so we can intervene at foundational levels (Baker, 1967).

Discovery of Bions

What is alive is in a constant state of movement, rest, and transformation. Reich, through his experiments, confirmed that principle. He watched under the microscope as organic materials, like sand, blood, or grass disintegrated and transformed into pulsating vesicles he named *bions*, meaning "life." The bion emanates a bluish color and has an internal motility, an effect of the energy within and without. Bions are basic life forms that pulsate, expand, and contract. We pulsate, expand, and contract in our cells, in our organs, and when we tune in, our entire body can pulsate with energetic movement. We are a buzzing, mobile organism wired to interact with the world to get our needs met. If we can sustain our fluidity of movement, pulsation, and flexibility as an organism from in utero, through our development and into old age, we will likely sustain our aliveness and our capacity to express ourselves in a multitude of ways.

Importance of Full Breath

Our experience of aliveness depends on the full movement of our breathing. Through our breath we oxygenate our organism and then breathe out carbon dioxide. Our breathing patterns are important to the health of the body and many spiritual and yogic practices from around the world emphasize the importance of the breath. So did Reich, and working with the breath is an essential intervention. When we armor, as our friend the amoeba, our breath constricts and we are tense. We communicate to our autonomic nervous system that we are threatened, and it activates the fight and flight hormones. We might live continually in this state of fear within our body, sending alarm signals on a moment-by-moment basis to our nervous system. Like the amoeba we feel attacked and threatened but now it originates from within and is a habit of the armored organism. When we inhibit our breathing we remain in a contraction without allowing the expansion of full breathing. So reinstating a healthy nervous system through open and stable breathing is a practical application basic to this treatment approach that promotes recalibration and therefore health in our mind-body.

Contact

Contact was a favorite concept of Reich's and relevant to my style. Orgonomy stresses the importance of patient contact with self and the therapist. Contact means capacity for present-centered energetic aliveness that enables connection to one's thoughts, feelings, and sensations and to the other. To have contact, we need a certain amount of energy with excitation above a minimal level. Contact can extend to contactful connection to the other. What does this really mean in our daily lives? When we feel in contact with another, there is an exchange of energy, feeling, body sensation, and excitation. An interesting personal, psychological, political, or philosophical conversation can engender an experience of contact. Our cognitions, feelings, and body sensations intertwine and we feel "alive" in the interaction. It can be a simple discussion between two people about prosaic items, like plans for dinner, an event you are going to, or a project you are taking on together, and you enjoy the mutual contact and exchange.

Contact with self is the critical underpinning of good contact with another. We can feel deep contact with self by observing or participating in a natural setting, listening or playing music, exercising, writing, cooking, or practicing other artistic pursuits. Whenever the body-mind is actively engaged and our senses are open, we can experience things with excitement. If our armoring is, for the most part, dissolved, our eyes can see clearly, our mouths are relaxed, our voice is free, and we can breathe fully thus allowing energy to stream throughout our bodies. We can see everything with crystal clarity and have sufficient energy to create and interact well. There is a level of excitation that illuminates everything.

We need to have clear eyes to see reality. Reich defines the armoring in our body by parsing the body armor into various segments. An important functional segment is the eyes. Often we are armored in our eyes from early on in our development. We may become afraid to look and see what is difficult to face. Armoring in our eyes means we have contact problems. We may hold tension in our head, overthink and lose connection with what we are looking at. Or we can distort what we see. Or our eyes are withdrawn, our vision blurry and we can say we are disconnected, spaced out, or *out of contact*. Or our eyes may glance furtively from side to side, never settling. If our eyes can handle the charge of energy and sensation, they can see reality clearly. Then our eyes can engage with another and contact can occur in relationship. This type of contact is satisfying as it is open-eyed and warm. There is presentness within the exchange that creates authenticity within the relationship.

We can't always be in absolute contact as therapists because we may have low energy or feel ill or be preoccupied with our own concerns. But good contact is the optimum goal. As we increase our capacity for contact we become more self-aware. That self-contact brings with it a capacity for authenticity. If we are authentic and congruent with ourselves, we are more likely to be authentic with our patients. If we can see them clearly, we can give feedback that makes sense. It is our willingness to engage in a more contactful, honest, spontaneous, and real way that makes this style of working refreshing.

Contact with reality leads us to a sense of responsibility for self, others, and our planet home. We naturally experience the preciousness of our earth and its resources: the life-giving properties of our plants, trees, insects; the coral reefs deep within the sea; and the uniqueness of every animal in our interconnected universe—we are on contact with the importance of all our natural resources and our contact demands our protectiveness.

The Direct Approach

Our frankness builds the patient's trust. As I developed as a therapist I became more and more interested in engaging in an honest and contactful way. The therapist's level of aliveness affects the quality of her interaction. If we respond in the moment to a patient's lack of aliveness or comment on his character defense, we are in the room, in the relationship rather than being on autopilot listening to a story. Reich engaged with intensity that came from his vibrant level of contact, authenticity, and frankness. Patients know when a therapist is stating something the patient recognizes as true. The therapist does not have to mince words. This method encourages the therapist to state clearly and directly, with neutrality, what is compromising the patient's health. It may be difficult for the patient to hear but that rough patch can be worked through and the patient can change. This approach takes the blandness and contactlessness out of the session.

This method takes courage as it depends on direct, no-holds-barred interaction. As therapists we have our own anxiety, fear, and historic limitations. It is essential that therapists do personal therapy so they can become the vehicle for change. Many therapists have not been in intensive treatment themselves, so they have not conquered their own limitations. Therapists can have fear of others, making it hard for them to kick up spontaneous thoughtful expression in session. Confronting or neutrally commenting on a chronic defensive style of the patient can incite anger, frustration, tension, or disappointment in the patient toward the therapist. The therapist must be able to tolerate tension and the feeling of not being liked. My style has become freer and freer in its willingness to engage all experiences in the session. That said, if my energy is lower, I may not engage with intensity. Or the patient may need a very different approach. Here is where contact comes in. We must be in good contact to know the right approach in any given moment or circumstance. Reich's style taught me to be fearless, as my goal is to help patients move through their struggles and suffering.

Deep Respect

One of the most important aspects of my therapeutic style is deep respect for the patient. Everyone has their struggles and pain, and even though they may have developed a character style that is alienating and destructive, they deserve respect. Life is not easy, and our patients need to feel our sincere compassion. I relate from deep, caring feelings for my patients. It might not look like their expectations, because I may not be gratifying what they want. I must decide what I believe is best for my patients. I will listen to them, as I could be wrong and they will teach me something different. I won't be a know-it-all, but I am comfortable as an authority. Many therapists shun that concept as there are modes of therapy that insist on following the patient and never taking the lead as an authority. My method states we must take the authority so we can help guide the ship through stormy waters. The therapist has to set the frame so the patient can learn what full responsibility is in the therapeutic setting. Once the patient develops in the process, he can take the reins and do his own work in session. He is on his way to becoming individuated.

Directness, confrontation, and clear limits can engender strong negative feelings in the patient. Sometimes there might be verbal or emotional wrestling in session; I call it *wrestling an issue to the ground*. I encourage therapists to endure it. Live with the ramifications of authenticity, tolerate the tension, tolerate the anxiety in the room, tolerate the backlash, and tolerate the loving contact, too.

I hope as you read my book you will try out some of these suggestions. When I do supervisory two-hour introductions with new students in practicum or intern sites they can feel the permission to be more themselves in the room with patients. They usually see questionable, obvious aspects of the patient but do not feel they can discuss what they see. When I suggest they comment directly on certain characteristics they see in session that may be relevant, they are often stunned by the freedom of the intervention. Caution is often stressed with new therapists, along with maintaining a supportive stance and empathetic listening, the meat and potatoes of many therapies. So they don't point out what is obvious in the room. In my sessions with new therapists, they respond to my directions with a feeling of aliveness as they are given permission to be more *out front* with the patient. This freedom brings a smile to their faces, along with excitement and anxiety, too.

I agree that we must always be sensitive to what a patient can tolerate and intuit deeply what will be most helpful. We must hold the patient in positive regard, establish trust through empathy and support, and exhibit a well-thought-out approach. Like the physician's motto, do no harm. Yet, we cannot be hamstrung by norms of psychotherapy that turn it into a palliative chicken soup model, one-size-fits-all.

Lastly, Reich's biophysical theories and techniques bring a wholeness to my work as a psychologist. I do not need to treat only the mental processes but can work with the body as well. The depth of feeling that emerges when the body is included is beyond words. It is a world of powerful, deep feeling, and expression. There is palpable relief when the patient can fully express grief through their sobs and screams of pain. To feel rage fully in their physicality engendering bright red skin, mean eyes, strong breathing, and a sheen of sweat. To reach their arms with longing as they lie on the couch, with warm tears and slow breaths that reach into their belly. These are the depth experiences in my daily patient practice; I offer it to you.

Note

1 I had experiences in spiritual retreats, specifically Arica and others, where I could clearly see the light field around people flickering on and off in a pulsatory movement. The Arica School is a *school of knowledge* founded by Oscar Ichazo in 1968. The trainings help create an opening and clarity that facilitates essential seeing. If you are in the right circumstances and your mind is clear, you might see this field and pulsation surrounding another person. You can also feel the field if you put your hand close to the skin of another and feel its draw on your palm.

Part II

Character Analysis

3   Character Armor

Defining Character Armor

Wilhelm Reich's theory of character analysis was one of his quintessential contributions to the field of psychiatry, psychoanalysis, and psychodynamic theory. A student of Reich's states, "Reich was the first to formulate a coherent theory of character. He showed that different character traits were dependent one upon the other, and that taken together they formed a unitary defense against all emotions that were felt to be dangerous in one way or the other" (Raknes, 2002, 9–10). Character analysis is the clinical technique for transforming a patient's character armor and its unhealthy consequences into a naturally functional approach to life. Character armor defines the ways of being that are defensive, problematic, and obvious to an Orgonomically trained clinician. Friends, family, or work associates may likely have aversive reactions or feel uncomfortable with those defensive traits although they may feel confused about their reactions.

My approach provides a set of instructions and a tool kit to inspire clinicians to add character analysis to their repertoire. The clinician can learn and practice this model exclusively or incorporate the somatic interventions as well. I believe that as we develop as therapists, we interweave our life experiences with various approaches absorbed over the course of our careers. So few modalities can or should be absolutely adhered to. Being a therapist is not a rote exercise in following a rigid protocol. Rather, I hold the practice of therapy much as I would any other art form. It requires autonomy, creativity, and courage. The therapist integrates her uniqueness and her soulful humanness gleaned from her life experiences as well as her hard-won knowledge, expertise, and finely honed skill set.

Let's discuss the essential tenets of the concept of character armor. This term refers to repetitive, stylistic, personality, attitudinal, cognitive, and behavioral patterns that develop throughout the lives of our patients and can be obvious to both the trained and untrained eye—if you are observant. The way a patient walks, talks, carries himself; her style of interacting, communicating; her habits; his relationship to his body; the way he uses his intellect; the volume of his voice; the way she laughs; the way she presents her body—all of these traits define the person's character armor. The composite picture of these character traits often mirrors how the person developed in her family of origin, the role he had in his family, the way she constructed herself to survive in the best way possible. Our character defines our habitual approach to life, how we are known and described.

Character style is set by adolescence. Our character patterns evolve within our family of origin. The lineage of our family—grandparents and great grandparents and the conditions in which they lived—influence how we are and who we become. Character formation begins with in utero experiences that depend on the mental and physical health of the mother, the influences of the father, and the context of the pregnancy. And there are other ingredients in the recipe. First we are all born with our unique genetic template that will define our energetic capacities as well as other basic ingredients. We are born into a community, a society, and a national culture. Cultural influences are important as they set standards, values, conditions, and expectations. Cultural and myriad other influences may conflate choices around sexual orientation. Gender nonconformity enters into the picture: a three-dimensional construct of nature, nurture, and culture as children are allowed to weave their own identity from the gender spectrum (Ehrensaft, 2016, 25). Economic conditions also factor into how we develop and who we become.

As we explore the term *character* we can see that many traits acquired in a lifetime result in effective survival skills that are healthy and functional in our adult lives. These character patterns have helped us succeed throughout our lives. We use them to defend ourselves whenever necessary if challenged or threatened. We learn that we can choose our defenses when needed and disengage them when not required for any given situation. We are not captive to our defense mechanisms but can be conscious and engage a defensive maneuver when required. As therapists we can highlight the adaptive mechanisms and support patients in appreciating their strengths.

Many character patterns are not adaptive and lead to destructive outcomes and difficult consequences. Character analysis determines what is functional and what is not in the patient's repertoire of character patterns, and brings them all into present consciousness so that appropriate choices can be made. When the character pattern is predominately defensive in nature we call it character armor, as it often thwarts the ability of the patient to become her best self as well as compromises all aspects of life, including intimate relationships. So the term *character armor* refers to defensive armor; specific and unique mechanisms to protect ourselves in the world that are not adaptive. Within our protective armor we may feel limited, isolated, and encased or irrationally on top of the world, god's gift to humanity. Character armor can skew one's sense of reality and therefore the way an individual relates. Our character armor keeps us from developing a real self as we rely on these defensive patterns rather than developing from within. Thus at one time or another we may feel like "we don't know who we are" and experience lack of meaning or purpose.

Character armor can prevent awareness, deepening insight, and a flexibility to grow and change. It becomes a rigid, paint-by-numbers way of acting. One patient called it her "shtick," a set of behaviors that felt old and tired. We need help in becoming conscious of how we are so we have options to make changes that could make a difference. Reich saw character armor as a significant barrier to accomplishing a satisfying life in critical areas, as Freud defined, love and work.

A patient's character armor is present in the therapy room as well. The character defense is up and running to protect the patient from all that threatens him in the therapeutic setting: (including but not limited to) his disabling anxiety, challenging feelings, difficult, painful memories as well as current problems for which he is responsible. He does not want to be seen or see himself as weak, sick, vulnerable, out of control, or in pain. The character style runs past those feelings and diverts or controls or avoids or attacks instead. The character armor helps us function over our more difficult and challenging inner lives, conflicts, and tensions. It is a structure with fault lines running through it ready to crack open at any time. Yet we keep playing out our character defense because we don't know another option, nor do we even recognize it as a problem. The character armor is in the therapy room, running its number, but if the therapist doesn't know how to recognize it she will likely bypass it. Then therapy will not be as effective because the mainstay of the work, restructuring the character, will not take place. We could say, in the cliché phrase, we are rearranging the deck chairs on the Titanic.

I often explain to patients that their character is like a well-worn, comfortable, furry slipper. It is molded to your foot until you barely know you have it on. Getting rid of that old, favorite slipper is hard and uncomfortable, as the new pair doesn't seem familiar. The first step is to become aware that you have the slipper on and that it isn't your foot. You have to acknowledge the difference between you and your character style. You have to notice it first. Then you have to begin to dislike it. Then it becomes ego dystonic, no longer fitting your ego comfortably. You even cringe when you act the way you always acted before it was pointed out and understood. Finally it becomes alien and can drop away, and new ways of being take over. Reich understood that to dismantle the character armor is the first order of business. Without accomplishing that the therapist avoids the proverbial elephant in the room.

Understanding the character structure as resistance was another unique contribution to the field. Reich refers to these chronic character defenses as the main resistance to analysis, meaning that, by definition, the defensive character is static, entrenched, and resistant to change. He saw that the main resistance to analysis was revealed not by what the patient said or did, but by the style in which he said or did it. The problem was not the story the patient told but rather how he actually is, how he relates and functions. So the patient comes to therapy "to change or improve her situation" yet the very way she is blocks her ability to change. The character armor is so embedded and habitual that the patient is not yet conscious that her very style is the way she defends against the therapist.

This is a unique and challenging idea to grasp. This guidebook will help the reader become familiar with this concept through examples noted throughout the book.

A male patient, let's call him John, may repetitively exhibit a slick style or a *Teflon coating* that lets everything and everyone seemingly roll off him without effect. So he enters therapy because he is aware that some things are not right in his life. He tells you a significant problem yet claims it doesn't really disturb him. John may top it off and say it is the other guy's fault anyway that things aren't going well. You may comment on his behavior or attitude, and he blows you off with a grin and moves on in the conversation. It is this slick, Teflon style that will defeat the therapist and the patient unless it is pointed out, unraveled, and understood. What you say in terms of content is less significant. Because John's character defense is his resistance and will defeat anything you tell him.

Judy is a detached and ultra-self-sufficient woman, who comes to therapy but resists any therapeutic intervention as her detachment *is* the way she resists. Her detachment leaves her unavailable to self-exploration. She tells you something and when you respond she already knows what you are telling her. She has always known and handled everything herself. You, the therapist, have little to offer as she doesn't really need anyone to help her. This detached style creates a wall of disengagement and no feelings get out or go in. Until that defensive style is realized and dismantled, access to important, relevant painful material and its expression cannot begin. The detachment style served as a distancing device to survive neglect and her painful abandonment feelings. If Judy is self-sufficient she never has to need anyone. She does not have capacity to develop a healthy self-regulating core and identity as she is stuck in detachment and distanced from her real feelings. Judy will have recurring difficulties in intimate relationships.

There are essential developmental phases to be completed in order to have a healthy self-regulating core. I will comment on some basics of developmental psychology in the next chapter but suffice to say by five years of age, a Self should be well established—as the stages of formation have been unfolding—given good enough circumstances. The mature, developed Self is often referenced in the common parlance of psychotherapy as an *individuated* or *authentic* Self. Many of us never had an opportunity to develop a Self as we were too stressed or traumatized to have the resources and permission to discover our Self. We end up with a character structure that is devoid of the components of a healthy Self. We may lack access to our inner feelings, needs, desires and therefore do not manifest them in our lives. We don't know who we are and look to others to define us, manage us, and take care of us. Or we are disengaged from others in order to feel ourselves as separate but end up not being able to have relationships. There are many ways an absence of Self manifests.

One of the reasons to dismantle the character armor is to permit access to the core drives without the inhibitions. Then the Self can be discovered and with it, the capacity to have authentic feelings and insights, and the freedom to create a meaningful and purposeful life.

We develop our character as a way to survive our unique challenges. We master quietness or aggressiveness, helpfulness or defiance. We find the best recipe to handle the situation we are born into: the family, the culture, the political or economic situation, and our genetic foundations. Character formation is adaptive yet can become a confining, destructive modus operandi as well. We continue our habitual, defensive styles throughout our lives without conscious choice. These coping strategies become the defenses that block access to our memories, our important feelings, insights, and our deepest Selves.

Understanding the character style and making a correct patient character diagnosis is an essential skill in this method. Although everyone is unique, Reich developed a typology of character types that fits most propensities. The therapist can do a bit of mixing and matching. I have added character types from James Masterson, MD, as well to round out the developmental picture. I will cover those additions in Part III.

Reich added other defining features (to be discussed in future chapters) that add to the composite you are building to better understand your patients and how to work with them. There is a systematic delineation of types founded on the developmental progression of the patient. If the clinician can decipher the basic character, she knows how to approach the treatment, giving her the best chance of a successful outcome. It is not a mystery or a chaotic conglomerate of symptoms or an extended narrative of details and content unique to each patient. Every patient has his own story that defines what has happened. It is important to understand the set of character inclinations that grew out of the patient's life. Within this unique history and symptoms, the therapist can see a basic composite type that this patient falls into, in general. This typology is so helpful in understanding the patient and putting all the information into an immediate, organized form. In my trainings, students get better and better at crystallizing the essential patterns of patients that come in as demonstration clients. They feel in command of what they are working with. Again, it is not to categorize but rather to see clearly the various types and aspects of character so you can help the patient restructure and create a better life. The therapist hones a skill set that is invaluable.

> Another example is Susan, a self-centered, dominating, and controlling type. This female comes in with high energy and a louder voice, and immediately may complain and control the environment of the office. She will take exception to your paperwork and offer suggestions for improvement. If you intervene, she will shut you down or ignore you. Susan can be argumentative and controlling regarding all the details in her life and the therapy with you. If she doesn't like what you say, she will attack you, even demean you, if necessary. Susan dominates the session.

This patient differs greatly from Richard, a frightened, avoidant, and frozen patient. Richard does not say much. The therapist has to wait patiently for information, and Richard will retreat in fear if pushed. He doesn't give too much but holds his personal information secret. Once you understand him you can work in a way that honors his fear but exposes it. The therapist sees the lifelong dysfunctional approach that plagues Richard.

Once the clinician differentiates the patient's approach to life and the defensive structure, then that becomes the focus of the interventions particularly at the beginning of treatment. Although character analysis will always be on the docket throughout, as it is dismantled the patient is capable of staying open and brings in material freely without so much resistance. Clarity of character formulation is not emphasized in many training programs as important, and rather than focus on the process; the story goes on, the symptoms dominate, and the patient is hidden behind all of that. The therapist feels obliged to listen as if the very act of discussing current content or symptoms will be curative. The idea that the therapist has to "hold" these unwieldy discussions as therapeutic is not effective.

What I observe when supervising clinicians is that they are very astute in their observations. In case presentations they will describe the patient well, picking up on various characteristics: appearance, way of speaking, body language, personality traits, and other specific stylistic qualities as they introduce and describe the patient. They even note how obvious or striking some of these stylistic qualities are and that it tells them something important about the patient. Then that material is never utilized in session even though aspects of it are obviously problematic for the patient and point to something important to focus in on. It's as if all this information is stored within the therapist but never utilized as an entrée into what is obviously relevant to the patient and her problems. Budding therapists don't feel they have "permission" to speak what they notice. Many mature therapists, as well, do not state the obvious.

One student I mentored was describing a patient who had long, unsightly hair and was not well-groomed. His glaring appearance was never a topic of conversation, yet it made a noticeable statement and reflected many aspects of his character and how his life unfolded. The therapist was afraid to discuss his patient's appearance. Therapists are often afraid to comment on the obvious for fear of "offending" the patient. I teach that it is not offending to discuss the obvious so the patient can make sense out of long-term patterns that are not functional. We are more helpful when we are not afraid to do our job.

As we go over student cases, I recommend that they tell the patient that they notice, for example, that the patient speaks very softly and looks down or sideways frequently and investigate that. Or that the patient seems evasive in his eyes, or that the patient speaks so quickly, rushing past what she is saying, or that the patient laughs when speaking of a serious matter, or that the patient smirks when he speaks, or that the patient dominates the session. These interventions can open up the discussion, pointing out real live habit patterns that are actually survival defenses and facades that prevent more authentic aspects from emerging. These very qualities, like evasion or manipulative aspects, usually are detrimental to the patient's functioning, are noticeable, and play out with the therapist in the office. I tell my students, say what you see. The clinician has to be thoughtful, therapeutically neutral, and the patient has to have a sense that you are speaking directly, with the best of intentions, and that you are there to help the patient. When you address the outermost layer of defense, you begin peeling away the false self, and the patient has more access to real affect and true expression. You and the patient learn in a here-and-now, alive way, how this style developed: his obsequiousness; her stubborn or guarded approach to others; his reserved, flat way of speaking; his numbness; her chronic rationalizing. The patient begins to understand herself without intellectualization but rather with real emotion and contact with historically relevant material; why she acts the way she does and the real-life consequences.

A big problem I see in professionals and students is that they are lost in the patient's stories du jour rather than working with the obvious character armoring. They feel trapped, hijacked by the patient, and become a captive audience. This patient behavior is often a manifestation of a conscious or unconscious need to control the session, tell stories, and keep the therapist off the trail of difficult or painful feelings, thoughts, or memories. No one likes to feel anxious, and we bypass it any chance we have. Therapists are often quite afraid to interrupt the patient, reticent to stop the patient from "going on and on." Aimless storytelling or narratives about events, talking about day-to-day items that are not really important to the problems at hand, complaining about others, and intellectualizing can be defensive in nature. These can be manifestations of a resistance to going deeper and entering the process with the therapist. I speak to clinicians about their fear of engendering negative feelings from the patient and will discuss this aspect in a future chapter.

Thus, the patient's character traits/style function as a unitary defense, blocking difficult experiences and feelings. Further, the character inhibits expressions that haven't felt natural to communicate due to one's past and present experience. Maybe a patient is terrified of vulnerability or of being angry, or frightened of his deep grief and depression. The therapist may think the patient is working on important material when he is focused on the current story, or even his history, but the defensive structure is actively in place so the deeper contact with feelings and pain, and the real issues are not surfacing due to the presence of the character defense.

These defenses Reich called character armor. Reich was able to show that this armor had its origin in childhood where the creation of a multilayered defensive structure began. In other words, embedded in the style, including its diversionary tactics, is the patient's entire defensive structure created throughout his lifetime. The patient's survival strategies and history are right there in the room, in the here and now. The intrapsychic structure has captured and is replaying the patient's development. This was and is a radical concept.

Reich states,

> Economically, the character in everyday life and the character resistance in the analysis serve as a means of avoiding what is unpleasant, of establishing and preserving psychic (even if neurotic) balance, and finally of consuming repressed quantities of instinctual energy and/or quantities which have eluded repression.
>
> (Reich, *Character Analysis*, 1972, 52–53)

Basic Structure of the Psyche: Layers of Experience

Reich defined the structure of the psyche as made up of the *core*, *secondary layer*, and *facade*. Imagine a circle with three layers. The facade is a thin outer layer, the core is the innermost circle, and in between is a thicker middle layer. The facade is our social personality that interfaces more superficially in the world. We all operate with a facade at times in order to conduct our business throughout our days. Hopefully we can drop our social facade with our self and intimate others most of the time.

The core is made up of our basic drives that in optimal situations are allowed to blossom freely without being overly inhibited by parents, school, work, and society. Our natural impulses to love or express aggression and anxiety emanate and stream spontaneously from our core out into the world. If an individual is raised in a relatively healthy family and society, these drives are allowed expression. Love is responded to, and communications and bodily expressions of aggression are accepted and listened to. Anxiety has its place to be experienced and expressed. The baby learns to trust that his expressions will be accepted and his needs met. As the child grows up she learns that not all feelings and needs will be gratified and learns to tolerate frustrations as well. Yet, her authentic expressions are respected, and she grows up comfortably expressing her feelings, emotions, and needs. In this optimal situation the core expressions make their way to the surface and out into the world of family, friends, work relationships, and love relationships. The individual develops freely a Self that is a composite of learning through life experiences, freedom to arrive at autonomous thoughts, feelings, and actions. The Self has been supported by others and develops a trust in a personal sense of self, meaning, and purpose. The individual with a Self has been free to create it with minimal inhibitions and lives in contact with his core drives.

The secondary or middle layer is made up of various contortions from blockage of our natural impulses. For example, if we have experienced multiple and continuous disappointments or serious rejections early on and therefore could not express needs and get them met, we would likely retreat and bury our loving feelings and ultimately become resigned to a sense of being unlovable. Consequently, we might feel angry and then when that feeling is stymied, we end up feeling hatred and we hide that with its opposite, a pleasing attitude. The secondary layer is made up of contortions of feelings that end up producing harshness, hatred, rage, guilt, shame, and a myriad of other conflicting feelings all bound up in the secondary layer and covered with a false facade. When feelings are tangled up and knotted, they create a state of constant tension, inner conflict, and distorted emotions, thoughts, and attitudes. The core feelings that express our basic needs—love, aggression, and anxiety—have been blocked and diverted into the middle layer. There they become tangled up and distorted. Therapy needs to unpack the middle layer and create order out of chaos by unraveling the knots so that feelings are less encumbered by tangles and the energy of the system can flow freely without obstruction from the core to the periphery.

The middle layer produces confusion and misperception of others. We may see others as critical, demanding, unfair, or threatening because we have all these tangled-up conflicts that get projected on to others, including the therapist. If we have contortions of emotions that we haven't sorted out, then our relationships reflect that confusion and it becomes difficult to sort out what's what in relationship dynamics.

The clinician needs to understand how this defensive layering process works. This discussion will be a bit dense, but it is important to understand how our character armoring is constructed because as patients or therapists we want to deconstruct it so we can feel better. Reich defined the creation of armor as the stratification of the layers of defense and created a schema of the structure of armoring. As I stated, it is an interlacing structure that is created on top of the natural, spontaneous healthy core streaming impulses of love, aggression, and anxiety that we are born with. These spontaneous impulses can become thwarted, inhibited, or warded off. As each impulse is inhibited, it at the same time inhibits an even deeper repressed impulse. These instincts can split up or dissociate: one part can turn against itself and the other continues out toward the world. Notice Figure 3.1, which shows a line (of feeling) with an arrow moving outward and then meeting resistance, splitting into two arrows, and becoming two opposing feelings. Some lines split and circle back, others split off with a line moving outward and splitting again. These lines that are blocked illustrate how our feelings and impulses, when inhibited, start moving against themselves and create a maze of compromised needs and impulses, and a state of chronic inner conflict. These reside in the conscious and unconscious mind. And they manifest in behaviors in the world that can be destructive or lead to serious depression, somatic complaints, chronic anxiety, and/or resignation (Reich, *Character Analysis*, 1972, 308–318).

Imagine the earth's layers, from the inner core outward, layer upon layer reflecting time, chemical interactions, and the flow of matter. We have similar layers within our psyche and unconscious and our own unique flow of plasmatic movement, feeling, sensation, hormonal and nervous system interactions, and time. To unlock the layers of the psyche we have to both understand the structure and work somewhat methodically to uncover and decipher the

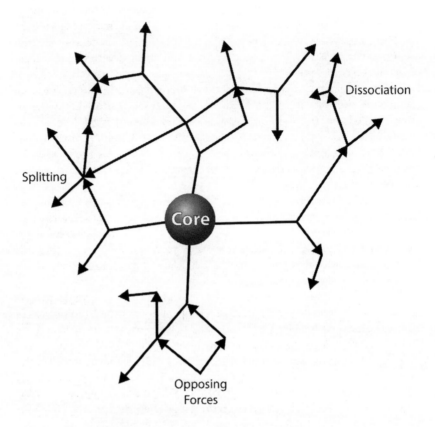

Dissociation

Splitting

Core

Opposing
Forces

Development of Armor

Figure 3.1 Schema of the Structure of the Armor

Source: Patricia R. Frisch, 2017, adapted from Schema of the Structure of the Armor in Reich, *Character Analysis*, 1972, p. 318.

depth layers and stresses within. The structural map helps us understand what we observe in the therapy room. Further it helps us organize our interventions so we are not delving into the subterranean layers when the patient psyche is located at the crust level.

Contactlessness: A Layer amid the Layers

Often as therapists we experience deadness in the room with a patient. We don't feel lively nor do we feel a flow of energy or contact between ourselves and the patient. Is the deadness coming from the therapist, the patient, or the field of interaction? I will digress a brief moment to introduce a concept that is important for our work. The "field" is the dynamic shared space that exists within and without the two or more individuals in the office. In field theory, Kurt Lewin described what is called an interactional field that is comprised of the psychology of individuals involved and/or the social environment itself and has a life of its own. Much like a family system, there is a larger space of interaction that plays its own unique role and all members help create the specific conditions. In this theory the therapist has to be aware of her contribution as well, to the conditions in the room. Therefore, when two people meet they create a third element of synergy that may be resonant or disturbing or somewhere in the middle. It is good to notice what we might term the general feeling or conditions "in the room" between two or more people. Sometimes we might say, "There seems to be a heaviness in the room." Or we might say, "Wow! We really understood and sensed each other, there was a flow of relating, a flow of energy between us." This concept is of particular importance in group or family therapy (Lewin, 1997).

Proceeding forward, it is important to notice how we feel with our patients. We may feel low energy that day and/or the patient may seem disinterested, lifeless, and bored. If we have differentiated our own condition and feel relatively stable energy, then we know it is a certain deadness or blankness coming from the patient. I will digress further here to explain the origins of this emotional layer, as it is important to understand it when you experience a patient as empty, flat, or barely in the room.

As I explained in the prior segment on character structure, we build our defenses to ward off painful feelings. As emotions are blocked, they branch off, in let's say, two directions and then circle back toward each other and end up going head to head (see Figure 3.2). This results in stasis, an unhealthy resolution that stops energetic movement much like a standoff in a war. Everything grinds to a halt and there is deadlock. The person experiences an inner deadness or apathy resulting in a state of contactlessness. Reich coined the term contactlessness as a critical layer of defense to be understood by the therapist. As the therapist and patient work through the layers of defense, layers of contactless will emerge. The patient may experience a layer of contactlessness as an inner experience of numbness or a feeling of frozenness or dullness. As difficult memories and affect are stored historically, sometimes the patient is overwhelmed with events and feelings and unconsciously screens out more globally, to make the entire experience go away. Often trauma is stored and then disconnected, or to use a technical term, dissociated, so it can be out of awareness. Contactlessness is an emotional and motility block such that everything alive is deadened. This layer will get worked through as well, in the treatment.

As therapists we often observe that a patient will experience deep and painful feelings associated with difficult memories and the next session he will have forgotten what he was working on. Or she will be detached from her therapeutic progression. He may state he feels empty and has nothing to say. Or she will feel a strong feeling and then go blank or get confused. She is likely

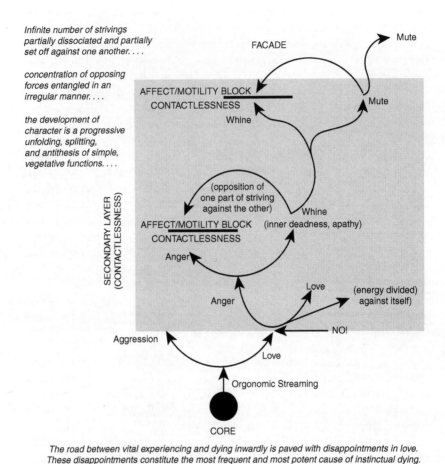

Infinite number of strivings partially dissociated and partially set off against one another. . . .

concentration of opposing forces entangled in an irregular manner. . . .

the development of character is a progressive unfolding, splitting, and antithesis of simple, vegetative functions. . . .

FACADE

Mute

AFFECT/MOTILITY BLOCK
CONTACTLESSNESS

Mute

Whine

(opposition of one part of striving against the other)

Whine

SECONDARY LAYER
(CONTACTLESSNESS)

AFFECT/MOTILITY BLOCK
CONTACTLESSNESS

(inner deadness, apathy)

Anger

Love

(energy divided) against itself)

Anger

NO!

Aggression

Love

Orgonomic Streaming

CORE

The road between vital experiencing and dying inwardly is paved with disappointments in love. These disappointments constitute the most frequent and most potent cause of instinctual dying.

Figure 3.2 Reich's Stratification of the Individual's Infantile Experience of Love

Source: Richard Blasband and Patricia Frisch, 2009, adapted from Reich's Stratification of the Individual's Infantile Experience of Love in Reich, *Character Analysis*, 1972, pp. 299–323.

hitting a layer of contactlessness that protects her from more painful feeling or memory.

Reich gives us an example. He worked with a patient with an overlay of agreeable helpfulness who also dropped repeatedly into a state of contactlessness. Reich was stymied by the contactless quality until he understood the origin of patient's attachment style and dependency. The helpfulness fulfilled the function of holding-in and suppressing his aggressive tendencies and more importantly compensated for his inner estrangement from the world. Behind the reactive helpful and sticky character style was aggression, and layered within and a deep feeling of estrangement (Reich, *Character Analysis*, 1972, 311–312).

When a patient feels deep alienation and inner deadness those feelings are very difficult to face. There is no aliveness or experience of energy toward life and the patient can feel desperate. Here the defense of contactlessness, which is mostly unconscious, helps to camouflage the deeply estranged experience.

This example illustrates contactlessness: a deep inner alienation from the world, covered with a readiness to be helpful as a defense. The defenses are structured: repressed demands, repressing defensive forces, and a layer of contactless psychic structure between the two. The contactlessness appears as a wall, the result of the contradiction between two currents pulling in opposite directions, thus establishing equilibrium. The blocking creates an immobilization within the system and deadness and apathy reign due to the opposing forces arriving at a standstill.[1]

As we create breakthroughs in the armor we can see an alternation between vegetative currents and emotional blocks. It is important to understand how the natural movement in the organism can turn into sustained rigidity. The goal is to reinstate vegetative streaming. In post-traumatic stress disorder, numbness can be lifesaving. Since continual oscillation from one direction to the other becomes intolerable, the individual gives way to numbness. "Wherever natural, adequate instinctual impulses are denied direct relationship to objects of the world, the result is anxiety, as the expression of a crawling into oneself and the development of a wall of contactlessness" (Reich, *Character Analysis*, 1972, 316).

As the patient explores his contactlessness, he can see how it pervasively affects all his relationships. Due to paralyzing and deep inner conflict, patients feel a profound inner alienation, isolation, apathy, inner deadness, depersonalization, and estrangement from others. These feelings can be traced back to this contradiction between deeper unmet needs, defenses of protection, and a compromise in the tendency to escape into oneself. Ambivalence is a direct manifestation of this paradoxical intrapsychic structure.

All psychic tendencies are dissociated into those operating simultaneously "toward the world" and "away from the world" in opposition to one another (Reich, *Character Analysis*, 1972, 317). As Reich stated eloquently, "The wall between vital experiencing and dying inwardly is paved with disappointments in love. These disappointments constitute the most frequent and most potent cause of instinctual dying" (Reich, *Character Analysis*, 1972, 317). The character analytic approach brings order to each patient's complex picture, as the history of his or her psychic structure is unraveled (see Reich, *Character Analysis*, 1972, 317–321 for full discussion).

Methodical Interventions: Work from the Facade to Core

Reich emphasized that interpretations that are out of sequence fall on deaf ears and actually sabotage the progress of the therapy. If one makes an intervention that refers to an early experience in childhood, like longing for love, and the patient does not feel connected emotionally to that experience, he will not emotionally absorb the intervention. Therapists may realize that their intervention was ineffective when the patient has no feeling connection to what was said. Then the intervention is not helpful; it is relegated to an idea to be stored in the mind. The patient may intellectualize about it but has no feeling connection to the material. Why? Because the outer character armor layers have not been dissolved. The interpretation is co-opted by the intellectualizing defensive structure and used as cannon fodder for further defense against authentic painful feelings. The patient needs to actually feel the emotions associated with loss of love, for example, otherwise he may know his story but have no access to the emotion and will remain stuck.

Many patients come to therapy having had prior therapies, know their story inside and out, yet feel little and are still difficult individuals to deal with. They still have obnoxious ways of relating yet have intellectualized their issues and their history. This is not helpful to their progress. Change comes from becoming aware of how they defend at the surface level so they can stop those habits and behaviors. Then they can gain access to why they have acted in certain ways and dig deeper into what happened. That knowledge is accompanied by heartfelt feeling associated with it. True awareness will elicit deep recognition and expression of sorrow or anger. Healing comes with true recognition accompanied by the feelings that were once repressed. Then they can learn to act differently. Don't make interpretations from your insights when the patient isn't ready. I know when I am off if I make an interpretation and the patient looks at me, nods, and may agree but feels nothing. I know then I was not in contact with the patient but was up in my head. Stay in contact with the patient so you know where they are.

As the outermost layers fall away—compliance, smiling and laughing over serious issues, intellectualizing, attacking, running, confusion, numbness, withdrawal—the therapist and patient are faced with the next layer of defense and resistance. Each are worked through methodically to the deepest layers of memory and emotion. Often surrounding the core are profound abandonment feelings, longing and grief for the loss of love and for the loss of their real Selves.

Understand that symptoms are a result of basic character patterns and resultant behaviors. Many therapies focus on the symptoms, diagnose the patient by their symptoms, and then treat the symptoms as the focus of therapy. Depressive or bipolar disorders or anxiety disorders, for example, are a conglomerate of symptoms that clinicians treat, many times with medications, without examining the character structure as the root cause. These symptoms directly relate to the character structure and, once delineated, make the symptoms understandable and treatable at its source in the character structure rather than addressing and treating the symptoms superficially.

Importance of Contact and Tracking

To observe and diagnose character, the therapist needs to be in contact with the patient. What does the term *contact* mean? The first requirement of contact is a minimal level of movement of energy with excitation. We discussed in an earlier chapter how the amoeba moves with energy and excitation toward and away from resources and threats. When an organism is free of blocks there is flowing plasmatic movement. When we are healthy, our organism allows for a continual ebb and flow of movement without stasis, punctuated with sensations, perceptions, feelings, and awareness of our body and our needs. We may have feelings of liveliness streaming through our bodies. The result of this movement and sensation in the organism is a feeling of aliveness. We have connection to our feelings, needs, and impulses without too much tension or feelings of blockage. Or we may feel sluggish at times and feel fatigued or less energetic; that is a normal ebb and flow. Anyone's ability to make contact is dependent, as I stated, on a minimal energy level with some excitation. If we are defended to the point of severe armoring in our character and correlated in our body, then our ability to make contact may be limited. Many of our patients have limited capacity to make contact or sustain contact through an entire therapy session.

When our contact is sufficient we can tune in to our patient simultaneously as we tune in to ourselves. We extend our personal level of contact to others and are able to gather impressions about others and our environment. Like the amoeba we can move toward what is pleasant and feel anxiety with elements that are disturbing. This is informative as to what we are sensing with a patient. When we are armored our contact is reduced and our ability to scan the environment and perceive with clarity is also minimized.

Reich discussed extending our contact from self and other, to encompass contact with the cosmos. When we are in contact with nature and the universe, so to speak, we can open to the vastness and at times, we experience ourselves as an integral part of everything. We fit in, we belong, and we feel at one with the natural world. We sense the sun, stars, soil, plants, and trees as integral ingredients within our cells, and we share in the intricate system of life. With contact, we feel a sense of responsibility for all things and feel sadness at the destruction of our beautiful natural resources. We feel from our core (core contact), and that results in cosmic feelings and a functional approach to our world. We can say we are in contact, feeling both the pain of our mutually shared existence as well as the joy of the life force that moves everything.

I have defined contact and contactlessness. Let me discuss one more of Reich's concepts—*substitute contact*. This term refers to our most superficial social behaviors and can be experienced as insincere or hypocritical behaviors. There is minimal movement of energy—not enough to have genuine interactions in the moment. One can feel substitute contact as it lacks authenticity. Some examples are affectations of style, jocularity, giggling, sales or marketing speak, insincere flirtation, overly intense enthusiasm, talking when no one is listening, childish chattering, droning complaints, and many other modes of contactless behaviors. These behaviors need to be commented on and stopped in session. The patient may feel anxiety when these behaviors are noted. He has come to depend on these ways of being to feel comfortable. When stopped, he will feel anxiety as he has limited ways to connect.

Developing good contact within and with the patient is a critical concept in this treatment approach. First we must be in contact with our selves, with our organism capable of movement, sensation, and openness. Then we can see clearly, with our eyes and our perceptions, the person with whom we are working. There is a level of excitation in us that brings our aliveness into the room and into the engagement. Our first task with our patient is to establish contact with them. Authentic contact feels good (Baker, 1967, 67).

Why? Because when there is good contact, there is an absence of defenses in both people. When we are in contact we can observe, read cues, and grasp what the other is thinking and feeling. We can see the patient and her defensive structure as it plays out. That is our job: to keenly observe and sense what is happening in the other so we can shed light. Establishing contact is the single most important aspect of character analysis. We must be very present, in the here and now, with all our perceptions, sensations, thoughts, and feelings engaged.

When an individual is armored there are defenses at play; the character structure is in the way of genuine contact. Maybe the patient feels inadequate, so the defensive response might be to dominate and play the opposite card. Then he is not really in contact with you but rather his character style is his way of relating and he may not be conscious of his chronic defensive mechanisms. One of our tasks is to comment on defenses and help bring the patient into better contact. When we notice a patient has moved out of contact we can comment and bring him back or have him understand why he moved away. So the therapist has to track well to recognize immediately when the other is out of contact.

> Let's discuss a couple, Liz and Henry. Liz complains about a repetitive couple issue. She was with her husband and wanted to tell him something important to her, and she was met with what she terms his chronic distractedness that she translates as disinterest and disengagement. Liz feels he lacks interest when she tells him something having to do with her feelings. This is a typical complaint of women with their male partners. Often in relationships energy levels can be off and one has energy for conversation and the other is tired. That is normal. But sometimes one partner, due to his or her character defenses, has trouble with engagement and the other may have a style that is off-putting. In fact Henry does avoid engagement with her rather than tell her directly that her approach makes him angry. He feels she is relentlessly intrusive. In character analytic couple's therapy we work with the character defenses of each person to illuminate how the defenses of each are in the way of genuine contact. Then each can dismantle his or her own defenses as each gains understanding of self and other.

Contact depends first on a minimal level of energy and excitation essential for contact. Then we hope for openness rather than defensiveness to perceive context and have sensitivity to respond appropriately. When we have character blocks we might respond but our response doesn't fit the situation. If there is something serious being discussed, like a friend is very ill, and the other person is smiling or is distracted, we can say she is out of contact with the situation. Her response is not congruent with the context at hand. There can be incongruous facial expressions, insensitivity, detachment, speediness; these qualities illustrate being out of contact with another. We go through the motions, living in our facade and not dropping deeper. Contactlessness is felt as a highly unsatisfying condition in relationships. Couples and family members long for real contact but few know how to attain that. The lack of contact creates deep disappointments in love (Baker, 1967, 69–70).

> Serena is a female patient obsessed with her relationships with men. She is telling a story about her latest escapade. She begins to look up, loses connection with you, and frankly begins babbling about who said what to whom. She is in a trance of words without staying in contact with the seriousness of her situation. Why is she drifting off lost within the story with great animation? Because as she talks she does not have to feel the discomfort with this repetitive storyline of countless relationships that have not stabilized, her unhappiness with her situation, and her deeper anxiety about relationship losses. So the trance-like stories disconnect her from her pain, and she is out of contact with you.

In therapy, our first job is to be in contact with our patient. Create opportunities for the patient to be in contact with you. Interrupt the contactless habits by inviting the patient to focus, stop the story telling, stop the rushing past his feelings, or confront his nonchalance about a critical issue he is superficially dismissing.

Tracking is a critical vehicle for the therapists. As therapists, we must watch what is happening in the room. Is the patient deflecting from what is important? Is she moving off a topic when her feelings are heating up inside? Is he controlling you or the topic and not wanting to relate to you and your input? Is she smirking and being slippery about getting serious? Is he looking down and melting into the couch?

The therapist needs to track the moment-by-moment activity in the session, track the exact cues. Don't ignore them; rather bring them up and establish genuine contact with the patient as you are discussing what is real in the room at any given moment. Then the patient can connect to what she is actually doing with you, the how and the why.

If you are sleepy—and we are allowed, at times, to have these various responses—then you know your contact will not be the best. Be aware of that. Are you mirroring what is in the patient rather than adjusting it? When we are good at tracking we can see the character defenses at play in the room. Are you sleepy because your patient is bored? Boredom is actually an absence of contact. We are never bored if we are truly present in most situations—unless it is a boring teacher in traffic school or we are captive in a stuffy room.

If our contact is good then we can track once we know how. The better we track, the easier it is to see the character patterns of our patient. The more we see those and gain clarity, the more helpful we can be.

Note

1 Contactlessness is the result of residual energy forming a wall, a static manifestation that creates equilibrium from the tension between the two opposing forces.

4   The Origins of Character Types
Changing Sexual Norms

Character Analysis: Summary

Character analysis begins with the therapist's contact with the patient. With close tracking of the patient's style and content, you can identify key problem areas that define the character style, the developmental picture that likely formed her approach to life, and how this composite manifests in the patient's current issues. This consolidation of information can occur in the first two to three sessions. You can grasp the basic aspects of the character and have a differential between two or three types to pick from. Before we go over Reich's character types in detail, let's summarize how you begin to define your patient's character.

In my supervision sessions with students and professionals I encourage them to hone in from the beginning. As they interview the patient in the first and second sessions with the goal of getting a broad and detailed overview of presenting problems, current context, and critical historical nexus points, they can arrive at some initial or provisional conclusions about the patient's character style and how these chronic patterns result in his presenting problems. I suggest the therapist summarize the salient points observed at the end of the first session and present them to the patient. It is similar to the approach of an excellent physician sleuth who notes the various symptoms, asks the right questions, combs through his mental database, and comes up with a likely diagnosis and etiology of the problem—although further tests will need to confirm his hypothesis. The difference is we focus on lifelong psychological patterns, how they came to be, and how they play out in the present. Those patterns and their consequences help explain the presenting symptoms. We can see—from an overview of developmental and historical markers—how the patterns originate and we can confirm our initial hypothesis as we proceed.

The patient wants to be seen and understood and offered an insightful analysis that goes beyond the therapist listening passively to her presenting problems and symptoms. As you suss out the character patterns and the critical problem areas, you can discern what is most important to offer the patient. The discussion of problems helps you see how the patient approaches life. You may spot a critical problem that the patient hasn't faced that indicates a character predisposition. The patient feels challenged yet relieved that the therapist is willing to speak in a forthright way about what she sees, hears, and provisionally concludes.

Lisa is a student in a supervision group I mentored. We discussed a case with the proverbial elephant in the room that was neither highlighted in the case presentation nor to the patient. This is a classic situation with professionals learning the method. Lisa presented a female, married patient, "Sally," in her late 20s, who comes in with a few presenting problems. Sally focused on her marital issues, difficulty in her relationship with her parents, and work-related issues. She had been in therapy before and felt she had many insights, but stated "the insights had no real effect" on her life. She had mastery of psychological jargon. The elephant in the room was that at 28 years of age, she was still living with her parents, along with her spouse, and had never left home for any substantial length of time. The family ran the business that she was a part of, out of the home. Lisa, in an earlier session, made one comment about this fact and it was met with dismissal. Lisa moved on quickly as she was headed off at the pass by the patient and felt "blown off" and feared approaching it again. The therapist went instead to more information gathering, because, as she stated, that direction was more psychologically comfortable for her. The session might have had more impact if Lisa had responded to the dismissal by saying, "I noticed when I brought up the subject of you living with your parents, your reaction was dismissive and you quickly moved away from my comment to something else. What happened?"

Stopping and calling attention to Sally's most important problem of dependence and noting how the intervention is received will facilitate a deeper recognition about the most critical issue and highlight her defensiveness in facing it. Sally's aborted development of independence and autonomy could be noted as an important theme at the start of therapy. Also, the intervention immediately focuses on her resistance to the therapist's intervention thus highlighting the therapeutic relationship straightaway and Sally's defining character resistance. Reich emphasized that the therapist should always notice the first transference resistance (Reich, *Character Analysis*, 1972, 33). There it was. As you note resistance, the patient may get in touch with what is painful underneath the resistance, how she hides her pain, and further, she comes more directly into relationship with you in a more honest way.

Through the maze of information gathering, Lisa held all the information without shadings of importance. Now three sessions in, Sally, who exhibits a critical style toward her husband and mother and has a "have-it-together" presentation, is covering a serious dependency problem that has not surfaced. Instead, Sally smiles, acts confident, and presents as if there is nothing really wrong as she denies her real problems. In character analytic therapy we comment on the style of smiling and acting like there is nothing wrong. That helps the patient see her style of defense to avoid facing significant issues. Lisa, with supervision, could understand how she was colluding with Sally's presenting character defenses and got lost in the weeds with the patient rather than pointing the therapy in the right direction.

Comment on the elephant in the room and don't run away. Highlight it and if the patient is resistant, highlight that. Note for the patient aspects of his style that he uses to hide his difficulties. How she defends against what is uncomfortable to admit. That will net you some excellent work right away, and you will be well on your way to establishing a meaningful therapeutic relationship that will have relevant present-moment intensity. The patient will go beyond cognitive insights to begin a process that interrupts and changes her basic character patterns.

Always look with your common-sense eye at the most significant problem and obvious character pattern presented to you. If there is a serious lifestyle issue presented, like being a young adult who never left the parental home, that is a significant problem in the maze of various other articulated difficulties. That is a problem that has a significant root; the patient was not able to separate and launch her life and shows regression illustrating an earlier impasse in her developmental progression. This information helps you hone in on a character diagnosis. Of course, a patient may have left home, graduated from college, and returned home to parents before launching the next phase. That is a different scenario as he did succeed in separating and meeting autonomous goals.

As you interview your patient during the first sessions, you are aware of how he relates both to you and his difficulties. Notice the initial style, the way he interacts, how he looks at you and how he responds to what you say. These aspects will give you a sense of his most dominant presenting characteristics. You will look to see if she uses control as her most important defining trait. Or does she retreat easily? Does she focus on others exclusively? Is he initially competitive and interested in asserting his power? Is he evasive? The therapist needs to define the character style and how that style manifests in the presenting problems. I will define the various character types in the next three chapters so that you will have definitive templates that will help you understand your patients better. From the beginning you have a bounty of information if you know how to decipher it. You are then able to relay this to the patient and start off with clarity on a grounded footing. The patient sees that your style is direct, engaged, and incisive.

When you begin with a new patient you want to establish an element of rapport so the patient is somewhat comfortable with you and can feel confident and sufficiently secure to commit to treatment. You offer clear insight and the patient senses she will be helped in tangible ways, but not colluded with in her obvious bad habits. As you establish good contact with the patient, he in turn has an initial sense that you have his best interests in mind and will help him if he does his part. So you calibrate your interventions so they are most suitable for each particular patient. You test the waters to see what he can handle and what is the most effective way to work with him. In the vast majority of situations patients readily accept my directness. I make the interventions in a clear, neutral, and forthright way.

However, if interventions are made from the therapist's reactivity, they won't fly. Interventions have to be unencumbered by the therapist's feelings so they can be received without static. If the therapist is fearful or overly cautious, then he will sideline what he really ought to be saying and the therapy becomes diluted.

I recommend therapists maintain their own personal therapy so they sustain deep insight into their own character defenses and continually work through their own traumas and painful challenges. The therapist must know what triggers him and when he is reacting to a patient's attitude, content, or style. Therapists need to know their own weaknesses and difficulties and keep those out of the room with the patient.

Establish the therapeutic relationship through a combination of sensitive contact with the patient while challenging her to look at herself right from the start. I encourage therapists to begin engaging defenses from the first session on. But to engage the defensive structure, a map is helpful. This will help you to gain mastery of these patterns and recognize them readily.

Reich's character typology is based on a developmental paradigm that anchors his types. I have incorporated the broad strokes of his typology and abbreviated his map of characters while adding from other resources to create my own concise reference of character types delineated in this guidebook. In order to understand these types, we will start with a basic summary of early development and theoretical developmental paradigms.

Stages of Development: Freud to Object Relations

We start life as a tiny embryo that becomes a fetus, floating in optimally spacious conditions for healthy growth and development. The physical and psychological conditions of the pregnancy affect the in utero experience. Through infancy and toddlerhood we make large developmental strides and are quite malleable and vulnerable to our parental figures and how they relate to us. Our brains are forming in these very early years and critical neural pathways are developed under the right circumstances.

There are critical developmental gateways and certain key growth tasks to accomplish to get us ready for the next gateway. At any passageway, we may experience interference and can lose ground as our development progresses. Ultimately, growing up and becoming an adult is a unique and challenging experience, a blend of many elements working together to create who we become.

We may move through our developmental passages in a fairly unobstructed way accomplishing development of a healthy Self—or not. If core feelings are acknowledged and unimpeded, we grow up with our aliveness intact and can express our true nature for the most part. We move from the delicious, fused, secure dependency of infancy to independence and autonomy starting in toddlerhood. If we have a safe, stable, and regulated environment we feel trusting and have a secure bond. Those feelings allow us to venture forth without too much looking back. In the course of our development, we carry the trust and security forward into our intimate relationships and achieve healthy sexual expression as part of that intimacy. Our sexuality is unimpeded as we grow up and we become comfortable with the sexual aspect of intimacy. We become our best selves without too many encumbrances. Even in the best developmental circumstances, there are challenges that need to be reckoned with and those challenges are necessary for the maturation process. That is one scenario, a fairly ideal one.

The other possible scenario is that our development is plagued with difficulties that steer us away from a capacity to develop the Self in the many areas needed for a full life. We are diverted, knocked off course due to inhibiting or uncontained family dynamics; parental clinging; parental loss or neglect; addiction; lack of a stable, regulated household; cultural mandates or discrimination; and so on. In those cases, we may learn maladaptive coping strategies in order to survive and reduce pain. Some defensive strategies do not stymie our development, and we can become fairly functional, albeit with plenty of baggage to cart away when we are ready to face it. Or our strategies for survival can be highly dysfunctional and we suffer greatly and those around us suffer as well (Frisch, June 26, 2014, blog, "Reich's Character Types").

There are multiple theories of development that delineate these various stages of how we grow from the tiniest seed, through infancy, toddlerhood, latency, and adolescence and beyond to become a functioning, mature, fulfilled adult. Multiple theories highlight different aspects of development in terms of what phases are seen as most important to healthy development. Since Freud began peering into the psyche, theorists have pondered what are the motivating, organizing principles that shape our development. These are big questions, and this book will not address them except to give a cursory sense necessary to our understanding of the roots of Reich's viewpoint and the roots of my amplification of his character typology into my system of types.

In order to help you understand Reich's system, I will provide an overview of Reich's developmental frame of reference for the types as a whole. Reich reflected elements of the analytic theories of his time, with Freud as his original mentor. Freud hypothesized early on in his career that physical symptoms are often a surface manifestation of unconscious and repressed conflicts. This was a revolutionary theory of the human psyche that deeply held conflicts in the mind could manifest in a variety of physical symptoms (Freud and Breuer, 2004). Freud, in his studies of the unconscious, determined that conflicts stemmed from inhibited, primitive wishes, impulses, and drives, predominantly libidinal drives held in the repressed cauldron of the unconscious. One goal of psychoanalysis was to make the unconscious conscious. He discovered that talk therapy itself, called free association, was helpful in alleviating symptoms, a revolutionary concept for the times.

The overarching conceptual context of psychoanalysis was Freud's redefinition of sexuality to include its infantile manifestations and later the child's desire for sexual relations with the parent of the opposite sex as described in the *Oedipus complex*, a term Freud coined. Oedipus was a fifth-century Greek mythological character who kills his father and marries his mother. The play *Oedipus Rex* written by Sophocles in 429 BC became a successful production in the 1880s and 1890s. Freud formulated the Oedipal desire as a universal, innate psychological phenomenon. This desire, by both males and females was, of course, unconscious and deeply repressed but nonetheless defined the third phase of development, according to Freud, called the phallic stage (ages three to five). The other five psychosexual stages, according to Freud, were oral, anal, phallic, latent, and genital. These stages define the source of libidinal pleasure in the different erogenous zones of the infant and child's body. An erogenous zone is an area of the body that has heightened sensitivity, and stimulation may generate a sexual response such as relaxation, excitation, or orgasm. According to this theory, resolution of the Oedipal complex occurs when the child identifies with the same sex parent. Unsuccessful resolution, according to Freud, led to neurosis in adult life that manifested in individual symptoms and difficulties in adult relationships. Earlier in his career, Freud placed great emphasis on the sexual origins of a patient's neurosis.

Reich's character types emanate from Freud's developmental paradigm that focused on the Oedipal-phallic phase of development. Reich classified his character types as essentially neurotic as they had reached the phallic stage albeit with Oedipal conflicts. Even attaining the phallic stage, he postulated that there could be blockages or fixations at earlier phases of development that form and alter the individual character types. He grouped pre-oedipal developmental problem areas originating in the infant or child's development within a larger category called the oral character. He also utilized the schizophrenic character category to address earlier phase problems. I will explain this type in a following chapter. Predominantly his typology is based on the assumption that the psychosexual phallic stage was achieved even if encumbered by earlier fixations. Development of capacity for healthy sexual functioning was the primary focus. For Reich, health was a function of a satisfying sexual life.

One place Reich diverged from Freud was to see the character itself as neurotic and label it character neurosis, a new concept he contributed. His theory included an examination of character formation as a significant aspect of neurosis. This understanding led to his formulation of specific character types that define various distorted patterns.

In Freud's classical analytic theory, it is understood that development is a function of drive gratification of the infant and child. Object relations theory (1920–1960) integrates early attachment development between mother and child as the primary organizing principle of development, in that the child is relational seeking, not just drive seeking. Object relations theorists focused on attachment as the most important motivational organizer.[1]

In the course of my clinical implementation of Reich's theories, I came to appreciate the relevance of early attachment developmental phases to my patients' problems. I felt an expansion of Reich's character typology was necessary to complete the picture. I saw many adult patients reflect serious difficulties that originated in these earlier developmental phases. They had trouble separating from parents, separating from relationships, and activating their lives autonomously. These fixations in earlier pre-neurotic stages overshadowed the neurotic issues of sexuality for some. They had not achieved the developmental goals of whole object relations, for example. Thus I include this theoretical and clinical contribution in my method.[2] Sexual health is an imperative. So is development of a whole Self. So I expanded Reich's developmental paradigm to include this developmental goal of health as well.

Reich's System

Here, in a simplified fashion, is Reich's theory of development as it is reflected in his character types. I describe his system without embellishment. You will understand how Reich evolved the types out of the basic psychosexual developmental stages defined by Freud and elaborated on by Reich. Reich's character typology gives us a map of how developmental passages combine with nature and nurture to influence formation of our defensive structures that over time define our consistent way of being.

Reich wove all these factors together and defined the inevitable fixations and resulting armoring as they occur during various developmental stages in both the psyche and the body. This tapestry defines how and where the energy can get concentrated or blocked. Symptoms occur when there is blockage at various points of development. The character can be defined by how dominant a given block is in a specific zone of development.

As I stated earlier, Reich saw neurosis, as did Freud, stemming from unresolved Oedipal issues, the phallic developmental phase completed by ages three to five and consolidated throughout adolescence. The focus was on innate instincts, drives, and need satisfaction as the primary motivating principles of development. Yet, Reich did see the importance of the mother and infant relationship and emphasized the importance of the mother's physical and emotional health during pregnancy and how that might affect the in utero experiences of the fetus. This angle on the mother-child relationship was innovative as he was looking at the energetics of the contact between mother and child: how the pregnancy developed, for example, out of the mother's expanded or contracted pelvis and how that might affect the birth and the infant-mother relationship. This was a radical departure from the analytic model.

On the other hand, Reich labeled his character types *neurotic* meaning their problems predominately originate in Oedipal conflicts in ages three to five.[3] He did not focus on earlier phase developmental problems except as the earlier phases add shading to the character. The lens of sexual development predominates in Reich's system.[4] His *oral character* covers all earlier developmental blocks but is not a well-developed diagnostic character type.

The stages of development, according to Reich, are oral, anal, phallic, and genital based on those erogenous zones. Elsworth Baker, MD, added the ocular segment as a major erogenous zone. In Reich's system, neurotic character designations depend on the degree of fixation at these various erogenous zones. In normal development each stage is passed through with mastery of critical tasks, hopefully absent of trauma. With maturity, these zones function in their pleasure-seeking capacity. Blocking (armoring) at any stage holds energy at that level, impeding it from reaching the genitals where full discharge can be attained. Therefore, symptoms are present wherever there is a buildup in energy concentration or blockage at a given zone (Baker, 1967, 17). Reich held that genital release clears excess energy from the system, and if there are blockages in pregenital zones, then symptoms are produced.[5]

The baby is born, and there are two primary points of contact at that time— the eyes and the mouth. The infant to age three months, although her vision is not yet developed, can focus on objects eight to ten inches from her face, and by eight weeks can focus her eyes on the face of a parent. The ocular segment is the infant's gateway to seeing and experiencing parental attention and love. The eyes provide the first information and stimulation even before they can reach, grab, or crawl. She looks into her parent's eyes and hopefully sees their soft eye contact. She likes what she sees and continues to look with wide-open, innocent eyes exploring without fear. One can say she is not blocked in her eyes. If she experiences mean, distant, or angry eyes from her parent, for example, she may adapt by going away in her eyes because she is uncomfortable. Then the infant's and child's eyes become armored; a block develops in the first segment. The eyes hold energy in a dysfunctional way as they become noticeably less focused, furtive, or distancing as the child grows into adulthood. The ability to make contact with reality and see clearly is diminished. The person seems hidden behind her eyes and you can't find them. She often experiences confusion and pervasive fear due to her diminished reality perception.

Stan, a professional therapist, presented a case. I will call the patient Fred, 59 years old. Stan liked this patient, as he was motivated and cooperative. Yet Stan felt he wasn't getting a handle on the case. Fred came from a difficult background with substance-abusing, seriously impaired parents who divorced early in his life, forcing him to shuttle back and forth between homes at a young age. Although Fred had a substantial cushion of inherited wealth from his mother, he was unable to sustain commitment to various endeavors. He progressed through law school but did not get his law degree. He moved on from law school to various other pursuits, established a decent business, but relied on his inherited wealth to succeed rather than his own activations. He complained of doing things he really didn't want to do, yet never developed pursuits he enjoyed. Underneath, he always felt fear and relied on others, currently his wife and adult kids, to stabilize. His eyes tended to be unfocused, cautious, and expressive of fear. He felt lost and in chaos, although those feeling states were not obvious on the surface. His earliest experiences with neglectful parents produced an ocular block, as he had to withdraw both from what he saw and from the absence of a genuine exchange with his parents. His contact with reality was impaired and never fully developed as the early trauma led to a loss of connection to reality. Although his inheritance got him by, he felt internally frozen with fear and relied on external structures, his dominant wife, and clinging to adult children as a way of grounding himself. He never established a whole self that functioned autonomously as he was impeded at the earliest phase. The therapist, Stan, although aware of the patient's self-esteem problems, did not see the character clearly. The overriding feeling of fear can be an indication of an eye block, marking difficulties in the first stage of development. Stan did not understand the degree of impaired development of Self that impacted all of Fred's life decisions as well as problems in his current family relationships. Fred had never stood on his own legs and made decisions but rather lived in a state of chronic dependency (although not readily apparent). His character stance of passivity, confusion, and wanting to merge with others developed through formative impasses made Fred who he is now. Once Stan understood the specific character traits and the developmental context, he could help Fred understand the origins and depth of his problem and how to solve it gradually, over time.

Moving on to the oral segment, the infant nurses at the breast and/or is bottle fed and as he feeds takes in nutrition along with full-body contact, warmth, and nurturance that includes eye contact. His oral sucking needs are met through nursing or the nipple on the bottle, as well as physical contact with his mouth on his parent's skin. Later he learns to bite objects, to chew and bite food, and his oral needs continue to be met with satisfaction. He becomes comfortable with the pleasure-seeking function of his mouth.

Another more unfortunate scenario may play out due to negative factors within his family leading to unmet oral needs. He might be left in his crib with his bottle to feed himself and there is no eye contact or affection with eating. Depression in the mother affects how the infant is nurtured as the mother feels drained and has little to give. The parents may be impatient when he is eating and not provide the connection and bonding necessary to make the experience of eating feel pleasurable. Or there may be tension and conflict around eating and thus the oral function is no longer satisfying but rather anxiety producing. The mother may want to stop breast-feeding before the baby is ready. The oral segment can be seen as erogenous as the baby has high excitation in his lips when he eats and discharges as well when he is satisfied. If this segment gets blocked from normal satisfaction, then the adult may have symptoms of oral problems such as overeating and orally driven compensations like over-talking or smoking. Other symptoms are the opposite of overeating as manifested in the picky eater who doesn't allow the pleasures of indulgence and is tight-lipped and rigid about food or oral pleasures.

> Lillian is 29 years old; she came into therapy with a serious anxious depression. She presents with a collapsed, soft-spoken nervousness coupled with hopelessness. Her body seems drained of life. Her lips are clamped shut. She is still living at home. Her mom has been chronically depressed and depends on Lillian for support. Dad left when Lillian was five years old. She feels obligated to fulfill her mother's demands and suffers intense anxiety when she tries to separate and leave home. This patient never felt nourished, but early on she learned to feed her mother. The situation led Lillian to feel deeply inadequate and worthless throughout her childhood and adolescence, causing serious symptoms in adulthood. Her oral block contributed to stunted development and a myriad of symptoms.

Erogenous zones develop either unscathed or interrupted. The anal segment can become either a point of conflict or an easy transition through potty training with ease. If parents disturb this function with their anxiety then there is anal armoring or blocking that affects the personality into adult years. During this phase the child separates more and wants independence. If during this phase the child is overly controlled and independence is not fostered, then symptoms will occur in the future.

The genital stage is also affected by the attitudes and behaviors of parents regarding sexuality. The comfort parents have with budding sexuality in the young child and as she grows into puberty makes a significant difference as to how the child resolves oedipal issues with the opposite sex parent.

Unsatisfied and Repressed Types

In Reich's model, developing through "erogenous zones" is not a smooth course. Blockages occur due to conflict and result in held-back energy. If there are pregenital blocks, energy is diminished in the genital zone. If the earlier blocks predominate then complete satisfaction in the genital zone is impossible to achieve. In some cases the individual cannot develop to the phallic or genital level. Or he will develop to the phallic level but with snags of energy stuck in the prior zones like the eyes, the oral segment, or the anal segment.

Emotional trauma leading to blocks may produce one of two results at any stage. Reich labeled the blocks *repression* or *lasting dissatisfaction*. In the former, the individual never develops a pleasurable functioning at the specific stage, largely through deprivation. In the latter, there is lasting dissatisfaction such that the person constantly tries to obtain once-known satisfaction. Remember, the block refers to the fact that the individual has been able to develop beyond the given zone but has been unable to give up that zone completely. The developmental blocks form the character style, symptom picture, and level of sexual function.[6]

Armoring is more complete in the repressed than in the unsatisfied stage. In the unsatisfied blocking, the semi-blocked energy is felt constantly as need. Drives are felt and impulses get through, but there is no satisfaction of needs—only longing for more.

In the prior example, as stated, the oral unsatisfied type falls prey to substance abuse, drinking, smoking, overeating, gambling, and shopping but never finds gratification. There is a constant demand for satiety, and when impulses are restrained anxiety results. In the repressed type, the individual defends against any expression from the oral segment. The oral repressed type lacks interest in food, has inhibited speech and visually may appear tight-lipped. He is the opposite of a pleasure seeker. This type is prone to regimentation and ascetic type mandates. The character type is delineated by armor in the oral zone.

Where there are no blocks, genitality is established and a genital character results. The closer a patient is to the genital level the healthier he is.

Changing Norms: Sexual Orientation and Gender Diversity

Oedipal resolution, in Reich's model, was the final critical developmental passage for the growing child into genitality. I suggest that the Oedipal complex and its resolution is not always the compelling feature of sexual development—as family structures come in a variety of packages. Sexual developmental dynamics are complex and can be viewed outside the Oedipal paradigm. Gay or lesbian couples, single parents, blended families, and other gender configurations raising children will provide differing sexual role model dynamics that affect the developing child. This topic will require longitudinal research to elucidate differing parental configurations and how they correlate with variables of developing sexuality.

In our current society, there is growing acceptance of diversity in sexual orientation and gender nonconformity. Sexual orientation is defined as romantic and/or sexual attraction to the same sex, opposite sex, both sexes, or more than one gender. Orientation can be seen as ranging along a continuum. Contributing factors are a complex interplay of genetic, hormonal, and environmental influences ("Sexual Orientation," n.d.). To ensure healthy sexual development, the child, adolescent, and young adult requires parental attitudes that reflect openness, tolerance, and acceptance so that they can explore, discover, and resolve their sexuality. The adolescent, in a healthy scenario, is free to explore configurations such as gender bending, LGBTQ experimentation, or gender fluidity if inclined. That said, parents can simultaneously create healthy home structures that support sexuality within a regulated environment of consistency and stability rather than neglect, or permit a free-for-all home environment without limits and boundaries that result in adolescent confusion, alienation, and other adolescent mental disorders.

Gender dysphoria (once referred to as *gender identity disorder*) or gender-fluid expressions (not defined as identity issues) may emerge by age four or earlier and evolve forward for many years—requiring thoughtful attention and treatment protocols currently delineated by experts in this particular field. If parents and society are not comfortable with diverse forms of sexuality and the shift from gender binary notions to a gender spectrum, or what gender expert Dr. Diane Ehrensaft refers to as the gender web (Ehrensaft, 2016, 24), then destructive inhibitions will result and the genital stage and adolescent sexual maturity will be contaminated with conflict, repression, guilt, shame, and anxiety.

In a July 1, 2016, article in *The New York Times*, titled "Estimate of the U.S. Transgender Population Doubles," the author states, "About 1.4 million adults in the United States identify as transgender, double a widely used previous estimate, according to an analysis based on new federal and state data" (Hoffman, 2016). Mental health professionals need to help young children, adolescents, and adults who do not fit into a one or the other binary gender box, or express a more fluid approach to gender, feel understood and supported. According to gender fluidity experts, some gender categorization is needed while mixing it up with gender diverse concepts as well, thus providing multiple options while providing structure. These are new conceptual/therapeutic paradigms that are evolving presently and require openness and flexibility that allow for acceptance of gender creativity. That said, the therapist must discriminate wisely as to the potential of multiple factors at play with each patient and do a comprehensive differential diagnosis, with the possibility of multiple diagnoses, to assess accurately the various contributing aspects of each case.

Healthy sexual development alongside healthy maturation creates relational capacity—the ability to engage with satisfying sexual partners and establish enduring relationships—either with same-sex, opposite-sex, or trans mates. One aspect of relational capacity is the ability to surrender lovingly, sexually, and with feeling, to one's partner—a point emphasized by Reich. It is important that parents not be sex negative. Rather, parents can demonstrate positive attitudes toward budding sexuality including flexibility as their adolescent's unique sexual development unfolds. The family can be a safe place to dialogue.

My method recognizes the potential for health and wholeness regardless of sexual orientation and/or gender expressions. This position represents a definitive departure from Reich's stance that pathologized homosexuality (LGBTQ configurations). Reich's general premises regarding healthy sexuality are valuable, yet some aspects are a limited product of his cultural and historic context. Notions of health and pathology must be altered to fit with changing times and new knowledge. Our culture and segments of the global culture are creating a sea change with acceptance and implementation of new cultural norms such as legalization of gay marriage and accepting gays, lesbians, and trans folks for military service, to name three sea changes.

For young or mature individuals, regardless of sexual orientation or gender identity issues and gender expression, the criteria for mental health still applies—and stands apart from this issue. Sexual identity confusion and/or gender dysphoria can be reflective of broader general problems such as confusion, dissociative trauma reactions, depression, substance abuse, sexual acting out, or other contributing factors that need to be parsed out similarly to other patient complaints and symptoms. We need to treat LGBT and transgender patients from a characterological and biophysical perspective. Regardless of sexual orientation and gender dysphoria, we treat the problems at hand—although those elements are an important and integral part of the puzzle. No matter what problematic issues and symptoms are presented—they need to be seen by the therapist, through the larger lens of character and biophysical health or dysfunction. These character problems are revealed regardless of sexual/gender parameters and must be treated as such. A healthy self and relational life, meaningful activation, wholeness, and life satisfaction are our goals. Character analysis and biophysical treatment is the method of treatment I suggest to dissolve defensive armoring and promote functionality and trumps all issues of sexual orientation and gender issues, although these are of critical importance in our analysis.

George, a 59-year-old gay man, came into treatment after many years of therapy. An intelligent, insightful man, he grew up in a small Midwestern city. He had put many of the pieces together regarding his problematic history yet still struggled with high anxiety and severe depression. He had always experienced himself as different; his disinterest in sports early in life left him feeling marginalized as he was not chosen for teams nor was he engaged in the "normal" athletic expectations of youth. He had other childhood challenges, as his mom was an obsessive-compulsive who lacked affection and nurturing capacities; dad was on the road traveling for business. George developed a serious depression early on from the absence of love and affection from mom and lack of connection with his father. He learned to cope by becoming mom's helper in order to get crumbs of contact. He became compulsively helpful at home but felt continuously anxious and despondent. His feeling of not fitting in and being "normal" in terms of small town norms caused a deep sense of inadequacy and unworthiness that lasted throughout his life—defended against by his arrogant, angry, and occasionally paranoid character presentation that covered his anxious depression. He also suffered with obsessive-compulsive traits due to his anal block. His strong oral block, due to absence of nurturance and affection, caused a deep depression that did not allow his energy to move fully to the genital level, which would have resulted in confident sexuality and natural assertiveness.

Another example of how character style, created by blocks in development, affect adult relational capacity is John, in his 40s, a successful financial analyst. He was in and out of relationships with women. He presents with an angular, handsome face with a boyish look; strong voice; and slightly aggressive style. He is critical and demanding, and no woman is exactly right for him. His family of origin had exaggeratedly high standards applied to income levels, intelligence, and appearance. His current relationship is with a different type of woman than his family is normally impressed by. John is feeling attached to her but is anxious and in conflict. The conflict unleashed his buried inadequacy feelings and feelings of being less than his father. He had been projecting those feelings onto his girlfriend. He was overwrought with guilt and could not stabilize nor could he decide whether to continue the relationship. He knew if he made a long-term commitment to this woman, his mother would not approve. Intimacy was a seriously compromised area for John.

Character analysis unlocks the patient from the prison of earlier patterning that continues into his present. Every aspect of the patient's life, from his potential to study and work to his relationships and his long-term physical health, are affected by early developmental blocks that stunt his capacity to mature and find meaning and purpose.

With a clear, organized typology of character types cohered around developmental impasses and other defining variables—starting from early infancy and solidifying in adolescence—we can approach our patients in a systematic fashion. As we learn about them, their life formation, their culture and family, we can distill the critical features connecting the way they behave with their historic crossroads that made them who they are. Having a typology of useable character types gives us an efficient instrument to jump-start the character analytic therapeutic process. Character analysis defines the specific approach for each patient and generates consistent momentum throughout a long-term therapeutic relationship.

Notes

1 These theorists emphasize how the psyche develops in relation to others in childhood. And that the experiences of those important caretaking others become internalized in the mind as objects in the unconscious that are carried within as parts of the self and can be projected later onto real life relationships. Objects in the infant's mind are determined by function and can be termed *part objects* with good and bad qualities because of the infant's experience of them. In healthy development of the psyche, the parts integrate and become *whole objects* rather than parts designated good and bad. Object relations theory prioritizes the developmental accomplishment of *whole object relations and object constancy* as the criterion that separates the designation of neurosis from *pre-oedipal personality disorders. Whole object relations* means the ability to see oneself and others as integrated with both good and bad parts rather than divided into split parts of good and bad. Whole object relations, as it is termed, is a critical mainstay of a healthy psyche. If we maintain in adulthood part good and bad self/objects inside, then we struggle with these good and bad designations and are plagued with feelings of worthlessness or superiority. We do not have a realistic sense of self or other.
2 I integrated object relations theory (1920–1960) predominantly the integration conceptualized by James Masterson MD (1926–2010) to my amplification of Reich's typology. I have included attachment phase problems and the attendant personality

disorders defined by earlier developmental phase problems not referenced by Reich. These earlier developmental stages are referred to as *pre-oedipal* (a term coined by Otto Rank in the late 1920s) or *pregenital* phases. Otto Rank was the first to create a modern theory of object relations and Ronald Fairbairn, a British psychologist in 1952 independently formulated it. Ferenczi may have originated this line of thought in 1917. The earlier developmental phases covering the first year to age three were not definitively researched until the work of Margaret Mahler in the 1940s and 1950s in the United States. She developed the concept *separation-individuation*, a critical developmental phase.

3   Reich's nomenclature refers to disorders considered neurotic and starting with Oedipal conflicts in the ages three to five.

4   The types are based on armoring in erogenous zones where energy is concentrated.

5   Whenever genitality is interfered with, the concentration of energy at the pre-oedipal erogenous zone produces symptoms from that zone. Only the genital release gives complete satisfaction. When energy is blocked from the genitals it can never be completely discharged. If energy is not completely discharged it can lead to symptoms due to bound up energy that is not released.

6   The degree of importance of the pregenital blocks determines if an individual remains a character type, for example, a Phallic type with an eye block or becomes more influenced by the magnitude of the blockage. Then the patient is referred to as a Paranoid type. As individuals retreat to earlier level of development, the characteristics of these stages color their presentation and functioning. Depression is an example of a full retreat to an oral repressed stage.

5   Introduction to Character Types

Overview

Understanding the various character types works well because they do not pigeon hole individuals in a black-and-white way. Most people fit into a defined character type with some consistency, yet we are all unique, and that uniqueness adds shading to an individual's character designation. Sometimes only a provisional diagnosis can be made as the character is covered over with symptoms of substance abuse or other addictions, physical illness, grief from a radical life change such as a divorce or a death, or severe situational depression. Patients may draw from two categories thus confusing the character diagnosis.

We gain direction and clarity by understanding the basic composition of each character type. We are not labeling our patients in a mechanistic way—each person is unique with their individual blend of genetics, family of origin dynamics, cultural elements, sexual orientation, and life story. In all phases of development, external situational factors have influence as well—war, death, relocation, medical issues, and socioeconomic context affect how development progresses. Each person brings her unique contribution to the greater whole and must be valued in her uniqueness. These types represent organizational placeholders, providing anchor points within the broader flow of details our patients bring to us (Baker, 1967, 99–152; see Figure 5.1, which is also in the appendix[1]).

Reich's character typology creates an elegant map that correlates with his schema of body armoring. This is a comprehensive and integrated approach to the mind-body as the character types organize the body armoring patterns and vice versa, affecting the entirety of the body including the autonomic nervous system. Current paradigms of psychological/medical treatment need to catch up with his thorough mind-body approach. Reich's character designations were innovative for his time and ours. His typology developed out of his Orgonomic research and clinical work, and integrates factors never before discussed in the analytic world, namely, that the character is defined by psychological development that informs the development of the brain and the body. If there are developmental ruptures, there will be biophysical blocks as well, that correlate with the resulting character type.

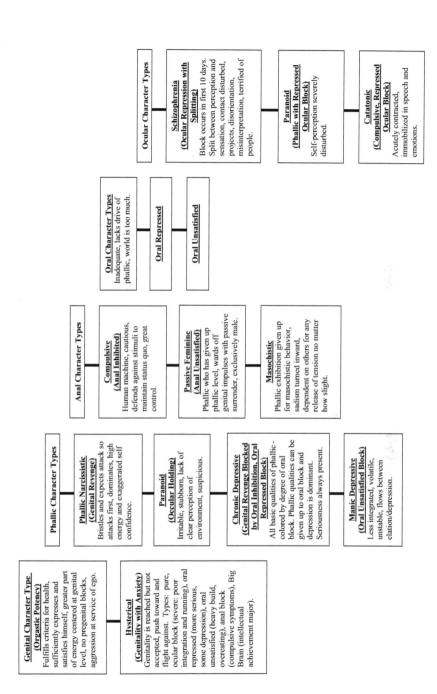

Figure 5.1 Wilhelm Reich's Character Types

Source: Partial Listing of Reich's Character Types adapted by Patricia Frisch, 2011; Baker, 1967, 99–152.

The character types presented here are abbreviated for ease of reference, not a complete compendium of Reich's types. I use the types that are most relevant and applicable to your clinical practice. Some of Reich's types are less relevant than others, so I have left them out. If you are interested in the full typology please reference Baker, *Man in the Trap*, and Reich's *Character Analysis*.

As we discuss Reich's character types, you may recognize aspects of yourself in the discussion. Again, it is not to categorize you but rather to give you greater self-awareness, insight, and the possibility of changing what is problematic.

A vocabulary of types is helpful to our understanding of our patients, providing the best way to intervene. Interventions are more effective when you understand the basics of who you are working with, the character type, and how the individual came to be that way and understand the symptom picture and behavioral cues as they relate to the character. Out of that distillation you can arrive at the most effective clinical strategy in relation to a specific type. So learning the types will greatly increase your skill level.

Genital Character Type

Let's start with Reich's description of a healthy person, which he labeled the *genital character*. Other theorists discuss health in relation to the *individuated* or *developed Self*. There is basic compatibility between multiple theorists on the qualities or capacities of health. I will cover Reich's delineation of health next.

The genital character type can sense, feel, and express sufficiently to be able to experience satisfaction in all areas of life. Because he is free to experience and actualize satisfaction, he does not accumulate body or character defensive armor. He is not regressed to earlier immature modes of gratification and thus functions in a mature capacity. His aggression through assertion is available for mastery of love and work.

Energetically and biophysically, the genital character has available movement, fluidity, and flexibility in the body. There is suppleness in the musculature and a lack of physical symptoms and stasis. The natural free-flowing energy is not stopped by extreme tension, flaccidity, over- or underdeveloped muscles, and chronic tension, for example, in the neck, shoulders, and back. Body weight is consistent with good health and well-being and not a preoccupation. The eyes are alive, open, and contactful. The mouth is soft and capable of relaxing without tension in the jaw. The voice is strong and expressive without constriction. The circulation flows to the extremities so the person can maintain warmth. The belly is soft and pliable to allow ease of digestion and elimination. The pelvis is mobile and able to feel full sensations. The breath is open, full, and consistent.

Sexually, this character type can surrender to a loving mate without problems and has sufficient available energy and capacity for contact to experience sexual satisfaction. Integrity in relationships is maintained. The term *genital character* derives from a capacity to have an open genital or pelvic segment.

Reich divided the body into seven segments of armoring starting with the head, the eyes, and moving down through the mouth, neck, chest, diaphragm, stomach, and pelvis. When armoring is dismantled in the upper segments, energy can flow freely in the pelvis and down the legs. Then there is a capacity for continuous, free flow of energy and sensation, and the person is capable of full sexual release. Thus the term *genital character*.

This character type is comfortable in her skin and responds naturally without self-consciousness or awkwardness and is capable of spontaneity and natural movement. Feelings are accessible, across the entire spectrum—from deep sadness and grief to appropriate anger and hate. The range of experience is from pleasure to pain, all willingly felt and integrated.

As Ellsworth Baker states in *Man in the Trap*, "Because his primary drives are fulfilled, he has a natural decency. He is unafraid of life, and therefore does not have to compromise with his convictions if his own are opposed. He knows what others want and can accept their needs" (Baker, 1967, 103). The genital character can be *fully responsible* in his life in all areas.

This healthy state allows for autonomy and closeness. There is self-sufficiency alongside a capacity to be comfortably dependent on others. This type has plenty of available energy and capacity to create, follow one's bliss, and live one's true meaning and purpose.

The genital character can regulate feelings without being overwhelmed with states of mind, emotions, or reactivity. There is an ability to contain difficult events and feelings without losing the Self.

The genital character, give or take our normal limitations, does quite well in the world and can achieve a relaxed, confident interface with the deep wisdom that engenders humility in the face of the grand adventure called life (Frisch, June 26, 2014, blog, "Reich's Character Types").

Hysterical Character Type

This summary of the hysteric type will include historic contextual markers relevant to Reich's theoretical evolution and the development of this specific character type.

Within the category of the genital character, Reich includes the hysterical character type, referenced as *genitality with anxiety*. This diagnosis has roots in ancient history and the Middle Ages where *hysteria* was discovered and designated as a medical condition believed particularly applicable to women. When Sigmund Freud began his seminal work in the field of psychoanalysis, hysteria was at the forefront of Freud's developing understanding that medical pathologies can be traced to the mind. Freud's launching pad was the work of French neurologist Jean-Martin Charcot, who investigated hysteria in depth. Serious symptoms like paralysis and fugue states (behaviors displayed but later not remembered) became an impetus for Freud's research, and he published a series of articles on hysteria and the mental etiology of these conditions. Freud delineated how hysterical symptoms are a conversion of psychological stress into physical symptoms, that is, paralysis, fugue, or selective amnesia. Freud and his student Reich attributed hysterical symptoms including overdramatic behaviors and emotions as the unconscious mind's attempt to protect from psychic disturbance.

Reich's discussion of this type is influenced by the times in which he lived. To remind, during the period of his mentorship with Freud and after separating from Freud (1918–1934), Reich incorporated Freud's analytic concept of libido or biological sexual energy, and after years of research expanded on it and scientifically validated the existence of biological energy. Freud, on the other hand, moved away from his earlier concept of libido and reduced it to a psychic concept without physical basis.

The recognition of the importance of sexuality as a necessary and healthy function of expression and release was revolutionary in the 1920s. Freud, the father of psychoanalysis, was focused on the etiology of mental illness and saw inhibited sexuality as a primary cause of psychological symptoms and a major contributor to hysteria. From his study of patients, Freud theorized that neurosis is caused by conflicts between natural sexual and other primitive instincts and social inhibition and frustration of those instincts. The Victorian Era was the backdrop, with its highly moralistic sensibility as well as a new cultural movement toward romanticism. This cultural context and shift influenced Freud and Reich. Reich's focus never strayed from his interest in biological sexual energy and through his scientific experiments he confirmed the existence of real energy in the body.

That said, the hysterical character is still relevant and is listed under Personality Disorders in the latest, revised *Diagnostic and Statistical Manual of Mental Disorders*, fifth edition, published in 2013 by the American Psychiatric Association. In *DSM-5*, this type is referenced as the Histrionic Personality Disorder, distinguished by "a pattern of excessive emotionality and attention-seeking" and includes eight further descriptors. This type also has higher rates of somatic symptom disorder. Other personality disorders also have propensities for somatization or displacing psychological problems into somatic symptoms. Many of the other traits Reich delineated for the hysteric type are listed in the *DSM-5* (American Psychiatric Publishing, 2013, 667–669).

Reich considered the hysterical character a genital character with anxiety. This means that an individual, either male or female, has reached the developmental phase of genitality and is not lodged in an earlier developmentally regressed phase that prevents sufficient maturity.

The hysterical character has the capacity for genitality but cannot embody it. That means, for the most part, that this character type does not have serious blockages or armoring throughout the segments of the body; thus this type has freed-up energy that flows down the body to the genitals mostly unobstructed. Therefore, there is a high level of excitation in the system. Yet he suffers from anxiety related to this free-moving energy and defends by running from real contact, focus, and depth.

Reich and others of his time defined the potential etiology as having difficulties around a person's budding sexuality during the Oedipal phase of development (approximately three to five years of age and expressed during teen years) usually with the opposite sex parent. There wasn't freedom to be affectionate and sexual in an accepted and supported way. Instead, these feelings and sensations were inhibited by the parent through turning away or disapproval. There are many ways this story could play out, and this is the traditional analytic playbook. The Oedipal phase difficulties are not the only obstructive influence affecting development of this type. As the infant and toddler developed, the dynamics of the family, including competitiveness and jealousy felt by the same sex parent or over-eroticized identifications in both parents may have contributed to earlier developmental difficulties before the Oedipal phase. Gender identity conflicts and gender nonconforming children may emerge as early as age three and must be factored in as well. I emphasize taking the whole picture of development, including family dynamics, into view so that your etiological understanding is not confined only to the Oedipal complex.

The hysterical character type exhibits a strong and compelling flight from contact that leads to chronic approach-avoid mechanisms, both in relationships and other areas of life. These individuals can flit from relationship to relationship, deeply terrified of commitment. The abundance of free energy natural to this type is not fully lived or discharged as it causes too much anxiety to be contained and utilized. Thus the individual has chronic buildup of energy, experienced as anxiety and acted out in flight, over dramatization, and other behaviors that release it. That buildup leads to constant agitation, restlessness, lack of focus, and immaturity. They are prone to some depression and moodiness and crave stimulation to alter their mood.

They are driven to seek attention and sometimes do that with flirting or seductiveness. Yet, intimacy is not in their reach because they are flighty and immature. Further, they alienate others as they are self-centered and threaten same-sex relationships because of their seductive style. When couples are out together, the hysteric will be flirtatious with either or both partners from the other couple and create tension in everyone else. These qualities apply to gay or straight individuals and couples. Underneath there are deep abandonment issues so they act out dependency needs in unhealthy ways.

This type can be very suggestible, often seeking definition through the other, and wants to please as a way of securing a dependency object. There is superficiality apparent in this type as the person's anxiety keeps her on the run so she has trouble digging deep. As hysterics have trouble settling into themselves, they are changeable in their behavioral directions, shifting course or feeling on a whim. They can be devaluing when not in a pleasing, compliant mood.

This type can be described as shallow, as the Self has not developed its full potential due to high anxiety. These folks can be vivacious in conversation but lack detail, knowledge, and depth. They rely on their appearance to feel good about themselves and put a great deal of attention on looking attractive. With this shallowness, they compensate with dramatic, exaggerated expression of emotions that fill them up and hide the emptiness. They have problems directing themselves intellectually or mastering their full potential in careers and creativity as their superficial values take precedence. They want immediate gratification and have trouble putting in the hard work of building something substantial.

Let's now discuss how their armoring manifests in the body. They are not prone to dense muscular holding but rather have very light armoring. Their bodies are soft and pliable usually in good tone. The tension shifts to various spots. As they can't bind energy with muscular holding and internal contraction, such as tension in the organ system, they are prone to symptoms including somatization. That means they feel physical symptoms and focus on those, usually having an array of physical problems, concerns, pains, and fears of disease.

Hysterics have developed to the genital phase, and if there are no significant earlier blocks, they will have significant available energy to discharge. Their major defenses are going out of contact and flight. As Baker states, they can exhibit "frantic behavior," being overly emotional or agitated and running around in flighty patterns. If they have a higher level of repression, they can be overly "calm" with more withdrawal, disconnectedness, and freezing up (Baker, 1967, 104–110).

There are shadings to all Reich's character types if blockages in the upper segments (eyes, oral segment) are part of the picture, and they usually are.

Let's meet Nancy, an attractive, stylish, slender female in her late 30s who entered therapy because of relationship issues, chronic anxiety, insomnia, and fearful concerns over a few physical symptoms. She had seen multiple practitioners from acupuncturists to psychics, "body workers," and multiple therapists over the years. (I will briefly digress to discuss multiple helpers including body workers. Often this type of patient will seek support with a masseuse or body worker, among others, who mixes deep tissue massage with psychological help. The masseuses tend to be intuitive types and are nurturing and helpful in relieving tension and can also offer many words of input and advice. From a professional standpoint often what is offered is not good advice. If a patient surrounds herself with a multitude of practitioners all giving input, the messages become chaotic, confusing, and overly gratifying in a not-so-helpful way. Hysterics are suggestible, so they take it all in without deeply processing its applicability. So I often intervene to stop that process of seeking help chaotically and investigate the what and why of the repetitive support-seeking behavior. I will speak more on this in another chapter.)

Nancy was a highly animated conversationalist, smiling and laughing with stories of aborted relationships. She was a college graduate, had developed a career in HR but was not particularly inspired. As she bounced around in her first session, I quickly commented on her flighty, entertaining style that belied her concerned feelings underneath. As the first session evolved we got to her fears surrounding her physical symptoms, her chronic anxiety, and insomnia. We discussed how she might want to run from therapy as she runs from life, and confound her relationship with me by seeking help with other professionals or healers. I told her that those behaviors would need to be curtailed so she could truly settle down with one therapist in a committed fashion. She balked at that as she found it unusual to be contained in that way. She had been on the run for her whole life. So my approach was decidedly different.

Therapy with hysterics begins with illuminating their tendency toward flight and stopping it. This type can be attracted to a nonstop conversation with friends eliciting advice from everyone as they are filled with anxiety that they have difficulty tolerating. This style is not helpful as their suggestibility creates constant inner and outer confusion.

Point out the superficiality and substitute contact for their smiling, animated brightness, and overly dramatic style of talking. Discuss their preoccupation with appearance. Often this type overexercises to ensure their ability to seduce. Help them understand the feelings that drive these preoccupations.

The hysteric often resists therapy because depth is difficult and he doesn't want to be contained; it interrupts the frantic flight path that is a defense against depression. As the containment stabilizes, then deeper fears and considerations can be faced and felt honestly. He can see that his attention-seeking and provocative attempts at superficial contact just leave him empty and more desperate.

Ultimately, hysterics have a good amount of available energy and capacity for aliveness without much armoring so when they get directed they can accomplish and create a substantial life path and enjoy the intimacy of stable relationships (Frisch, July 29, 2014, blog, "Reich's Character Types").

Phallic Character Types

I include a review so you can keep clear on the etiology of the types. Reich's types emanate from blocks in these erogenous zones: genital, phallic, anal, oral and ocular zones. These are correlated with classical developmental phases of growth, affecting the character and their biophysical/energetic progression. In the classical theory of the times, if an individual develops to the genital level, she has capacity for healthy sexuality. The Oedipal phase (three to five years and consolidated in adolescence) has been completed with resolution of Oedipal issues, meaning competition and jealousy with the opposite sex parent resolves and the individual can move on to healthy relationships outside of the family matrix. I have established a broader view of this phase that is inclusive of a variety of family configurations and sexual and gender orientations yet can include basic dynamics of healthy sexual development. If an individual does not make it to the genital level, the phase before is the phallic level. This developmental level connotes distortion in attitudes toward sexuality. The genitals are not seen as a vehicle for sexual love. With the phallic level, there is an aspect of revenge and competition. There are other issues beyond just the sexual one indicated, and they will be revealed as we discuss the character types. The Phallic character has ample available energy like the genital character but with distortion as their developmental progression was interrupted (Frisch, July 29, 2014, blog, "Reich's Character Types").

Narcissistic Character Type

I will begin with a discussion of healthy narcissism. We all need and wish to feel good about ourselves and experience a consistent and stable sense of our self-worth. Our self-perception of inherent goodness, wholeness, and integrity can translate to a sense of deserving to be creatively expressive with a willingness to promote ourselves in our world both socially and in the work realm. This is called healthy entitlement. Therefore, we can have a reasonable agenda and activate it, allowing our expression of Self to speak in a variety of ways. These efforts represent healthy stable narcissism without destabilization from negative self-talk and inaction. Further, our healthy narcissism allows us to be in relationship with others in a reciprocal fashion that supports others as we support ourselves. We saw these healthy traits in the genital character previously described. Remember, when we have achieved a mentally healthy condition, life becomes simpler. There is more complexity to living when individuals slip into neurotic or disordered patterns.

The narcissistic character type has an obvious style and a well-known brand, the *top dog*, which many of you may recognize in yourself or others. First and foremost, the narcissistic type has exaggerated self-confidence and exudes a sense of superiority. He demands to be in control and does not want to subordinate to anyone. His inflated self-confidence can lead to poor decisions.

Plus, his inability to focus on details due to his exaggerated self-confidence leads to inflated but unrealistic plans and expectations that easily fall apart.

The narcissistic character type can be quite self-engrossed and self-maximizing. His predominant and consistent focus is on his own needs, concerns, and wishes. He is an excellent self-promoter who loves the limelight and vies to be seen as special. He expects his needs to take center stage in his relationship to others. He is often upset if those needs are not mirrored perfectly by his partners, friends, or colleagues.

Although Reich did not look to earlier developmental issues, I have added those phases into my method and delineation of character. A particular earlier developmental phase will help illuminate how this type is formed. *The world is their oyster* is a good phrase representing a developmental phase from which the Narcissistic character did not graduate. This phase of development occurs when the toddler is still within the orbit of the parent, having not yet separated. She feels imbued with the power of the parent behind her, so the child feels the world is hers for the taking. There isn't yet the recognition that she is at risk if she moves too far out of mom or dad's sphere. Then she would experience her separateness and that can be a shocking realization at first. In the next phase of development, she realizes she is differentiated and shuttles back and forth between the parents for resources. She begins to absorb that she is, at times, separate from her parents. But while in the parental orbit, she remains empowered and feels omnipotent. Narcissists can be seen as holding at this phase and, given *the world is their oyster*, they are filled with a sense of omnipotence. They believe they should get what they want when they want it—and that they are entitled to it. They command, control, dominate, and cajole to get their needs met and there are no limits! Others are an extension of them and not seen as separate. For example, if they like something, their partner should like it, or if they do a chore a certain way or have an attitude about an issue, their partner needs to match that exactly for there to be peace. They can be critical and demanding at times, as they want things to be perfect to reflect their internalized quest for perfection. This can be troublesome in relationships!

Narcissistic types go about working everyone to get maximum gain. And they can be charming, with a charisma that others, who don't have those qualities, are attracted to. Sooner or later these traits are obnoxious, especially to individuals who are attached to them. Narcissists can have a glow, due to their power, that attracts fireflies to their light. Because of that, they can control and dominate others. Those others get burned as the narcissist takes what she wants and then moves on.

Narcissistic characters can appear successful—well-known athletes, political figures, or entrepreneurs; they function well in complex situations. The grandiosity of success can result in impulsive and poor decision-making that can undo the success (as we see in the news, many land in prison, humiliated). Sexual acting out is pervasive with these individuals as they believe they are entitled to anything they want and ignore the potential consequences. The less healthy phallic may slide into alcohol and drug addiction, or depression, and becomes less functional depending on the configuration of earlier developmental blocks. Less functional narcissistic types cannot accomplish as much because their egos are weaker and their decision-making more flawed. These types don't succeed by external standards but think they are the cat's meow. They can be filled with bravado without any basis in reality, thinking their ultimate success is just around the corner—a corner not even close to their vicinity. I will say more about this lower-level narcissist in a later chapter when I expand on Reich's typology.

Narcissistic types can have grand visions and live the big life. They are status-seekers and covet power symbols to ensure their need to be recognized and emulated. Narcissistic types thrive on winning. They want admiration, are competitive, and are concerned with their image, burnishing that to maintain a sense of self-worth and dominance. Thus, they live in a world of idealized others and devalued others. They inflate others—look up to them, want to emulate the more powerful—and then devalue those who don't impress them. These feelings of inflation and deflation are also internal and relate to how they view themselves. They are on top of their world, or they are failing, not keeping up, not good enough.

They often accomplish a great deal as they have available aggression, and that is a positive aspect of this type. On the other hand, they often neglect their close relationships because they need to maintain their status position and that absorbs their focus. Their relational skills are compromised as they are usually too inflated to be sensitive or empathetic. They can be limited in their contact as they are quite self-engrossed. And, usually, internally they are competing, feeling envious, and comparing who is better or worse off. And there is the overriding concern for what they can get from another.

Narcissists often utilize an attack mode to dominate and control, which is sometimes masked in a sophisticated style. They will use attack if necessary to maintain their advantage, to control and dominate. They can escalate in a conversation and overtalk and raise their voice and increase their speed to establish superiority, resulting in others backing down. Or they become argumentative and rude in order to assert their top-dog position. Narcissistic types have a great deal of anger as they compensate when they feel internally insecure, like when they feel they are losing their upper edge, feel criticized, or have a competitor. They have to maintain their edge or they can drop into their feelings of insecurity. They will get angry to maintain their position and cover up their hidden feelings of weakness. They often deny their inherent insecurity because their defenses work well. This type does not want to stop the speedy, aggressive push forward in order to slow down enough to make contact and self-examine.

Narcissists are extremely sensitive to criticism. If they even feel the slightest criticism, they will act defensively. If they anticipate an attack, they will attack first. They have fragile egos and don't do well with challenge and feedback. They can rear up defensively and dominate the conversation through fury, or withdraw punitively. They lack flexibility to engage and drop their defensive structure, because they need to keep their egos protected from demotion.

Sexually, certain issues emerge for the narcissist. Reich's healthy genital character type expresses sexuality in the service of expressing love, affection, and closeness. Sexuality can be visceral and intense as well. When we move to the phallic narcissistic male, he likes to manifest his potency through aggression and can express revenge in sexuality. He can be competitive, asserting power over his partner and wanting to show off his prowess more than express vulnerability with his partner. The male can wish to primitively pierce to prove his potency. The phallic narcissistic woman can be competitive, with a need to cut down and diminish her partner. She can be relentlessly critical and is therefore effective in her ability to dominate and then discard the other she is with.

Biophysically, narcissists have well-proportioned, athletic bodies with high energy and vigor. They can be good-looking, physically striking types and attract others to them due to their chiseled face and good looks. Attractiveness can lead to parental indulgence, specialness, and advantages outside the home.

With their substantial energy, they can be expansive in their actions yet bristle easily due to their high charge. Because they build up energy easily, they can be impatient, irritable, and overly aggressive in benign situations. They can move from charming to arrogant and from warm to cold withdrawal.

The narcissistic character's armoring is focused in an inflated chest; armored diaphragm with upper body, shoulder, and neck armoring; and tension in the legs. The chest cannot give in to the breath or yield to softer feelings. There can be other blocks that can dominate the picture. For example, if there is a significant eye block, then the character turns more paranoid. If the oral block dominates, then the narcissist experiences depression. These blocks help paint a more thorough picture with shadings that illuminate each particular person within the character type.

Narcissists seek therapy when their empires break down. Maybe they lose a good job or their marriage, get demoted, or otherwise lose their status through loss of wealth, position, or power. Then they begin to feel their weak, fragile, dependent underpinnings. They are habituated to control and dominate at their work or in their families. Suddenly, the hierarchical status symbols are waning. Aging, loss of image, illness, loss of control: all these types of situations challenge the narcissistic character. They are not flexible in adjusting to losses that affect their identity. They can fall into depression, lose motivation, and become unstable and anxious. Or they throw temper tantrums and rage at their weakening defenses. They have been bolstering themselves with external approval and externalized identity and when that shifts, they experience alienation, fragmentation, loss of self, and depression.

> Daniel is a successful real estate developer. He came to therapy due to difficulties in his marriage at 55. He is an attractive British man, polished, with a good sense of humor and a strong air of confidence and superiority. Yet, he lacks empathy and sensitivity. His confident glow gets the better of him. He travels due to business and enjoys his trips, although often drinks too much. One of his kids identifies with his dad's superior stance and can exhibit the same problematic lack of empathy. His wife feels ignored and unseen. She has difficulty getting his attention and then becomes hostile and provocative. Daniel has been compensating for his difficult history with a father that was also consumed with his own superiority and inflated sense of power. His mother was shy and distant. He emulated his father and had a meager connection to his mother. He learned in therapy how the lack of nurturance affected him, causing pain and feelings of sadness and loss. These feelings were inhibited partly due to British cultural norms. The Brits are known for their reserve, their stiff upper lip, and capacity to function over pain without dramatization, as that type of expression is unacceptable. The British can be prone to depression and alcoholism that originates in the emotionally inhibiting

culture and the preponderance of drinking as a societal norm. Daniel came to understand the reasons for his walled-off style of insensitivity and self-centeredness as he began to delve into his own losses. He could see his character pattern of superiority as a defense against his vulnerable feelings.

If the eye block dominates, the narcissist does not see reality clearly and becomes fearful and aggressive, falling into our next type, the paranoid.

In working with the narcissist, the Orgonomist dismantles all defenses listed earlier. As this type is extremely sensitive to criticism and will fight all the way to keep her position of dominance, the therapy can be quite engaged. As these defenses relent, the individual can feel more deeply into her underlying issues. The person can examine his inner demand to be special and one-up, and let this false power position go. Then he can relate better to others, and his aggressive approach will fall away. With good therapy, the narcissist's natural, exuberant high energy can be put to good use relationally, creatively, and spiritually (Frisch, August 22, 2014, blog, "Reich's Character Types").

Paranoid Character Type

The paranoid type is a phallic but with a severe, repressed ocular block. The block in the eye segment overrides his phallic status and defines him, meaning his eye block becomes his definitive feature and overrules his attainment of the phallic level. As this type usually does not seek therapy, I will be brief in my explanation. It is important to understand paranoia as an outlook that can be seen subtly or in an exaggerated fashion in many character types. This type does not look internally for the source of his problems but rather looks outside for the cause of his discomfort and discontent. We can say that his perception is distorted so he projects his inner distortion onto the world. Everyone else and everything else is responsible for his problems and disappointments in life. He can be arrogant in his assessments and feels righteous indignation about his causes. The levels of distortion may vary from slight to extreme as he views the world from his distorted lenses.

Paranoid types can be irritable, suspicious, with mood fluctuations and anger bouts as they blame others for everything. It is part of their presumptive thought process to see ulterior motives attributed abundantly to everyone and everything they come into contact with. The paranoid feels offended easily, misinterprets, feels insulted and slighted. He negatively projects on to others, meaning he attributes his own hostile, suspicious, or jealous ulterior leanings on to others and reacts. He has difficulties in relationships as everyone is against him or not to be trusted.

As heightened fear with aggression drives this type, he is prone to make drastic, irrational decisions. He literally moves out to the margin of society, out to the countryside and lives off the grid, thinking that isolation makes him safe. He may pull money out of reliable investments due to a preoccupation with doomsday scenarios and the advice given by other paranoids. He is prone to irreverent, irrational political views founded on exaggerated fears. Many political demagogues incite those fears to gain a following. He lacks trust and that manifests in chronic suspicion and contempt for conventional institutions such as the medical establishment, financial institutions, and regulations of any kind.

> Sal was the embodiment of this type. Married and in his early 50s, he was prone to making radical decisions without consulting his wife. He would unilaterally buy gold and stockpile it, never getting consultation. He trusted no one. He was ruled by his philosophy that saw danger around every corner. He would never seek conventional advice about anything. His wife was helpless in the face of his fears, and their relationship deteriorated. He did come into therapy from time to time and that helped temper his fear and aggression that led to impulsive moves. He was healthy enough to tolerate confrontation without bolting, and that is a good sign.

This type can feel persecuted in an exaggerated conviction that he has been wrongly treated. Out of this delusion comes a heightened, grandiose mission justified by feeling wronged. We can see this acted out in today's world screen where seeds of persecution and paranoia lead to extreme delusions and grandiose missions. The profiles of Europeans and Americans who have become involved with terrorist organizations begin with alienated, often isolated individuals with paranoid features.

Paranoid thinking can be seen in other character types who have significant eye blocks, but the paranoid ideation is not as pronounced as the paranoid type who has a *dominant* ocular block coupled with available energetic aggression. We have to be willing to point out those paranoid characteristics even if the paranoid clues are subtle. I am often quite frank in commenting on paranoid thought processes. If a patient has serious paranoia and is making up outlandish stories, then I will say what I think. It does no good to pretend that what they are saying is anything less than outrageous. Sometimes a paranoid patient can accept that intervention and feel relieved to have a way out of their delusional nightmare. The more serious types are not interested in your opinion and would rather blame and be right.

The Chronic Depressive

Phallic types who cannot maintain their dominance over their lifetimes or who initially did not get their emotional needs met in their families of origin will become chronically depressed. They falter and cannot sustain the phallic narcissist level due to their difficulties maintaining their aggression and become the chronic depressive.

The chronic depressive is a phallic type but due to dominant holding in the oral segment, namely, the mouth and jaw, this phallic type suffers from depression. He has all the basic features of the phallic but, because the block is predominantly in the oral segment, his energetic movement and expression is clamped down resulting in depression. Reich stated that this diagnosis is predominantly in males, though I have seen this character type in females as well.

A healthy oral segment facilitates *taking in* with pleasurable sensations through a wide-open, soft, receptive mouth. Also, we *give out* through our oral expression in the form of voice: words, sounds, and expression of feelings, facilitating relational communication so that we may pursue our needs in the world. This segment, if restrained, reduces both what is taken in as well as expressed. If the lips are tight and thin, and the mouth clamped down, then not much goes in or comes out. There is a lack of sensuality with oral repression. The more the block dominates, the more one experiences depression. The chronic depressive struggles between his energetic phallic narcissist features and the oral repression that drags him to an earlier developmental zone. He has maintained his phallic station, but has a lowered energy level, and as the oral block dominates, he gives up the Phallic Narcissist type completely as the depression overrides capacity for animated, free flowing energy.

The chronic depressive has a history of unmet needs and losses that fuel the depression. Early on, he may have missed breastfeeding or resonant connection and nurturance. So he clamped his mouth closed and harbored disappointment, sadness, and then anger in his jaw. He may have been misunderstood in his youth and wasn't free to express himself in the myriad of ways necessary to grow up unrestrained. He didn't feel deeply supported and seen. As a result, he couldn't fully become himself or utilize all his energy and intensity in his own behalf. He may have realized what he lacked but did not have the confidence to express his frustration or anger overtly, and instead felt guilty. If he expressed his dissatisfaction, he might risk losing what he did have, so he suppressed his natural expressions. Underneath, he felt grief, loss, and sorrow at not being loved and those feelings were held back as well. He might have appeared as a more serious, diligent, quiet, and well-behaved child trying to please and caretake his parents.

The chronic depressive can defend against his vulnerable feelings with righteousness and indignation or with ideological stances as he expresses his personal aggression in these more subterranean and muted ways. He feels disappointed underneath, but has difficulty taking those feelings seriously. As a result, he may feel chronically irritated and frustrated, as his life is not satisfying and he lives with pent-up aggression. He has problems manifesting as he lacks the necessary aggression in his own behalf, essential to activating intentions in the world.

This type is quite sensitive to his own feelings and the feelings of others as his phallic narcissistic traits are minimized by depression. The chronic depressive has lively contactful eyes and can make good contact. His eyes are an expression of his sensitivity and at times heightened feelings. He frequently experiences anxiety as feelings churn within, and he is acutely aware. He is a serious, highly responsible individual. He can be generous—he often caretakes others. His caretaking impulses ward off his deep longings. He takes care of others rather than expressing his needs to be loved and cared for. He has a long history of self-sacrifice. He doesn't want to rock the boat so he learns to adjust to circumstances and not demand too much for himself. This is his bind.

He may not appear depressed and sometimes he isn't, as he can be quite engaged in his life. He can have a good sense of humor although often directed against himself. But inside he battles with his depression. He is strong but restrained. It is the restraint that is his weakness. He can't quite realize his own agenda—come out into the world and claim who and what he is as a phallic narcissist can. His oral repressed block is a retreat that tempers his phallic power and brings on the depression.

The chronic depressive has a serious temperament. When the depression is activated, he can feel low energy. He will have cognitions that go along with depression, for example, self-blame and criticalness. As phallic narcissists blame others, the chronic depressive blames himself and takes all the responsibility. He accepts others' weaknesses but doesn't offer the same tolerance toward himself.

He is extremely honest and responsible in all aspects of his life. He has a strong drive and is often is very competent, even with his lowered energy level. He is usually above average in intelligence, organized, and conscientious. He can have compulsive traits due to the drag back from the phallic to the oral and then anal levels. This can show up in hyper-orderliness and meticulousness. Yet he does not function up to his capacity. Since he does not live up to his natural energy level, he feels inadequate and then guilty. So he gets caught in a loop.

The chronic depressive does have ample determination and doggedly keeps going. He longs to expand, express, and feel free from the psychological weight he carries, but has strong inhibitions against his desired freedom. He does not let himself feel pleasure on a regular basis and modulates his entitlement. It's as if he has to take care of others first and is reluctant to give himself what he wants. This is why chronic depressives make excellent caregivers and are enablers. *He survives by being needed.* He ignores himself by focusing on others as a way of deflecting his own anxiety and depression.

Allen, a middle-aged, good-looking, heterosexual male, came into therapy for his chronic depression. He is a talented writer but has not succeeded in consistently producing works for publication. He had published one novel but then was stymied predominantly by his caretaking propensities. He was in a long-term marriage that was fairly healthy and productive. After his marriage ended he got into another marriage where he was the sole provider and caretaker of an impaired mate. Allen became seriously depressed, unmotivated, and despairing. He was not getting his needs met but felt guilty when he wanted more. His feelings were quite repressed and his mouth grimaced over them. After a few years of diligent therapy, he is out of that unrewarding relationship and setting limits on caretaking friends and family. He has returned to writing and is generally feeling buoyant and happy for the first time in a long time.

Therapy helps to mobilize and expand the chronic depressive's energy. In bodywork, the chest is mobilized so he can breathe more freely. With the expanded breath and energy, he can feel his inhibited rage that has resulted in depression and release it. Also, his deep sorrow, loss, and grief can be felt through crying. His oral repression begins to give way and his mouth softens. With these changes, his energy is freed so he can direct it toward his own life and creative activation. He realizes his longing for pleasure and love and can go after it. His negativity can be transformed into pleasurable life experiences. His natural drive helps him to work intently in therapy—he sticks with it and gains the benefits (Frisch, September 26, 2014, blog, "Reich's Character Types").

Manic-Depressive Character Type

Like the chronic depressive, a phallic type distinguished by *repression* in the oral segment, the manic-depressive also has an oral block, but it fluctuates between repressed and *unsatisfied* responses. The oral unsatisfied type has had some taste of pleasure but then it was not sustained. This type longs for oral pleasure but never feels satisfied. The repressed type didn't have satisfaction and shut down interest in getting needs met. In this case both the repressed and unsatisfied elements are engaged, first one and then the other in an on again off again rhythm.

The manic-depressive character type is referenced typically as bipolar disorder. This is an overdiagnosed label these days. I notice that many people are referred to as bipolar in everyday conversation. Of course, there are legitimate diagnoses in *DSM-5* for vegetative bipolar disorders requiring medications to achieve basic social functioning. I would suggest that the manic-depressive *character type* be the focus rather than the symptom picture as that would change the conventional treatment approach. It would encourage less pharmacological interventions and a more therapy-oriented approach when suitable. What I am discussing is a character type that embodies features of volatility, psychological instability, and impulsivity with repetitive mood swings from inflated elated moods to depression. The description goes beyond defining mental problems solely from a symptom approach, that is, a mood disorder, and encompasses a broader palette for understanding the individual and her problems. A character type develops out of repetitive, stylistic, behavioral, attitudinal approach to life; a method of survival and defense founded on nature and nurture aspects.

The manic-depressive has reached the phallic phase with an unsatisfied oral block that leads to oral unsatisfied traits of expansion, and then the oral repressed block steps in with a contraction and depression ensues. The manic-depressive is unstable and less integrated than the chronic depressive. When the oral repression loosens and expands, a manic phase ensues. Thus manic traits are unleashed making her demanding, impatient, and erratic. She tries to fill up her oral craving as that desire is unavailable when she is depressed and the oral block is in a contracted phase. So she feels free with a heightened energy. She may overeat and drink, be talkative to the extreme, go on buying binges, smoke, do drugs—all leading to an accelerated level of activity as she tries to gain satisfaction. She is not used to the energy and she becomes disorganized quickly. Due to this restless quest she is excitable and can be loud, displaying exaggerated self-confidence. It is difficult to be rational and focused under these circumstances. Therefore she exhibits poor judgment and faulty decision-making. Due to her unrealistic inflation she can become dogmatic and rigid in her views and push headlong into situations with disastrous consequences.

Another contributing factor to the manic-depressive's poor judgment is his eye block. This type suffers from lack of clarity in the eyes that leads to misperceptions. The eyes go out of focus, particularly in the manic phase, and contribute to distorted points of view. During those times, it is hard to reach someone in a manic phase as he feels intensely all-knowing and sufficiently out of contact to ignore input.

Then inevitably the high ride is over and the oral block contracts. This is because expansion and contraction or pulsation is the nature of all living things. Everything in the universe expands and contracts and so do we—our cells, our organs, our nervous system, our energy levels, and so on. When the oral block contracts, the manic-depressive falls into a depression with the attendant discouragement and hopelessness. Her body and mind slow down and inactivity takes over.

There are variations in how extreme the swings are. Some individuals have subtler shifts between mania and depression; others fluctuate wildly from one to the other. Some tend to be more depressed, others more manic as their steady state. As individuals age, these phases can be more entrenched and the repercussions more debilitating.

> Jennifer started treatment with a dynamic style. She was overweight but attractive with brilliant red hair and an animated smile. She was a successful entrepreneur with productive ideas that led to successful enterprises. She also suffered from bouts of depression that left her bedraggled and discouraged. She had a difficult history with a psychotic mother and passive father. She was ready to work with all of that. We had to rein in her shopping sprees as she could spend money impulsively when she was feeling upbeat. She often got carried away buying for her daughter and smothering her with clothes. She would binge eat and drink as well, and those habits were always on the table for discussion and limitations. She was prone to hot ideas and had to be contained regarding grandiose scenarios that she wanted to act on. Fortunately she was dedicated to therapy and worked long and hard on her issues. Jennifer spent many a session in rage and grief about her difficult past but as she worked through these feelings, her mood stabilized and she no longer had extreme ups and downs.

Therapy for manic-depressives focuses on containment and internal organization and regulation. This individual must understand his intrinsic dynamics so he can see his swings, make adjustments, and not cooperate with the swings. The manic fluctuation needs to be recognized and contained so that the issues of loss and feelings of longing underneath can be explored. When in the depressive phase, energy can be mobilized by breath and movement. The individual learns to get needs met in a productive way. Healthy habits have to be sustained as the character is unraveled in treatment. Then this individual can become stable and in control of his moods. The oral segment is opened up so that the repressed block is diminished along with the depression and the person can experience healthy pulsation and pleasure without volatility and craving. The eyes are worked on to increase contact and clear perception. As the individual settles down in therapy, distortions can be ironed out and the person develops a stable self, with appropriate creative expression and satisfaction in relationships (Frisch, October 25, 2014, blog, "Reich's Character Types").

Anal Character Types: Compulsive Type

The compulsive type is a highly controlling personality. These individuals are quite anxious and contain their anxiety through various controlling behaviors. They want to feel in control of everything and everyone as a way to feel in charge and less threatened. It is an untenable relational position as others respond negatively to their need to manage everything. The controlling quality leads to rigidity as they are tied to specific ways that tasks need to be accomplished. They become stubborn as they lack flexibility and must maintain control no matter what. They do not give in and fear letting go of their control. Self-control is critical to their sense of having mastery over the challenges of life.

As Baker states, "The compulsive is the human machine" (Baker, 1967, 124). This type is extremely cautious and conservative as he maintains a robotic interface with all aspects of his functioning. He does not want to rock the boat and experience too much stimulation and destroy his equilibrium. Compulsives are tidy and lead an overly ordered life that can include extreme organizing rituals. Everything is thought out and planned and the need for events to become routine is paramount. If routines are interrupted the person does not cope well. This type is the opposite of spontaneous or impulsive. There may be set ways of dishwashing and loading the dishwasher, and it is highly uncomfortable to have it done in a slightly different manner. The anal type needs extra time to prepare, and if he does not have ample time he will feel anxious or panicky. It may take him extended time to shower and dress and gather himself together. Thus getting ready to leave the house may take an inordinate amount of time.

His attention to detail and avoidance of anxiety or panicky feeling leads to ruminative or repetitive thought processes. He is doubtful about decision-making and will obsess as he tries to decide on the best strategy. Everything must be thought through and through and through again. Add the caution and things need to be analyzed over and over to make sure that a decision is suitable. He tends to be indecisive and distrustful of others. No one else can do it right for him.

There are no priorities in terms of thinking things over, meaning whether the items are ordinary and mundane or something of important intrinsic value, they are given the same weight. So creativity usually falls into a maze of more prosaic worries and thus never gets expressed. Creativity is bogged down amid the ordinary details of life.

Compulsive types can be frugal and downright stingy. They keep everything they have close to them and are not giving. They do not expand but rather contract around their possessions, holding on and retaining at all costs. The compulsive can be obsessed with material objects, coveting items and focused on the management of material possessions. They are not generous with time, money, or feeling for others.

These traits are seen classically in terms of the anal function and fears of soiling or "making a mess." Because of this anal holding, possibly due to too early toilet training or parental negativity around this phase of development, the phallic stage is achieved briefly but is given up for extensive holding in the anal segment. There can be severe anxiety early on as the child tries to control what is beyond his capacity, in order to please his parents. The developmental phase of separation and individuation and development of autonomy are important tasks to be mastered at this phase as well. If parents discourage the impulse to separate and explore and establish a sense of self, then the child's independent spirit can be squelched. Therefore, attempts at too early control create tension, muscular tightness thus armoring throughout the child's body.

The pressure produces anger, frustration, and rage and the aggressive feelings are held back too. Thus the compulsive finally reaches the phallic stage but with held-in aggression that is not tolerated within nor expressed externally. The individual reverts back to the anal stage. This type becomes the epitome of the good adolescent but lives without available emotion under severe pressure.

If the compulsive defenses are weakened there is a type that expresses the opposite style with messiness, sloppiness, and lack of attention to detail. This subset can be irresponsible about money and other aspects of life, including self-care.

Compulsives throughout their lives have a difficult time accessing the flow of feeling, as they are robotic and mechanical. This type has little contact with their emotions as feelings are bound up in their rigidity. Their bodies are rigidified as well, which goes along with their overly controlling style. Their face can appear awkward and stiff.

A couple came into treatment with much distress. The woman in the relationship was a compulsive type and would not stay out of her husband's personal spaces. She managed everything from how he folded his towel in the bathroom to how he kept his home office. He was always angry and expressed that with his own style of provocative behaviors. He felt deep down that he couldn't really manage without her "parental" guidance and she hid her weakness and dependency needs by acting like the strong woman in charge. They were caught in a fused relationship with neither having autonomy and space to discover the truth about themselves. These dynamics needed to be clearly spelled out and the character of each delineated. Through awareness, behavioral suggestions, and deep understanding of self and other they could revamp their relational and individual dynamics.

Therapy for compulsives is helpful as it loosens the grip of the control and exposes their fear of stimulation, movement, and letting go. Point out the caution, the doubting, and their stubbornness. Later in therapy, the hatred, rage, and sadistic impulses have to be confronted and expressed. Aggressive impulses are held back in an internally aggressive way, so that bind needs to be loosened. Expose the ruminating tendencies that will expose their fears. These patients can be tortured by the tedium of the rituals and the emptiness of it all. Set limits on all ritualizing and compulsive behaviors, delineating all of them openly. Stopping the repetitive and empty behaviors will free up anxiety and deeper feelings that had been bound in controlling maneuvers. The patient comes into contact with her important inner conflicts. She needs help in redirecting her time and energy toward her own pursuits and creative manifestations of the authentic self.

Ocular Character Types: The Schizophrenic

In our daily interactions with intimate others we look into their eyes and may feel responsiveness, a steadiness and presence in their eyes as they look at us. We have a sense that we are in "eye contact." Yet for most of us there are limitations in our ability to make satisfying eye contact. If we extend our circle out from intimates we might notice how difficult it is for people to look with a steady gaze or to have clear eyes that are readable. Some ocular holding is common, meaning that our eyes—including our ability to see clearly, perceive reality, sense reality through our physical sensations; tolerate eye contact from others; and come forward through one's eyes—have been compromised. We count on the integration of the ocular segment with our other capacities of sensing, perceiving, feeling, and thinking to give us a clear grasp of reality.

Reich stated that a serious eye block starts in the first ten days of life. He was referring to the mother-infant dyad and how the eye contact evolved between the two. Did the infant look into warm eyes that enveloped with safety or was the caretaker distressed, distracted, or expressing meanness in her eyes? The absence of early attachment synchrony is a factor in the development of an ocular block.

The ocular segment is critical to our functioning after birth and is the earliest way we begin to orient along with our oral needs. And so an ocular block would result in our first developmental difficulty. As we develop toward latency and puberty, our biophysical characteristics mature. As in other character types, puberty is when the character type is fixed and symptoms solidify for the most part. The eye block does not necessarily inhibit development to a higher level of functioning (phallic level) but will color the functional capacity depending on how serious the ocular segment block is. Individuals with an ocular block do not retreat to that level (as does the anal character), but rather keep developing with those limitations. More severe types may retreat to some extent to the ocular level and have psychotic symptoms along with more extreme withdrawal and shutting off from the real world as we know it.

The term *schizophrenia* has a long history in medical nomenclature and is a current medical diagnostic category in the *DSM-5* that defines a severe brain disorder in which people interpret reality abnormally. Classic schizophrenia may result in a combination of hallucinations, delusions, and disordered thinking and behavior. Research has discovered a strong genetic component in the development of schizophrenia. Classic schizophrenia defines a disorder that seriously affects normal functioning and is chronic and stabilized according to current guidelines with massive doses of medications. Many schizophrenics with heightened symptoms can live with either low dosage medications or none at all and benefit from psychotherapy (Bollas, 2015). In fact, this was recently confirmed by an article on the front page of *The New York Times*, entitled "New Approach May Alleviate Schizophrenia," which said, "Study advises therapy and reduced drugs" (Carey, 2015). (This research published in the *American Journal of Psychiatry* and funded by NIMH is a rare, exciting turnaround in clinical practice guidelines. The study found statistical effectiveness in the trial with low dosage medications [20%–50% lower], early intervention at first episode—usually in late teens—with talk therapy, family education, and help with education and work.) The article affirms the importance of a holistic approach that views pathology through the lens of the personal rather than throwing massive drugs at a problem in a generalized way.

The schizophrenic character type can mimic similar social behaviors and traits seen in some individuals who might be diagnosed on the autistic spectrum or with Asperger syndrome (as it is still known). Individuals with Asperger syndrome do not have intellectual, cognitive, or language delays but do have the social and communication limitations of those on the autism spectrum. The autistic spectrum defines dimensions of severity across multiple indicators from mild to severe social communication symptoms noticeable in early childhood. The adult with a higher functioning capacity might be misdiagnosed as Asperger or attention deficit disorder when he is actually a schizophrenic character type.

Reich utilized the term *schizophrenic* differently to define a character type distinguished by the stage of the developmental difficulty and the severity of the block in the ocular segment. Reich discussed this type as reaching the phallic level albeit with early developmental arrest in the ocular segment. I will discuss schizophrenia again in another chapter on developmental passages when I cover the earlier pregenital attachment phases and disorders attendant to those phases. This comprehensive understanding of the components of the Schizophrenic character type can give direction to treatment.

Don't be alarmed by the term *schizophrenic character type* or think it is an unusual type that you rarely interact with. There are many extremely successful schizophrenic types in business and technology, for example, or in artistic realms. This type can be extremely intelligent, creative, with heightened capacity for imaginative thinking. They can be dogged, industrious, and work compulsively; they can be driven to accomplish and work on projects for long hours until they are completed in a way that suits their high standards. Yet, they exhibit oddness at times, a contactless quality, as if they are often lost in thought. In the social area they are less confident and tend to be introverted. They can seem ungrounded, confused, and lack relational skills as they have difficulty reading social cues. The schizophrenic type has minimal interest in his appearance and grooming and is less interested in the physical aspects of his life. He can seem idiosyncratic and you feel you can't quite pin him down.

The most significant area of armoring for this character type is in the brain as the occiput region connects through the optic nerves to the eyes. The schizophrenic has a brain contraction and therefore retains high-energy charge in the head and withdrawal in the eyes. Further, the contraction in the brain lowers stimulation to the vegetative centers in the brain, including the hypothalamus and particularly the respiratory center. The normal pulsation of the brain is constricted. Therefore the brain tissue and supportive glial tissues are impacted. This constriction contributes to the eye block as there is too much charge in the brain and head. The energy flow does not circulate down toward the chest, organs, and limbs, therefore creating an implosion in the cranial area. Schizophrenics often feel tightness in their head muscles and occipital regions and those areas are painful to the touch.

One of the major symptoms of schizophrenia is the split between perception and sensation. Thus excitation, which normally leads to sensation with perception is disrupted and split apart. Perception of self comes from contact with an excitation and the subjective experience of that excitation that results in consciousness and conscious self-perception. If there is a malfunction in self-perception, then consciousness is limited. Consciousness includes our capacity to orient and engage in social reality. If the dysfunction is severe, then thoughts and perceptions are separated off from the body. This results in confusion, disorientation, and projections on to others and a lack of clarity in all areas.

That means that the way sensation is codified in the mind is separate from perception. So schizophrenics can discuss their sensations as separate from emotional or cognitive connection. They may feel sensations acutely but as stand-alone events related to nothing else in their life. A schizophrenic can describe "electrical currents in their legs" and in extreme cases attribute those sensations to a message from god. Or their perceptions don't integrate with their sensations so they may perceive things out of context or not related to their feelings. They may perceive or fear a physical symptom and what it might mean but have no sensation to back it up. It is a purely cognitive conjecture. Thus their communication about things can seem odd or disconnected from what others generally perceive.

The schizophrenic cannot "see clearly" and integrate the rainbow of feelings: fear, love, anxiety, or anger due to chronic misperception of reality. As they exist more in the thinking function, cut off from their body, they don't have sufficient access to emotions. In order to feel, we need an organized, integrated perception-sensation function.

Schizophrenics go off in their eyes. Their eyes can appear receded, vacant, trance-like, and are seemingly not connected. If a schizophrenic is overly stimulated, has more sensation than he can tolerate, he will immediately remove himself by going away in his eyes therefore losing further contact with reality. Sensations and stimulation may lead to distortions or delusions in his way of feeling. The ocular block results in disorientation, dissociation, and withdrawal of interests.

The schizophrenic breathes at a minimum due to lack of energy flow to the respiratory center of the brain. If you sit with these individuals in session, you can barely see the inspiration or exhalation. They keep their energy level down with their repressed breathing style. The lowered energy level due to limited breathing reduces sensation and stimulation so they don't need muscular armoring to hold the excess energy. The lack of body armor permits heightened awareness as it is not bound in muscular holding throughout the body. So the schizophrenic can be acutely alive and aware of his environment through one function like perception or another as in sensation, albeit with a limited movement of energy so he can feel more comfortable.

This type also has a tight throat and therefore can have a raspy voice or sound constricted when he speaks. He doesn't express emotions easily as his throat is chronically, partially closed up, inhibiting his ability to vocalize and emote. He can be shy and timid, withdrawing easily if threatened.

Due to the ocular block, the schizophrenic has poor contact within himself, others, and the external environment. He can project and misinterpret because his vision is compromised. With distorted awareness he misinterprets and lacks perspective, so he doesn't read cues from others, doesn't relate well in social situations, and can be lost in his head thinking with distorted perceptions. He can lack a capacity for empathy.

The defining emotion for the schizophrenic is fear. He is fearful about most things partly because he is out of contact, misinterprets, and has sensations devoid of perceptions that ground him in reality. He can have an imagination that takes him to fearful places. He can be terrified of others, feel threatened, and then feel hatred due to the threat he misperceives. To diagnose the schizophrenic the therapist must see fear as the predominant feeling in the patient.

The schizophrenic has weak boundaries psychologically and biophysically. As his energy is lodged predominantly in his head and thinking function, his body is less developed. The armoring is in the head; his body has little armoring and therefore has less muscle mass. The more extreme the eye block, the less armoring in the body, as the armoring is in the brain and eyes. So his body may seem weaker and appear to spread out in the office, limbs askew. Psychologically he does not have firm boundaries as his thinking spreads out to engulf others without limits. Baker states, "The energy field is extremely extensive and widespread and seems to have no boundaries. . . . His field is diffuse and weak because his organism is unable to hold it together with his low energy level" (Baker, 1967, 145). He doesn't know where he ends and you begin.

> Shana came to therapy at 19 with encouragement from her concerned parents. She was accepted to college but felt so much anxiety and fear that she ended up having to return home before the year ended. She collapsed at home in a depression. She was also smoking pot somewhat regularly. She felt lost and inadequate. Shana was consumed with circular thinking and fearful rumination as she surfed the Internet daily. Other than that she was doing nothing. She had a muted, weak voice, a slender body, and unfocused eyes. She looked disheveled when she came to her appointment. Therapy was about first unwinding her anxiety and fear to discover the contributing elements. The first order of business was to stop her pot smoking—a form of self-medication to numb her high anxiety. Stopping pot helped her to become more connected to reality and her feelings. As we unraveled her situation, Shana explored the disconnectedness she always felt with her parents, who were aging hippies who still smoked pot and led unconventional lives. Their lifestyle was difficult for her growing up as she felt ignored and was not helped to form regulated habits that would have contributed to her sense of confidence. Therapy helped her create form and substance in herself and her life that enabled her to become independent and return to college.

The schizophrenic can lack aggression due to his confusion and lack of strength both psychologically and physically. Confusion is a major characteristic. His confusion weakens his aggression, as he doesn't know what he really thinks and feels. This confusion stems from his eye block as he is unable to define his reality. He suffers from an unintegrated quality and can seem disorganized. The interface with reality is less than orderly as his focus on the brain and thinking can predominate over a hands-on sense of reality.

A small portion of schizophrenics can be prone to exaggerated paranoid thinking due to their lack of visual and perceptual clarity. Their paranoia can lead to an attitude of grandiosity and righteous indignation perpetuated by an inflated, all-knowing attitude. They project fear and anger outside themselves and onto others, including institutions. For the average schizophrenic with paranoia, he may have doomsday scenarios that result in paranoia in the financial realm. He can be fearful of conventional institutions or become vulnerable to hoarding and other schemes like stockpiling gold. Or he can be mistrustful of the government, conventional medicine, educational authorities, and other conventional institutions of authority; paranoid thinking can also manifest in political extremism.

These fears can lead, in an extreme form, to isolated, marginalized types who feel deeply inadequate and live in their minds with enhanced projections on the outside world. They long for power as they feel that they don't fit in and feel rejected. Often they feel inadequate in love relationships as they do not extend themselves to create normal relationships due to their insecurity. They defend against their deeper pain by engaging in compulsive Internet use and social media to compensate. Here they lose further contact with reality and dive deeper and deeper into delusions.

In the most impaired cases we see the lone gunman acting out his paranoid, grandiose fantasies and distorted perceptions. Through mass shootings he captures a sense of power and publicity that compels him beyond his small life and becomes a suicidal mission as well.

Some extreme political fanatics or zealots are paranoid schizophrenics—out of contact with reality, slaves to their ideological thinking that turns into religious fanaticism and bigotry. They can become righteous zealots that justify heinous actions for the sake of their cause. It is not only the paranoid schizophrenic who may act out in society; the psychopathic personality disorder, the phallic paranoid character type (Reich), the paranoid personality disorder, and the devaluing narcissist can also be implicated in these types of crimes against society.

Schizophrenics may be inclined to use marijuana, but that is not a good idea. They are already out of contact in their eyes and pot makes it worse. Many "pot heads" are schizophrenic, diffuse in their dealings in life, "spaced out" and floating as if in a cloud above reality. Pot can encourage marginalization from society. Habitual pot use must be discouraged and particularly with this type.

Many of the character types can have an ocular block. If the eye segment is quite problematic, then that defines more the character manifestations. For example, a hysteric may have a significant eye block but retain her hysteric qualities, but if the eye block and characteristics of the block dominate, then she might be labeled a schizophrenic.

Therapy teaches the schizophrenic to increase his capacity for contact and regulate his life better, enabling more grounding and confidence. Therapy can challenge the paranoid assumptions. Work on the relational deficiencies helps to unlock the buried pain. Treatment helps the schizophrenic communicate better and feel more connected to others and that relieves symptoms (Frisch, November 15, 2016, blog, "The Schizophrenic Character").

One subtype you may see frequently in your practice is the catatonic schizophrenic, so I will define that subtype here.

The Catatonic Schizophrenic

You might think this name *catatonic schizophrenic* refers to the extreme version of patients seen in mental wards but actually this character type is common among average neurotic people. This type is an anal character but with a significant eye block. Many of the features of the anal compulsive are at play, adding the schizophrenic elements of confusion and fear. The predominant characteristic of the catatonic schizophrenic is immobility, just like the anal character but with heightened fear due to the ocular block. Remember the schizophrenic's major emotion is fear. The catatonic schizophrenic is particularly terrified of movement, excitation, and stimulation. This type can be extremely functional in the real world, holding down a job and a family.

The catatonic has the doubting and caution of the anal type. So decision-making moves slowly with extreme caution and ruminative thinking. She can feel numbness in her body as there is a high degree of tension and muscular holding. This leads to emotional frozenness. This type is quite immobilized even when functional. They don't like to feel too much, have too much excitement, or demand too much of themselves. They like life to move slowly, without too many obligations to keep stimulation down to a minimum.

Initially in treatment with the catatonic there is a limited range of feeling as there is frozenness and contraction that doesn't permit contact with feelings. Over time the therapy can progress so she can tolerate movement, excitation, and feeling.

> Kathy, an intelligent college graduate, age 45, had a muted expression with vacant yet furtive eyes when she started therapy. Her voice lacked substance and was raspy. She was overweight and low energy. She originally came in because she felt lost. She was working at a job where she was overqualified but never considered seeking an appropriate job. She was in a relationship that had little life to it, but felt it was best to stay put. She responded often in therapy with the statement, "I don't know." She was quiet in session as she had minimal access to her feelings and thoughts. It was helpful when we discussed her fear and its roots in her family of origin. She had been so frozen around her historical events that thawing those out brought a trickle of tears to her eyes. She began to experience herself in the room with me and could tolerate more feelings of movement. If she went into confusion, we would stop there so she could see that she had moved behind that defensive style to ward off painful recognitions. That knowledge has helped her get under the vacant, confused layer. She began to understand her terror of change and movement, and how she warded off stimulation.

With schizophrenics in general the therapist has to be aware of the fear component so they understand and accept their high fear quotient. Then as the work creates an expansion of their system, the energy can move more into their bodies, their eyes can clear, and they can feel more confident. They become more grounded in reality, in relationships, and feel more connected to daily life.

The Substance Abuser

Substance abuse and addiction can occur in all character types. Substance abuse is a way to medicate uncomfortable feelings, curb anxiety, and in general deaden the stimulation that comes from interfacing with life challenges.

Reich would say this symptom comes with an oral unsatisfied type who needs constant oral gratification to self-soothe. Substance abuse is regressive in that the patient is slipping back to an oral stage of development and passively gratifying as a coping strategy. Most substance abusers either stop their development when their addictions start or sabotage or destroy gains they have made in their lives at the point the addiction takes over. Many marriages have failed because of alcohol or drug use that contaminated and ultimately destroyed the relationship and family. Careers have crashed and burned up due to impulsive decisions made on drugs and the lack of responsibility that comes with chronic drug and alcohol use.

Alcoholics tend to mediate anxiety through drinking and then become addicted to alcohol. For some the social stimulation at a bar draws them as they might feel too isolated without a place to hang out and have social contact.

> Jim, 55 and divorced, found himself at the bar in his favorite restaurant usually five times a week. He craved the social connection of hanging out where he was known. He would often binge drink with six or more drinks. When he drank excessively he would feel hung over. His health was compromised. His parents were alcoholics, and alcohol was always part of his life and contributed to his failed marriage. He could hold down a job responsibly and had succeeded financially, but his life was a circular process of working and drinking with less and less meaning. He was avoiding his loneliness and doing nothing substantial about it. When he agreed to attend AA meetings, his life began to turn around and we could go deeper in our work together without alcohol clouding our field of inquiry.

Pot smokers usually exhibit difficulties mastering life. Their daily marijuana smoking can mute their engagement in life. If the habit starts too early, the young person may never launch to college, a career, or establish meaning in his life. If older, his life can be like a broken record stuck on one song. The immaturity is obvious, although he often thinks he is very "cool."

There are very serious addictions to Oxycontin, heroin, methamphetamines, fentanyl, cocaine, prescribed opioid pain medications, and many other drugs that have come on the market. Drug use creates an aborted life that is preoccupied with sustaining the addiction.

I have seen therapists in training work with individuals who have not stopped their addictive behavior. Substance use must be continually addressed, as therapy cannot begin if repetitive use of any kind is still operative. If a patient is medicating himself, then he is not available for introspection and cannot tolerate the necessary feelings and anxiety. The therapy becomes a sham. One therapist didn't realize her patient had broken the agreement not to smoke 24 hours before session and came to her office multiple times stoned on pot. I don't feel an agreement to not smoke 24 hours before the appointment is helpful as the therapist is colluding with the patient's addictive behaviors. Other clinical students know their patient is smoking pot regularly, but ignore the topic. If a patient is not willing to face that he has a drug or alcohol problem, then the patient is not ready for therapy.

I recommend that patients interested in serious therapy commit to AA programs to achieve sobriety. If a detox program is necessary, that comes first before therapy. If the patient is not addicted but drinks in excess, then the therapist can see if self-regulation is possible. The therapist has to be vigilant to make sure drugs and alcohol excesses have not crept back into the therapy room. Often patients hide their excesses from the therapist and continue to use secretly. That becomes an issue in the therapeutic relationship. We are not the police, but behaviors that derail the therapy are our business. So are the lapses in integrity.

Note

1 I suggest laminating this partial list of character types for use as an easy reference guide. The chart can be accessed for printing in the online appendix for this book at www.routledge.com/9781138562363.

Part III

Expanding Reich's Diagnostic Typology

6 Integration of Masterson's Disorders of the Self Diagnoses

Why Expand Reich's Types?

Indigo, a 41-year-old, heavy set, attractive, provocatively dressed woman, talked fast, in a pushy fashion, demanding attention and controlling the therapy hour. She had been spinning the therapist around and around for more than a year with her volatile feelings regarding a series of relationships. She was dominating and refused to be contained in therapy. She went from relationship to relationship, discussing these with her therapist as each one ended in heartache and drama. Meanwhile, her career was in tatters, leading to financial problems as well as difficulties managing her alcohol use. One could spin with the symptoms, give advice in the attempt to control the patient, or the therapist could figure out what is really going on and settle on the organizing principle. What does this configuration of symptoms define? Once you can see the gestalt of the symptom picture, you have a case formulation and an inherent game plan rather than working session by session blown by the winds of the current situations and improvising on an ad hoc basis. That mode of therapy can lead to feelings frustration and impotence in both the patient and the therapist. Patient character patterns and therefore behaviors are repetitive and although insights may abound the patient stays stuck.

Another case, Cindy, was presented through a description written up by a professional-in-training. During trainings, cases are presented so the clinician can get help. Professionals discover that if the patient can be understood through the lens of their most important defining traits and problems, the patient's issues can be seen with clarity and the case organized effectively. In this case, the professional was confused and the therapeutic approach haphazard. Cindy, age 40, was a medical doctor practicing an alternative modality with little success. Cindy lived in constant fear and suffered from severe, chronic anxiety. She was preoccupied with her own symptoms and worried about potential diseases and risks to her health. Her fear guided her down various paths of risks and cures. Her coping strategy was to obsess and ruminate about everything. She became obsessed with managing what she concluded were food sensitivities through extreme controlling measures. As her dominant feeling was fear, she felt afraid of most things and utilized compulsive behaviors to gain control, but that approach did not help her anxious state. She had not faced her driving state of fear, but rather tried to gain mastery by her obsessive attention to details. This resulted in odd behaviors that could be rationalized as appropriate unless you looked with our clear lens at the whole picture. The therapist was lost in surface feelings having to do with her history of obsessiveness and old issues with mother and sister. The patient presented family of origin issues as her central presenting problem. All the while, Cindy's pervasive fear—acted out in compulsive controlling behaviors—were noted but ignored in treatment. What do these dominant traits suggest in terms of a character diagnosis?

Let's try to place Indigo and Cindy in one of the stages so we can figure out the nature of their problems. Only then can we help. By defining character or personality patterns and how they develop, we can understand the underlying drive and therefore know how to intervene in an organized and consistent way. We can be effective rather than watching in dismay from the sidelines.

By viewing patients through their personality or long-term character structure you can make sense of an array of symptoms. We can look at our own symptoms and see the essential defining structure and make sense out of our confusing myriad of feeling states. We need an organizing reference template of character types and how they develop.

Reich's paradigm of character is a sufficient and comprehensive clinical system unto itself. Yet I felt his emphasis on psychosexual stage development with focus exclusively on the neurotic phase and Oedipal conflicts was in need of amplification. In my study of James Masterson, MD, (1926–2010), and his institute's contributing clinicians, I discovered a clinical compatibility with Reich's approach that encouraged me to integrate certain elements. Masterson's organization of personality disorders allowed me to bridge his Disorders of the Self (DOS) types to Reich's.

In my practice I see patients that do not fit into Reich's neurotic categories, for example, Indigo. A clinician might think that she is neurotic but actually her development was stymied much earlier. She is an example of a patient that fits the DOS borderline personality classification due to an earlier impasse in her development. I was thrilled to discover Masterson's description of DOS personality disorders as it was compatible with Reich's approach and helped me conceptualize my method. I filled in the blanks left by Reich's system with the addition of types defined by early attachment problems. Interestingly, as I was writing this book I learned from the current director of the Masterson Institute that they also teach elements of Reich's character analysis to their postgraduates. I was thrilled to discover that they see the compatibility. The Masterson Institute does not teach Reich's somatic component.[1]

The next chapter describes Masterson's personality disorders. My purpose is to supply the clinician with critical additional personality types that complete my character typology. Then the map of types is comprehensive and suitable for a thorough differential character diagnosis that sets the therapist up with a suitable game plan. Although the two systems don't blend perfectly, the wise clinician can pull from both to have a comprehensive road map of types. I will not cover Masterson's work and other developmental theoreticians' work in a comprehensive way. Please consult the list of reference books for a complete and thorough understanding of the early developmental stages, attachment theory, and the theoretical structure of the personality disorders listed.

Summary: Stages of Development—Zero to Three Years

According to the research on early childhood development, the need for attachment is the quintessential motivator of a child's behavior. It dynamically affects the development of critical areas in the brain. The developmental stages occurring before age three are referred to as *pre-oedipal* (a term coined by Otto Rank in the late 1920s) or pregenital phases.[2] The earlier developmental phases covering the first year to age three were not definitively researched until the work of Margaret Mahler (1897–1985) in the 1940s to 1960s in the United States. She and others conducted directed child observational studies including testing and interviews of normal and pathological children's development up to age three. Mahler developed the concept of separation-individuation, a critical developmental phase. Many other researchers and clinicians contributed to the studies on bonding and attachment, including the famous contributions of John Bowlby (1907–1990), a British psychoanalyst who studied the bonding behavior of animals. Mary Ainsworth (1913–1999), a colleague, studied infant-parent separations and came up with secure and insecure attachment patterns. Knowing your patient's early attachment history gives you necessary information to formulate an immediate take on how and why the patient formed his basic style and behavioral responses. Further, specific attachment history will give you perspective on how your patient will respond to you and relate to others.

The growth period before the Oedipal phase is critical to healthy development, and ruptures in this period create significant disorders; the central core of the person does not develop to completion if early development and attachment is compromised. I will utilize Margaret Mahler's stages knowing that other theoreticians might emphasize a slightly different phase development process. The phases begin with the *normal-symbiotic phase*, until 5 months, and move into an extended *separation-individuation phase*, 5–30 months (including subphases). The first subphase of separation-individuation is *hatching—* awareness of differentiation and development of body image (5–9 months). The second subphase is the *practicing* phase (9–16 months). The third phase is *rapprochement* (15–24 months), and the fourth subphase is consolidation of *individuation* and the beginning of object permanence (Jean Piaget, Swiss psychologist [1896–1980]) and object constancy at 22–30 months (Mahler et al, 1973).

How do these stages of development affect the development of personality disorders or character types? Much like Reich diagramed how blocks in erogenous zones affected development of types, these phases, if not adequately completed, create personality liabilities that continue into adult life.

> Where there is sufficient maternal libidinal investment in the child's growing self, normal development will occur. Where the mother's libidinal investment is insufficient, that is, where there is neglect, abuse, trauma, chronic misattunement, or persistent emotional pressure on a child to submit to a relational bargain primarily designed to serve the mother's psychological needs as opposed to the child's, a Disorder of the Self will result that will manifest itself as a stable diagnostic entity with its own structural characteristics.
>
> (Masterson and Klein, 2004)

The infant is born into the symbiotic phase, zero to five months. Some theorists believe there is developing interactional capacity and beginnings of physical cohesion at this point (Daniel Stern [1934–2012]), but this phase connotes the infant in a most insular condition merged and protected by the mother and father. This phase is characterized by an innocent vulnerability, an absence of boundaries and ability to regulate internal and external stimuli. The mother and father play the critical roles of protecting and managing the interface with the external environment as well as meeting all biological and psychological needs. As there is no cortical control the infant depends on the parents to provide those functions. With secure attachment, the mother can model and then transfer the regulatory capacities slowly to the infant who experiences this maternal modulation. Parental regulation creates optimum conditions for the cortical areas of the brain to grow. If in this phase there is lack of protection and synchrony with the mother or father, disturbed patterns are formed starting now. We will look at how a non-phallic, or early phase schizophrenic type, can develop from this period. Each of these phases of early development is critical to an outcome that is either normal or impaired.

There are significant genetic and environmental contributions to mental disorders and those aspects must be considered as well. Substantial research has been done on the genetics of schizophrenia, alcohol addiction, and other mental disorders that must be considered as we diagnose our patients. I will not cover that research in this book, but when the therapist takes a thorough history and examines the family of origin mental health picture, important information is gleaned for consideration. All information needs to be factored into creating an accurate clinical picture.

> Nathan, in his 60s, had long, dingy, unkempt hair and a disorganized appearance. His eyelids looked partially closed, as if he could barely tolerate the stimulation of the session. He lived in a rural setting in a guest house and maintained the grounds of the same property for over 30 years,

living modestly in isolation. He rarely had social contact and had an odd quality. He was a chronic pot smoker. He came into therapy with anxiety and depression due to loss of his job. He had never made plans for his future retirement and did not have a perspective on what was next. Fortunately for most of his life he had lived in a contained situation where he felt safe so he survived fairly well. His character diagnosis was a nonphallic or early phase schizophrenic type.

Cindy, on the other hand, would be diagnosed as a schizophrenic type but rather than early phase, could be seen in Reich's typology as a schizophrenic who made it to the phallic level with very early ruptures in the earliest phase before separation individuation. Fear is at the basis of all schizophrenics. So when we see fear as the driving force that overshadows all else, we need to look at the schizophrenic character type. This type has trouble with basic regulation as their impairment started so early. Cindy, however, had the basic energetic push to get through medical school and continue a career—albeit unsatisfactorily—so we would see her as a phallic catatonic schizophrenic. Diagnosing character types is challenging as it is an intricate puzzle much like medical doctors pondering a symptom picture to figure out the disease. But once we have it, we have an organizing principle; a way to intervene, structure our interventions, and explain to the patient why she is doing what she is doing.

In the symbiotic stage there is no differentiation, as fusion with the parents is still in operation. It is a critical stage that depends on continued resonance between infant and parents. The totality of the infant's dependency needs being met by parents sets the stage for the beginnings of trust; the infant can let go and merge with the parent in a healthy scenario. James Foley writes of the importance of synchrony within the dyad. This phase and the other stages of early development depend on good enough attunement between infant and parent. Is the mother able to read the cues from the infant and be consistently responsive? Are the two aligned, such that the infant's needs are met in a relatively facile manner? This phase begins developing the baby's capacity for emotional self-regulation.

The separation-individuation stage at 5–30 months engenders critical milestones in the developing infant, toddler, and child. The first subphase—hatching/differentiation and development of body image—is 5 to 9 months. The baby is mirrored by her parents and develops a sense of self through their joining and mirroring. The child's body becomes hers rather than owned by the parents.

Vicki, at 19 years old, had never known a time when she was at peace with her body image. She had fought with her weight since she could remember. Her mother was obsessed with thinness along with a constant focus on Vicki's appearance. She had been under her mother's thumb all her life. Her mom would tell her what to wear, buy her clothes, clean her room, and regulate her food growing up, introducing her to dieting at a young age. Her mom never let her pick out her own clothes, even as a very young child. Vicki did not have the opportunity to decorate her room or choose the activities she wanted to do. Rather, she adhered to her mother's directions to ensure good relations with her and avoid conflicts. This was the relational bargain Masterson references: keep mom happy while sacrificing differentiation. Vicki struggles with binge eating and vomiting as a way to regulate her weight. She is plagued by an internalized critical voice that is demanding and self-disparaging. She is in college but has no idea what her interests are other than pleasing others to make friends. She feels constantly insecure. In Vicki's case, she mirrored her mom rather than her mom mirroring and joining her. Vicki never developed a sense of self, but was forced to stay fused with her mother and we could see her struggle defined by Closet Narcissistic DOS. She had no chance to develop through the phases of separation-individuation as her mom coopted her body image and all her basic choices throughout her development. She was taught to mirror others rather than listening internally and creating inner definitions of self.

The second subphase, called the practicing phase, occurs at 9–16 months. I reference this phase in an earlier discussion of narcissism. The baby exists in the omnipotent orbit of his parents and he feels secure and empowered within the orbit as he practices diverse skill development. His hands are free to manipulate objects; there is locomotion and upright stance. This is a period of relational engagement, and toward 10–14 months communication and emotional signaling skills are developing (Foley and Hochman, 2006). In the first year of life the right prefrontal cortex in the brain is developing and initiates emotional control and social functioning (Allan Schore). Narcissistic personality DOS can't evolve from this phase as the individual does not complete separation sufficiently and maintains the entitled "world is my oyster" attitude.

Susan, 35 years of age, came into therapy with work-related issues. She was employed as a director and her senior VP boss had mentioned that her peers complained about her dominating style. She was a slender, attractive, stylish woman who exhibited competency in many areas of her life. Yet, she had an arrogant, pressured tone and was demanding and impatient. She stood in the waiting room and commented if I was a few minutes late. She insisted on a specific time for her appointment and then changed it repeatedly. She didn't want to follow the protocol of therapy scheduling and wanted special conditions regarding the cancellation policy as she "had important appointments and demands on her that she may need to cancel and did not want to be charged." She tried to manage the therapy hour, talking fast and avoiding feedback. Susan was sensitive to criticism and defended herself vehemently. She had little interest in introspection as she prided herself on her confident competence and superior ability to meet challenges, as she often reminded me. Although a narcissist is sensitive to criticism, she needs to see and understand her grandiosity and how that style alienates others. It feels good to think of oneself as superior; yet that defense can lead to loneliness and ultimately crushing deflation. The therapist needs to understand this type so characteristics can be pointed out. Over time, the patient learns about her style and faces the consequences. She discovered that her character patterns are unlikeable and ultimately resulted in painful relational problems.

The third subphase is rapprochement at 15–24 months. During the first years, the brain grows rapidly, doubling in size. This growth continues until 24 months. Rapprochement is a process whereby the toddler shuttles back and forth between the parents and the outer environment. The child moves toward the parent for emotional and pragmatic supplies and then moves out to the activity he is engaged in. This is an important phase of confidence building that some toddlers and children never complete, thus developing a personality disorder founded on this particular incomplete phase. In this phase if there are attachment problems, the child does not face forward, looking excitedly toward her next activity. Rather she continually turns back around to watch the parent with anxiety that never leaves her when she goes on to separate and be on her own. She is unable to participate in her activities with ease but rather experiences distress and preoccupation with her parent or later with her dependency partner.

Here we meet Indigo, a borderline personality disorder, locked into seeking gratification from men and not knowing how to be independent and autonomous. She lives on a roller coaster of failed relationships and lack of responsibility due to extreme dependency needs laced with ambivalence and rage.

In this phase, parents are sometimes experienced as wonderful and, at other times, not so wonderful. Those two feeling states are not yet joined into a whole. In other words, the child has not developed sufficiently to view the parent as made up of both good and not-so-good characteristics. Borderline personality disorder is described as having a lifelong rapprochement crisis, meaning they have difficulty maturing, seeing others as whole, separating, and activating responsibly. They are still seeking supplies and wanting gratification from others and can't leave home physically or psychologically.

Sharon, 55 years old, divorced 12 years, came into therapy overwrought with feelings of chronic anger and anxiety. She was still blaming her husband for not providing sufficient money and continued to rage at him by email and phone message. She had not developed a career path but relied on her child and spousal support to survive. Now her two daughters were gone, along with the funds. She raged at her husband's selfishness and felt entitled to be supported for many more years. She could not see herself as independent and self-supporting nor had she developed any real interests outside the home. She had once done secretarial work but had not pursued it. She depended on her adult children for emotional support and kept her daughters close and attached to her. They had problems with autonomy as well. She would criticize her daughters if they had goals that made them less available to her. She would text them repeatedly if she felt anxious.

The fourth subphase is consolidation of individuation and the beginning of object constancy at 22–30 months. Object constancy and object permanence are learned understandings that if your parent is not visible or heard, he still exists in the form of an internalized representation. If a parent leaves, she will return and has not disappeared. The ritual of peek-a-boo begins the development of that awareness. The child learns to hold the parental image within and remains feeling connected and safe without the person's presence. Then when the parent returns, there is a smooth transition filled with happiness at the reunion. The child has held the parent within and has been comfortably secure if the parent is gone for a reasonable amount of time depending on the age of the child. Many adults suffer anxiety, even panic, upon separation and have difficulty carrying a loved one within. It's as if when the person leaves he disappears and the other feels alone and bereft. We develop the capacity to carry our loved ones within and feel secure in our dependency needs, yet are able to function autonomously.

If early phases are resolved well, the person achieves whole object relations. The psyche grows from a fused oneness, to the accomplishment of separation-individuation and the formation of a consistent and reliable individual identity. Initially, internalized others are split into intrapsychic parts before finally being integrated as whole. I mentioned this earlier as the toddler sees mom as separately wonderful and not wonderful. The split parts, intrapsychically, are a normal condition of psychic development and reconcile, we hope, into wholeness internally and externally. This is experienced subjectively as a sense that mom is whole and acceptable even though she has aspects that the child does not always appreciate. The child feels internally whole as well even as she recognizes she has strengths and weaknesses. If this phase is not consolidated the split parts remain and the patient is referenced as having a defensive structure of "splitting" that results in many unfortunate consequences. DOS personality diagnosis is distinguished by the presence of splitting. If we maintain in adulthood intrapsychically split good and bad parts applied to both self as well as our internalized objects, then we struggle with these good and bad designations and are plagued with feelings of worthlessness or superiority. We do not have a realistic sense of self or other.

As a practicing therapist it is extremely important to understand this concept as you will see it often in the office, and the condition of "splitting" is one of the most challenging aspects to treat. It is imperative that you understand this developmental phase and the consequences if it is not accomplished. The presence of splitting is obvious as the patient's chronic inner dialogue is marked by self-hate or self-devaluing images. He will project this good and bad split onto others. In his relationships, others are seen as bad, mean, selfish, and so on, and he blames, disparages, and slams up against others as they act out these projections. Or the person sees the other as gratifying, idealized, and she folds into the other. The most important way you can differentiate the level of maturity the patient has achieved is by the presence of splitting. If there is splitting, she has not passed the bar of the first 3 years and will *not* move on to neurotic status.[3]

> I dreaded sessions with Al, as he would blame me for all that went wrong in is his life and was convinced his assessment of me was accurate. "You could have warned me about her. You always act all-knowing but you did not know much in this case." "I am not comfortable with you; you don't know how to truly empathize with me." "I can't trust you as you are never able to comfort me but rather point out my flaws." "I get along with everyone well except you." "Why do you look at me that way? You are trying to control me." These blaming or disparaging comments are an example of a devaluing style that makes the therapist feel incompetent and inflates the patient. The patient blames the therapist rather than look inward at his own pain. The patient sees the therapist as all bad and himself as all good. That can fluctuate the other way as well. It is a sure sign of splitting. It is important that I help him experience his inner pain that comes when he does not feel mirrored.

In the first and second years of life important structures in the brain are developing that help with emotions, socialization, and motivation. Abilities to regulate emotions are developing in the cortical areas of the brain that influence lifelong patterns of behavior (Allan Schore). If there is an established, trusting resonance between the infant, baby, toddler, child, and parents, then healthy emotional attachment is developed ensuring basic emotional and behavior adaptation.

In our examples of patients listed earlier, we can see their serious problems with basic regulation of feelings and behaviors, whether it is Indigo's emotional volatility plummeting her into relationship after relationship, or Cindy's inability to mediate her fear so she acts out with extreme methods of self-control and control of others. Nathan's lack of motivation, pot addiction, and isolation have stopped his life from having intimate relationships and freedom to plan new directions. These are examples of early aborted development of basic skills needed for healthy survival. If we know where the ruptures likely happened, we can organize an approach that fits their problem. The patient's presenting style and dynamics alert us to character type and therefore where their development went askew.

By three years of age, if all goes well, the inner state of the psyche is whole, meaning all parts or splits in the psyche are integrated and include object permanence and object constancy. At this stage, we enter the phase of the oedipal conflict (three to five years old) and potential neurosis if it is not resolved. This is the developmental phase that Reich emphasized.[4]

Masterson's Concept of the Self

Masterson defined DOS diagnoses as rooted in disruption of the early attachment phases therefore permanently impacting the developing self. The developing self affords a self-identity that is continuous and steady over time. Although we may have many roles we engage in, the self integrates all of the roles into a stable entity. This stable self can feel what it needs and express those needs. The self maintains self-esteem across time and circumstance. Self-esteem develops from a sense of mastery of tasks and challenges in reality and is built over a lifetime. Living without a self feels like we don't know who we are, where we are going, or what is meaningful, and we cannot manage in relationships. We heave up and down like a ship, tossed by strong winds.

Masterson's concept of the false self is similar to Reich's facade. The false self does not emanate from the real self but rather is a compromise that is adaptive but not authentic. The false self is based in fantasy and not reality as reality may be filled with painful feelings to be avoided. The self is based in experiences of mastery of reality; the false self hides from reality and perpetuates defenses that deny painful recognitions.

Qualities of the developed self are similar to the characteristics of Reich's genital character: healthy entitlement, capacity to self-activate and assert, consistent self-esteem, ability to hold and soothe painful feelings, and capacity to create.

What I am going to say next is critically important as it links the mind and the body definitively and describes the importance of our earliest experiences. The concept of self is linked to the earliest development of specific areas of the brain and nervous system that depend on healthy attachment experiences. It makes sense out of patients' biophysical and psychological complaints of lifelong symptoms of stress, anxiety, and reactivity or chronic difficulties managing volatile feelings states. Dr. Allan Schore integrates neurobiologic brain development and attachment theory with the development of the self. His brain research demonstrates the neuronal structures that support the establishment and continuity of the self. He discovered that maternal regulation ensures the development of the right prefrontal cortex that becomes the center of the self (Schore, 1994). This center contains and regulates the emotions and allows for healthy relational capacity. This brain structure, if formed and stabilized through healthy attachment, informs the developing intrapsychic structure and creates an adaptive capacity to regulate stress. The right prefrontal cortex, neurological center of the self, is wired to and dominates the limbic system, the area where our most primitive emotions and reactions emanate. Its role in adaptive emotional and social function and its influence on the autonomic nervous system sets the stage for solid mental health or character dysfunction as well as impacts the physical health of the organism establishing its ability to cope with stress and trauma.

Schore's theories support Reich's understanding of the development of character and body armor and its effects on mental and physical health. Masterson's comprehensive theory integrates Schore's research. In both Reich's theoretical system and Masterson's developmental paradigm, the mind and body are united. Development affects how the body-mind is organized, adapts, and functions. Developmental ruptures and blocks can result in a lifetime of serious suffering, chronic unhealthy personality patterns, and physical disease.

Notes

1 Masterson treats chronic personality patterns rather than symptoms and confronts the character defenses and accompanying dysfunctional behaviors directly. Because of the elegance of Masterson's integration of object relations, theorists, and the developmental neurobiological research of Allan Schore, MD, that supports Masterson's emphasis on early attachment developmental impact, I felt his conceptualizations filled in the blanks not covered extensively by Reich's typology. Dr. Masterson and his institute's theorists created a comprehensive early developmental paradigm and clinical approach, and it is predominantly his analysis I reference. For the sake of thoroughness and clinical applicability, I have included attachment phase problems and the attendant personality.

2 Otto Rank was the first to create a modern theory of object relations. Ronald Fairbairn, British psychologist, in 1952 independently formulated a similar theory. Ferenczi may have originated his own object relations inquiry in 1917.

3 These theorists emphasize how the psyche develops in relation to others in childhood. The experiences of those important caretakers become internalized in the mind and are carried within as parts of the self and can be projected later onto new relationships. In healthy development, the parts integrate and become whole rather than parts designated good and bad. This accomplishment provides the ability to see oneself and others as whole with both good and bad parts. Whole object relations, object permanence, and object constancy are critical to a healthy psyche. These gains are consolidated throughout adolescence.

4 The other critical goal of connoting resolution of the early developmental phases is the achievement of whole object relations. This means that the psyche has moved from early fusion with the parent to the beginnings of differentiation and later separateness. Simultaneously the psyche grows from a fused oneness with the other to internalized parts of others as differentiation occurs. These internalized others are split into intrapsychic parts before finally being integrated as wholes. The split parts intrapsychically are a normal condition of psychic development and reconcile into wholeness internally and externally. This is experienced subjectively as a sense that mom is whole and acceptable even though she has aspects that the child does not always appreciate. The child feels internally whole as well even if she recognizes she has strengths and weaknesses.

7 Masterson's Pre-oedipal Personality Disorders

Disorders of the Self: Narcissist, Devaluing Narcissist, Closet Narcissist, Borderline, and Schizoid Types

This chapter will cover Masterson's major Disorders of the Self (DOS) personality types in a condensed and skeletal fashion eliminating his extensive elaboration as well as the subsets that fill out the basic types. I encourage therapists to study and become familiar so you learn to recognize all character types with ease. This skill will come through application of the method over time and clinical experience. Right now I want you to gather a sense of the basic stylistic and etiological parameters of each type. The fine-tuning of your recognition and depth of knowledge will come later.

DOS patients will present either with overt significant symptoms and lower-level functional impairments, with a mid-range symptom picture, or as highly functional types that do not exhibit obvious symptoms yet are diagnosed as a DOS due to a repeated pattern of failure to fully activate Self and reach their full potential as well as difficulties establishing healthy love relationships. The upper level types meet the DOS criteria in terms of their intrapsychic structure and defensive organization.

DOS patients struggle in many of the following areas of functioning. They may have chronic separation issues, immature attachment, lack capacity to individuate, have difficulties in self-regulation emotionally and behaviorally, and lack autonomous capacity. Emotionally they are prone to bouts of anger, impulsivity, explosive tantrums, and sullen withdrawal and are unable to self-soothe and contain their reactivity. They blame others as the cause of their distress and identify as victims. Their contact with reality is distorted and they can project aggressive and malevolent motives onto others and then attack and devalue them viciously.

In many functional arenas such as school, work, or family life, their performance is inconsistent and below their inherent capacity. Relational problems are apparent, and they often demonstrate defenses of clinging and distancing and can be manipulative, overly dependent, and immature. As parents, they create unhealthy environments for their children. They can isolate and hide, and engage in few—if any—other relationships. These patients have inconsistent self-esteem and often identify difficulties with responsibility and self-activation. There are degrees of impairment ranging from high- to low-functioning levels. Many DOS patients can appear and function successfully in specific areas and confine their acting out to failures at work and/or have compromised relationships. These upper level patients undermine themselves before they reach their full potential.

> Sandra, a highly successful entrepreneur in her late 40s, enters therapy distraught over a long-term, on-and-off relationship that lacks commitment or direction. She had been desperate, depressed, staying in bed for days; she drank too much and felt, at times, suicidal. She was prone to chasing symptoms in her body and had quite a few maladies. Sandra would cling in the relationship and then distance, feeling rage, but was unable to end the unhealthy relationship that had become self-destructive. Given the issues she delineated in her family of origin, I could see the backstory that led her to this point. Rather than focus exclusively on her story and symptoms of depression, I look at the character picture: her anxious, dependent attachment style; her immaturity, her need to cling to the fantasy of being taken care of; and her repetitive volatile histrionic feeling displays that result in self-destructive consequences. Underneath, her feelings of emptiness and a lack of self were pervasive. Looking at this picture I create a provisional diagnosis of borderline in the DOS category.

Then with further interviewing as well as confronting the acting out behaviors I can see if this provisional character diagnosis holds. This understanding of her character structure gives me a working set of assumptions as to how to proceed.

The pre-oedipal types can be distinguished from Reich's phallic types in a few ways. These types are not neurotic so have *not* developed unscathed into the neurotic Oedipal phase delineated in the developmental stages outlined in the prior chapters. DOS patients lack a whole object framework and have what is called a split psyche with good and bad parts. They project "badness" or "goodness" onto self and other, including the therapist. When the patient views herself through her bad lens, she can hate herself and may refer to herself as a "worm" or "disgusting and unworthy." A neurotic patient may have unfavorable opinions of self under certain conditions but will not identify with that status across all parameters. The neurotic may have a disagreement or be annoyed with the therapist, but can see the therapist within a realistic perspective, as a whole person rather than in a distorted way—as a projection screen for his internalized split parts. The DOS patient can have extremely lopsided views of the therapeutic relationship and is not able to mediate those distortions. If she sees you as a threat, those feelings have to get worked through, but it will not be easy for her to realize that the problem resides in her distortions. With the neurotic, that reality-based shift to engaging the therapist as a real and whole person, is easy to reinstate. The neurotic has various dysfunctional defenses but lacks the split psyche.

All of the disorders mentioned in this section are listed in the *DSM-5* and are categorized around symptoms. Many clinicians diagnose from the list of symptoms reported and then treat the patient's symptom picture. I suggest *not* matching up the list of symptoms reported in order to diagnose, but rather developing an understanding of the patient's character disorder that may include some of the symptoms—but you are looking wider and deeper. Personality or character disorders are pervasive and chronic emotional and maladaptive behavioral patterns with typical, repetitive defensive structures. These manifest across time and characterize the patient's approach to life. They are often immediately recognizable upon interviewing the patient and absorbing the details of the presenting problems, obvious stylistic traits, and historical markers. The therapist can assess quickly and run that information through their internal experiential database and come up with a hypothesized character type—in a session or two.

Narcissist

This type is less functional than the phallic narcissist (neurotic) but has some of the same basic traits. This type craves to be acknowledged, admired, and seen as special and harbors grandiose fantasies that he is potentially better than his current reality indicates. The DOS narcissist can be entitled, demanding, and self-indulgent and may exploit others to get what he feels he deserves. He can lack empathy as he is exclusively self-concerned and does not sincerely care for others. She can be jealous and envious and take on airs of superiority. This type is also plagued with feelings of shame, inadequacy, and defectiveness if she loses power and status.

> Amy, 35, an attractive Asian woman, came in distraught with a sense of shame at her lack of success in her new business. She was experiencing panicky feelings and daily stomach aches, and she had difficulty surmounting these overwhelming feelings. She choked up and froze as she tried to pursue her various goals. Amy had always been the prized child, the one her parents and siblings gave the future mantel of success. She had some initial success with her new business, but lately it had diminishing returns and immobilization was setting in alongside her feelings of inadequacy and not measuring up. She was tortured by feelings of envy accompanied by dark shame at not being good enough. Her expectations had always been high, and now she felt on the bottom rung of the ladder of success. She disdained failure and mediocrity; if she couldn't be on top, she was worthless. I could see the deep self-annihilation and the split between her grandiose identity and her sense of shame, failure, and worthlessness. Her delineation of her current struggles, coupled with the cultural family of origin mandate, led to a character diagnosis of DOS narcissist.

Developmentally, the narcissist is stuck in the practicing phase of separation-differentiation in a fused state with a parent or parents. This type was subjected to the idealized projections of the parent(s) who needed their progeny to complete what the parent or parents were unable to achieve, or the parent may need the child to be an extension and mirror the parent's grandiose accomplishments. The parents lived through the favored child, joining with her and living through her. The child could not have an independent development of her own intrinsic sense of self with her own needs and instead had to live for her parent. Classic examples are the "ballet mom" or "the sports dad," the helicopter parent or the vain parent who insists on vain values, social or financial status, promoting and idealizing achievements that may not be intrinsic to the child and young adult. The narcissistic child or adolescent will pursue those images to get the adulation and gratification from the parent yet sacrifice the development of his authentic self. This type was often overindulged by the parent and given more than he realistically needed. The child and adolescent or young adult did not have to work for the gifts, but received them without earning them or having the gifts tied to a realistic assessment of her accomplishments.

The narcissistic DOS child did not get acknowledged for her genuine developing self so was left to contend with a lifetime of emptiness having never developed a real self. Grandiosity, arrogance, and superiority provide a defensive facade to hide the sense of inner fragmentation and emptiness. The parents resonated with their own projections but not with the reality of the child or young adult. When the narcissist tries to pursue her real self, she may experience depression and abandonment feelings as her uniqueness was not historically rewarded. The parents instead showed disappointment and withdrew their interest when their child did not achieve what they felt was important in terms of markers of "success." The child might have been criticized, devalued, and rejected because she did not achieve the narcissistic status goals demanded by her parents.

This adult expects to fuse with significant others much as her parent fused with her. She might expect her significant other to match and mirror her in gratifying ways and could become angry if he does not comply with her demands. If she chooses a mate who reflects well on her in terms of status, looks, power, or wealth, then the relationship enhances her personal glory and identification with those status symbols, but at high personal cost.

Underneath his grandiose self, this type has difficulty retaining self-esteem and inner stability as he can be easily frustrated, lose control, and have distorted reality perceptions. On the other side of his split, he feels unworthy and inadequate when he is not in his grandiose self-identity. He easily crashes into inadequacy with any loss of status. From that perspective he can view the other or the therapist as critical and demeaning, and feel attacked. He is no longer in the glow of the highly regarded therapist and views you in the faded light that he views himself.

Therapy with DOS narcissists can be rocky as they bounce back and forth between their split halves. When they fuse with you as the "best therapist" who admires them, they feel better and can tolerate self-examination. If they feel inadequate and sense you are neutral rather than admiring, they can react harshly and attack. They are easily slighted and often feel offended. To defend against those feelings, they reinstate their grandiose position and devalue you. They must stay on top at all costs.

Mark came into therapy on top of his game. He acquired wealth from his own business efforts, continuing to garner positions that reinforced his power in the world of finance. Yet he suffered from periodic debilitating depression that snuck up on him. He was divorced with three kids and was in a new marriage. In therapy he was quite testy, as he did not want to explore painful subjects like his family of origin or his divorce or his loss of contact with his children. His tendency was to blame others for his problems and then attack in a vitriolic way. His blaming tantrums escalated in session to the point of extreme distortion, and inevitably derailed his treatment. Narcissists can be challenging, and it is important to get underneath their defenses so they can feel met and not criticized, but if they can't tolerate accessing their internal pain they will continue to project on others and use denial as a primary defense. I did not succeed in my task with this patient. At times we do not succeed and have to accept our own limitations as well as the limitations of our patients. We won't succeed with everyone.

Emily, 32, is another example of how narcissism is perpetuated by an overly idealizing and fused mother. She described a lunch with her mother, who would gaze at her with admiration, infatuated with everything she did or said, always treating her as if she was so special. The mother played out a child-like attachment. Emily at times cringed with this adoration and created some distance from it. Then Emily noticed her mom became angry if Emily didn't fall into mom's merging pull. Mom became upset when Emily did not join with mom's need to idealize. This is how abandonment feelings begin. A child learns that if she displeases mom by being her real self, mom withdraws. Emily had grown up with her every need met, and came to be quite entitled in her adult relationships. She expected her every need to be mirrored and blamed her mate if he did not mind read her expectations in any given situation. She demanded full compliance with her requests, and if compliance was not achieved, she could become enraged. Then if the mate became angry, she would feel abandoned similar to the preceding script with mom.

Devaluing Narcissist

Devaluing narcissists had an even more treacherous childhood with harsh criticism, verbal and physical abuse, and severe neglect. They had to rely on withdrawal, serious isolation, social aggressiveness, and a viewpoint of para-noia to manage the constant threats in their environment. Later in life, this type will utilize devaluing as their major defense. Once aroused, they are quite reactive and will harshly denounce others, using ridicule, shaming, and humiliation to maintain their fragile sense of power. They are prone to para-noid projections and cannot be reasoned with. Once they feel even slightly diminished they will come out fighting with lethal insults, devaluing the other without hesitation. This type demonstrates little insight into self and relies on blame and retaliation. They lack empathy as the other barely exists except as a belittled extension of themselves.

This patient, although not frequently seen in treatment, is obviously extremely challenging. He will frequently project his inadequate self on the therapist and attack aggressively, mimicking his own childhood treatment. This defense serves the same purpose as the grandiose defenses of the narcis-sist, to reestablish equilibrium if challenged. The challenge for the therapist is counter-transference. This patient's defensive need to belittle with harsh aggressiveness is unsustainable in treatment unless the therapist can set limits and dismantle this brutal defense. The therapist must be very strong and not collapse under the relentless demeaning. If the therapist can find a way to crawl under the defense to the painful suffering this individual endured, pro-gress can be made. Hopefully there is still some humanity left in this person with which to connect.

There is a version of this type that looks less lethal on the surface as these individuals can be successfully engaged in the world. Their ability to func-tion in the real world allows them to conquer domains even though they lack relational skills and respect for others. They can be highly intelligent and magnetic in their fields. They can wield power in corporations or in politics or religion, and can lavish money on others in ostentatious ways. They can intimidate others into submission. They make their way sustaining their power positions through brutal devaluing of others while simultaneously impressing them with their prowess and magnetism. A fall will happen—as their instincts are basically unhealthy and sooner or later they will make a series of highly visible mistakes that take them down. The all-powerful, grandiose sense of self believes it can get away with anything and everything, but life has a way of crumbling even the most inflated. Aging, too, levels the playing field.

Closet Narcissistic

The closet narcissist is an interesting type as his narcissism is not as obvious as the narcissistic personality disorder described earlier. Rather than the blatant grandiose, self-centered, exhibitionistic narcissist, the closet narcissist is sub-tler and lives underground as she serves the grandiose narcissist in order to get her narcissistic needs met.

This dynamic is often most noticeable in couples. There is one star per-former or dysfunctional dominator and an accomplice hiding behind the more overt individual. The lead performer enjoys having someone to dominate and control, someone he commandeers to serve his needs and boost his ego. The more subservient partner gets to share the light of fame, fortune, success, or, more often, simply false bravado founded on nothing. The closet narcissist gets to feel important and special as she idealizes the other. The closet narcissist feeds off the projections she places on her mate; maybe his educational credentials, her powerful position at work, his accomplishments, her glamorous looks, his impressive motorcycle, or her false sense of pride and cockiness built on the surface without substance or foundation. The closet narcissist feels weak and deflated inside and relies on the other to feel a sense of cohesion. She can tag along on a ride with the dictating spouse and live a life that appears special; one that the person is unable to accomplish on her own. The closet narcissist lives the other's life; takes trips decided by the mate on his terms for "their" benefit and the closet narcissist goes along because she can't decide what she wants anyway.

This template can grow out of being raised by a narcissistic parent or parents. If one had a grandiose larger-than-life parent, the child usually looked up to that parent and liked the glow he or she created. The parent may have accomplished little, but acted important or special. Often the parent was enamored and impressed by superficial values, materialism, good looks, power, presentation, and generally undeserved inflation, and the child learned to emulate those values.

The child could not grow or individuate as no one was truly interested in what mattered to her. The parents were more interested in promoting their own needs, and the children were extensions of the parents and did not exist in their own right. That inhibited the child's growth as an individual in her own right as she suffered the abandonment of self-engrossed or neglectful parents. Parental grandiosity can set a precedent of loyal submission and caretaking modes in the child. The child learns to serve the parent as demanded. The child is an extension of the parent and exists only for that reason—the trophy child filling the empty, yet camouflaged hole within the parent.

The closet narcissist inherits the internal emptiness as he has not had the opportunity to grow the self and accomplish the tasks of establishing his own identity. He can feel like an empty shell when he is not feeding on the other's glory. When he feeds on the other, he can feel entitled and experience the narcissistic good feelings of specialness, power, and perfection. When he stands alone, the emptiness strikes and his lack of identity and self-worth are illuminated.

The closet narcissist is prone to fits of jealousy and envy, and can be aggressive toward self and other. If her narcissistic identifications are threatened, she can feel angry, vengeful, and antagonistic. She wants to rein supreme, be competitive and special, and will not give up her fragile identifications easily. Even if it is a less obvious power position, she still identifies with specialness, privilege, and pride even if positioned through another. She can, at times, hate herself because she hasn't grown an authentic self and knows she is a fraud hiding behind the other. When she suffers a narcissistic injury, she can feel humiliation and shame at being found out.

As in all character types, one can grow out of a defensive pattern and develop one's true nature. Each of us deserves to be authentically who we are as we listen carefully to the tune of our own being. We have to focus on who we are and not hide behind others as a mask. We can establish our own self-worth through self-trust, discipline, focus, and loyalty to our self above all. Then we shine on our own, live freely as we are, make the demands we need to make, and have our lives be a manifestation of what we love to be and to do. We can make a contribution to others from the light we generate from within and our light is our own—not a reflection of another's source of energy (Frisch, February 15, 2016, blog, "The Closet Narcissist Disorder of the Self").

Borderline

The borderline DOS, although commonly referenced in psychiatric diagnostic manuals as a series of symptoms, has a unique developmental quagmire described by Dr. Masterson and other object relations theorists. The borderline is defined not by symptoms but rather by character structure and its related developmental conflicts that never resolved in the psyche and therefore result in inadequate functioning.

Individuals with borderline personality disorder have not developed an authentic self. Rather they live in their defensive structure and facade—what Masterson called the "false self." They sacrificed their real self for a pathological relational bargain with parents. Some borderlines, depending on their level of functioning, are unable to mature, achieve goals, or be creative. They can be irresponsible, have serious intimacy problems, separation stress, depression, and anxiety.

Individuals with borderline personality disorder can create volatility in their relationships as well as in the therapeutic relationship, as they can act out frequently and dramatically. The description *acting out* means that rather than think about, feel, and explore their problems and emotions and discuss them with friends, family, or the therapist, they instead display their unmediated emotions, impulses, and reactivity. Frantic, angry, sometimes violent displays of emotion; suicidal gestures; impulsive decision-making; and/or substance abuse are examples of acting-out behaviors. These feelings and behaviors are not understood and contained. Instead, destructive actions toward self and others are repetitively played out.

Borderline patients have a bad reputation, as lower-functioning types can and do act out with dramatic symptoms, giving them notoriety in clinics and clinical seminars. Higher-functioning borderlines do not act out with such flair and drama. The clinician may find the higher-functioning type harder to diagnose. Do not rely on the caricature of the borderline to diagnose; instead delineate the intrapsychic structure and defensive strategies to determine the diagnosis. Higher-functioning borderlines may simply distinguish themselves by their chronic difficulty activating their *full* potential. Lifelong patterns that undermine their potential and bad relational bargains may be the critical distinguishing features of this diagnosis rather than reliance on a dramatic symptom picture.

The borderline individual does not establish a mature identity and rather lives without a "reality ego." Her life can revolve around fantasy hopes and dreams, rather than be based on realistic assessments that create realistic behaviors and activations. She is notably immature, seeks pleasure, and avoids reality.

This type is prone to dependency relationships all of her life and lives in a regressed mode, counting on others to finance her and take care of her in a myriad of ways. The borderline can feel entitled to get from others, denying her weaknesses, her lack of independence, and her dearth of self-sufficiency. Her entitlement can lead to outbursts of rage when it is thwarted. She has difficulty taking responsibility and organizing her life to move forward with plans and tasks. Rather she often counts on others to handle her life. With young adults, this is often described as failure to launch. A bright student goes away to college only to panic, get depressed, and struggle to stay or leave and come home. Or the young adult does not find her way after graduating high school and stays at home with parents without creating and following up with a game plan geared toward independence.

Borderline relationships are fraught with upheaval. Borderlines mobilize the defenses of clinging and then distancing, and the less functional types distance more than cling to express their displeasure at not being gratified. They express their immature regressive tendencies by seeking solace from others. If they are not satisfied with the gratification received, they can viciously blame the other as mean, wrong, and a bad person.

This type is waylaid in the rapprochement subphase of separation-individuation. This phase, in healthy development, describes the young child who can engage and play on his own, having completed the fusion phase of infancy and is beginning to feel his separateness. He ventures forward at the playground with confidence, returning to the parent or viewing the parent briefly as a way to feel a sense of security. This shuttling back and forth from activity to parent and back to activity is a normal process in this phase of development as the parent both encourages his independence yet remains a secure, stable object that provides the child with consistent refueling. That process enables the child to develop confidence and feel secure with stable, loving parents while at the same time venturing forward on his own. The child continues his path to independence knowing his parents do not need to cling or distance from him as he seeks autonomy. The parents understand their child and always support his uniqueness.

Borderlines do not ever fully separate, as they are too anxious and have chronic fears of abandonment. The abandonment trauma originates with parents who either disengaged too early, demanding premature self-sufficiency due to their personal preoccupation outside of parenting, or were dissociated, troubled, and anxious themselves and did not supply the child with the fuel she needed. Or the parents suffocated and engulfed the child, due to their own anxiety or neediness, and did not support the child's autonomy. In these ways, the child was abandoned; not loved in a way that contributed to her developing health and maturity. Rather she was a pawn in her parents' pathological life.

Then, as adults, borderlines will continue an immature life that lacks autonomy and self-sufficiency, often depending on relationships in the same way they acted with parental figures. Underneath their dependent, gratified contentment is emptiness and fear of abandonment. It is this abandonment fear and panic that can produce the desperate acting out. Their moods are unstable, and they can have raging angry tantrums with violence, screaming, and loss of control. They are triggered by feelings of fear and loneliness when they or a mate tries to separate and pursue self-activation. Those events set off depression as borderlines fear being alone and abandoned unless they are clinging to the object and regressing. They have chronic separation anxiety and fear of loss.

The borderline often comes from a family where regression is encouraged and individuation is not. Many borderline mothers produce borderline children, and the fathers can be distancing narcissistic types. The father does not engage the child encouraging confidence and autonomy while helping the child expand out of the maternal orbit—a healthy father's parenting task. Rather, the father ignores and neglects the child, leaving the parenting functions in the hands of the borderline mother. The mother may collude with unhealthy dependency, as she needs the child to remain close and take care of her. The mom may manipulate the child to keep her in an emotionally and physically caretaking position. In fact, the child receives support for giving up her autonomous functioning. The child and adolescent learns that if she stays close to mom, gives her what she needs, and holds back disagreement with mom's ideas and directions, then she can feel secure and "loved." If the daughter thinks about venturing out, she is not prepared. Independent pursuits seem threatening and challenging, plus mom may likely distance and express disapproval if her daughter does try to go out on her own. Separating violates the unconscious bargain between mom and daughter and the consequences are dire, resulting in a lifelong failure to mature. These two approaches of the mother—(1) rewarding regression and (2) withholding good feelings and punishing when the child or young adult wants to differentiate—are internalized. The borderline adult is left with this intrapsychic conflict inside: rewards and good feelings when she is regressed and a feeling of badness when she tries to grow up and be responsible. The borderline then has deep self-loathing and can feel ugly, inadequate, and worthless.

These internalized good and bad parts are projected onto others. Seeing others as good or bad is a borderline process. There are no gray areas; they may feel good about you if you give them what they feel entitled to. And they can turn on a dime and hate you, think you have betrayed them and have been unfair, and see you as their enemy. They lack reasonableness to moderate their black-and-white thinking. Instead they reinforce it by talking to others, getting validation for their irrational feelings, and then acting out their hatred. The black-and-white disparaging views exist within their psyche in a painful way and they can disparage themselves ruthlessly or project those splits on to others.

This good-and-bad dichotomy plays out in the therapist's office. The patient may try to entice the therapist to gratify her dependency needs and the therapist may feel compelled to collude with her regression. If the therapist does not gratify but rather confronts the lack of responsibility, for example, then the patient may feel abandoned and compensate with rage, seeing the therapist as "mean" and not supportive. Therapists unconsciously collude by giving too much advice, not expecting the patient to act responsibly in all situations, and tolerating acting-out behaviors. The therapist may fear the patient will judge him harshly and leave him if he confronts.

> Naomi was in her early 30s when she entered therapy with an intern supervisee. She had a history of marijuana use and volatile relationships, and had not finished her education nor established a career path. She chose recently to move back home to live with her mom. She was used to throwing angry tantrums with mom and that relationship always yielded high drama. The first order of business was to set the rules of treatment and the expectation that the patient would commit to weekly therapy and abide by the structure of therapy: consistency, timely payments of her bill, making her sessions, and following the cancellation policy if she couldn't to attend her session. Sessions were kept at exactly the duration allotted and not extended for any reason. The main goal was containment of the acting-out behaviors and keeping the strict therapeutic frame as well as confrontation of the destructive consequences of her various behaviors.
>
> Of course, her marijuana use had to cease so she could be conscious and aware of her thoughts, feelings, and actions. As Naomi cooperated with the guidelines and stopped her marijuana use, therapy was off to a good start. If she stays committed to treatment, she will mature, learn to be independent and responsible. Therapy can be successful if the structure of the therapy is held firmly in place, leading to Naomi experiencing deep feelings of loss that unconsciously resulted in her destructive behaviors. That release of feeling as well as cognitive and behavioral changes within a solid therapeutic alliance allows the patient to develop understanding of the true origins of her problems while developing capacities to live a productive life.

A borderline can dissociate and lose connection with her self and reality. This loss of self happens more often with this type than other types as she can be overwhelmed with anxiety and lose contact. Therefore it is critical that substance abuse not be tolerated. The dissociative defense needs to be addressed in session when the patient drifts off into contactlessness. Patients need to learn about their chronic ambivalent dependency that leads to raging tantrums within their relationships. Therapists need to learn that any and all maladaptive defenses in the treatment room need to be confronted. The initial containment works as patients became aware of how they distract themselves from feelings of emptiness and loss by creating dramatic interactions to fill the void.

This patient will pull for gratification as she wants to feel taken care of and avoid the looming abandonment depression. When the therapist does not comply with that expectation, the patient can see the therapist as unkind, withholding, and negative. The borderline sees herself in her split as inadequate and worthless and the therapist as the horrible mother or father who is rejecting and abandoning her. She will rail against you until the split begins to repair and she can see herself and you without distortion. Then the patient faces into her deep abandonment depression without acting out to avoid it, and the deep grief from the loss of self can resolve. Acting out stops, reality is faced, depression is worked through, the split resolves, and the patient moves forward in a whole, authentic way.

As the borderline heals and becomes whole without good and bad parts, she has capacity for health. She can create healthy relationships and attach. She has a good quantity of energy to apply to activated plans and go forward with maturity and confidence in her various pursuits. As she is capable of feeling, she brings an emotional depth to her life (Frisch, September 10, 2015, blog, "Borderline Personality Disorder").

Schizoid

The schizoid is most notably an isolated, self-sufficient type. His relationship situation can vary on a spectrum of having relations with family and friends to one that lacks any social contact.[1] The schizoid is introverted and more comfortable with solitary activities. He spends his mental time with an active fantasy life as a substitute for contact. He appears detached and unemotional about most of his personal issues and can seem cold and disinterested. Beneath this appearance, the schizoid is sensitive and has deep longing to belong but may not appear that way on the surface. He has suffered pain in his life and therefore is frightened to move too close and get hurt again. So he may appear aloof.

As the schizoid, like the rest of the DOS types, has a split psyche, he has a distorted view of himself and others. He can feel bad about himself and then project the badness on to the other. He can find himself in a relationship where he becomes controlled and co-opted by his mate. His longing for relationship may put him in the dyadic dynamic of the master-slave as Masterson defined it, with the schizoid in the slave position. Or the projection on the mate or the therapist can be that the person is not safe and is, in fact, dangerous. That distortion results in the schizoid, in turn, feeling extremely unsafe, alienated, rejected, and unvalued.

The schizoid's history is fraught with feelings of alienation, fear, and lack of safety. These individuals experienced little gratification unless they were serving their parents' needs in some way. They felt used by their parents' demands for help, assistance, and support. Their parents did not relate to them as a separate people with needs of their own. If they weren't being used, they were ignored or hurt by the parent. Some suffered from violence at the hand of the parent or neglect and emotional abuse. The schizoid, unlike the narcissist or borderline, had no access to emotional connections and communications with family. There was no support offered, but rather he might endure violent beatings and harshness from parents. The narcissist was overindulged and gratified with the fusion and mirroring. The borderline was kept close and valued in a regressed position, although, at times, she would endure punishment through emotional distancing if she moved toward autonomy. The schizoid was used and then cut off. The parents did not acknowledge or appreciate the schizoid child and offered few supplies or affection. The child could not find a way to connect with his disinterested family.

The schizoid developmental attachment rupture occurs after the practicing subphase and before rapprochement in the separation-individuation stage when good and bad feeling states are congealing. The schizoid learned to retreat and fears closeness as unsafe. This type can have distorted reality perceptions, including paranoia, and lack the ability to tolerate frustration. He keeps a distance to create a safe position that is maintained by self-sufficiency. He can appear standoffish and arrogant but that attitude serves to maintain safe distance rather than a superior defensive stance.

Therapy with schizoids can be challenging, as there is an absence of content and feeling in the room. They don't generate material easily and there can be extended periods of silence. The therapist is tempted to overtalk to create stimulation. This patient can be content to have simple interpersonal contact and, underneath, feels relief from extended isolation. Highlighting the therapeutic relationship can be helpful. Schizoids can develop loving or erotic feelings for the therapist as they are subject to an active fantasy life that can include the therapist.

> Hank is in his mid-50s and has a successful career as an architect. He was devoted to his work and overworked at the office on weekends. When he was not at his office he spent time by himself. He was dedicated to projects at home as well. In all the years of his life and career, he had one long-distance friend he rarely saw. He did feel lonely at times, but stayed busy as a coping strategy. He tended to be withdrawn in session, introverted, and had difficulty staying in contact with his therapist. He came in due to feelings of emptiness and depression that, at times, overwhelmed him. Yet, he was so self-sufficient that it was difficult to make inroads.

The schizoid needs the therapist to be patient as relational bonds are built slowly. Comments regarding his outermost defenses of self-sufficiency are helpful as well as noting his fear of being engulfed and co-opted. Those observations help direct the schizoid to his deeper feelings of profound aliena-tion and isolation, or his anger about feelings of engulfment in the other. The higher-functioning schizoid, like Hank, longs for intimacy but is frightened to get close to another. The more impaired types steer clear of longing for friend-ship and relationship.

The schizoid swings between being controlled and co-opted if too close or isolated, like a satellite circling the earth in dark outer space, and this is his dilemma. His fantasy life creates an opportunity to circumvent the isolation through fantasy relationships and experiences.

Many schizoids are highly functional in their careers and appear social and relational at work events or with a few friends. They are often highly intel-ligent and successful as they focus well. Others may drift to the margins of society, if lower functioning, as they are more comfortable in a state of with-drawal and retreat. They may feel safer existing on the perimeter of commu-nity (Frisch, December 20, 2015, blog, "Schizoid Disorder of the Self").

The Early Phase Schizophrenic

In my typology I have described Reich's phallic level schizophrenic. There is also an early phase schizophrenic type, a pregenital type described both by Orgonomist Dr. Robert Harman[2] and developmentally delineated by the Mas-terson Group psychologist Candace Orcutt, PhD. Please read her excellent discussion of etiology and treatment of this type. The coordinates of the pre-genital schizophrenic fall developmentally in the symbiotic phase of develop-ment according to Mahler's work on childhood psychosis and amplified by Dr. Orcutt. The schizophrenic has more serious impairment and diminished ego capacity, as he does not experience sufficient differentiation developmen-tally. This type can have psychosis with thought disorder and may have her first breakdown at launch in adolescence when she attempts to leave home. This type may have psychotic projections on the therapist coming from the symbiotic developmental phase as the patient does not succeed in the first subphase of separation-individuation, the differentiation subphase. This ego fixation at the symbiotic level results in a need to establish or reestablish a symbiotic bond as a way to cope with separation stresses, usually evoked in adolescence—using merger and fusion with the therapist and others as a way to regulate the fear of disintegration.[3]

The early phase of symbiotic development of the infant is noted by per-meable boundaries and the need for maternal regulation to help manage the external stimuli. When there are ruptures in this first phase, early impair-ments result in the early stage schizophrenic, a type that exhibits a spacey, non-cohered quality with weakness in their capacity to function, organize, and assess reality.

Therapy with pregenital schizophrenics is a delicate matter with interven-tions that are minimal, so the patient can cohere and therefore exist in the room. The therapist helps the patient regulate stimuli as the patient grows

through the developmental passages not accomplished properly from the symbiotic state into formation of good and bad states into whole object relations
and can emerge over time into a whole self.

Early phase schizophrenics, due to their distorted contact with reality, may
acquire an inordinate number of pets to provide emotional comfort with safe
relationships. Often, patients engaged in these devoted relationships with
their multiple pets—cats, dogs, horses, birds, and so on—may acquire massive
debt to sustain the enterprise. These patients can be stubborn about altering
their situation that seriously compromises their well-being. This is an example
of the contactless and lack of boundaries that occur in this character type.

> Elizabeth entered therapy at 28 in a serious state of confusion. She had
> dropped out of college and had been waitressing ever since. She had no
> idea what she wanted in a career and felt frozen in nebulousness. She had
> trouble feeling her emotions or physical sensations, so she had no compass
> to direct her. Her mom had back trouble and other illnesses when Eliza-
> beth was growing up and was unavailable to parent. Her father was distant
> and gone most of the time. Elizabeth felt lost and wandered about in her
> rural neighborhood without structured activities. If she had a feeling, it
> was a low-grade fear. The work progressed slowly with her learning to
> focus on herself and feel what was going on inside. The therapist helped
> the patient reinstate structure in her life that grounded her from the lost
> and scattered way she was experiencing her life.

Strategy

When you take an initial history listen for specific character traits outlined
here and historic family of origin patterns that can guide you to an initial
hypothesis as to the character type and the differential between a neurotic
and a Disorders of the Self. DOS types have early attachment problems resulting from the dyad between themselves and the parent, and they have deep
crevasses in their psyche demarcated with self-loathing, calmed by immature
gratification-seeking or fantasy inflation. You might notice if the parents were
narcissistic, grandiose, and shallow, producing someone with inflation and
sensitivity to criticism or wanting to be seen as special—resting on top of a
shaky footing. Or you might notice if the patient is regressed and never able
to separate and take responsibility with immature borderline parental figures
who did not grow up either. Or is the patient self-sufficient with an absence of
social connections, with a history of lack of safety and neglect with marginalized schizophrenic or schizoid parents or a mix of each?

Although there are multiple character types discussed in both Reich's typology and the additions I have added, you can become familiar with them and
see clearly these various types in your office. This knowledge will ground your
direction with each patient, and you will be less likely to be caught off guard
with the events in the office and in his life. Of course there is often the surprise

factor in our work when a patient has a reaction we do not expect or takes action that stuns us in the moment. Psychotherapy is not orderly work as its magic is in the mystery, and there are unknown variables at play in each and every individual's life.

Notes

1 Schizoid DOS is a personality disorder and not to be confused with schizophrenic character types discussed later or by Reich as one of his phallic types. Schizophrenic character types do exist like other types alongside a more genetically based schizo-phrenic. The schizophrenic in my method develops from family of origin dynamics that may include a genetic component. There are seriously impaired and hospitalized schizophrenics that may have a strong genetic component. Much research abounds on schizophrenia and various viewpoints weigh in.

2 Dr. Robert A. Harman, an Orgonomist, in his article "Procrastination as a Symptom of Catatonic Schizophrenia" in the *Journal of Orgonomy*, Spring/Summer 1997, page 10, separates the early schizophrenic from the neurotic phallic schizophrenic character designation and gives it his own classification that I agree with. So here there is a close alignment between the Masterson Group and Orgonomy on this character type.

3 The early phase schizophrenic type is described by Master Institute theorist Candice Orcutt, PhD, who references Mahler's study of childhood psychosis and expands on treatment strategy (Masterson and Klein, 1989, 110–145).

Part IV
Therapeutic Guidelines

8   Create the Frame

Establishing a Stable Container

A successful therapeutic relationship is founded on a clearly defined and substantive initial foundation with a defined treatment structure and understanding on which both of you agree from the start. The treatment contract can cover purpose of therapy, therapist's modality and explanation of treatment, goals, confidentiality, fees, schedule of sessions, cancellation policy, challenges, and a legal arbitration agreement, to name a few. Too many therapists prematurely jump into therapeutic issues and have not set the stage, or set it up but don't stick to it. The loose structure leads to lack of consistency, misunderstandings, and disagreements that unravel the therapy. If the therapist wavers with the setup, then there are leaks that sink the boat either early on or when the therapy gets more challenging. Without clear guidelines neither the therapist nor the patient know exactly what they are doing and what to expect.

A professional came in for a consultation. She admitted that her patient, after a year of therapy, had stopped paying for her sessions. She owed a sizable amount and the tab was mounting. The therapist continued to see her rather than both patient and therapist face the fact that she needed to pay for therapy in order to continue. Often financial issues are challenging for both therapist and patient, so they are left in the shadows and not discussed. The therapist was embarrassed to admit that her patient was accruing all this debt to her. After our session, she discussed the issue with the patient and the patient terminated. This may seem like a radical example of a broken therapeutic frame, but I have heard many stories of this nature.

One supervisee was undecided whether her patient could continue to see her old therapist, too. Patients lobby hard for a compromised structure. "Could I come once a month?" "Could I continue to see my old therapist, too?" "I may have to cancel if a work issue takes precedence." "I also see a coach." It takes time for new therapists to understand the vulnerable nature of the therapeutic relationship and that it is easily tossed about by the varied nature of the patient's impairments and the therapist's own internal psychic triggers and weaknesses. That is why the therapeutic structure is needed. Therapy has the best chance of success only if the right conditions are created.

Carl Jung used the term *container* to define the context that holds the unruly elements of a relationship. The container, like a bowl that holds cherries, keeps the elements together in one place so they don't scatter hither and yonder. The container in the therapeutic relationship sets the parameters and by its nature creates safety, stability, and consistency for both the therapist and the patient. It emphasizes a serious commitment to the process that can become arduous as the work becomes more emotionally challenging. The therapist must educate the patient from the start, that this is not one more growth encounter from which the patient can drop out, moving quickly and defensively on to next—if he wants real and lasting change. The patient gets benefits from therapy when she can stick to it and not run away to multiple healing modalities that end up creating too much input and confusion. If the patient is prone to this type of seeking, the therapist creates a container for this patient to stop running. As the container creates structure, it is healing in itself as many patients come from chaotic families without a semblance of regulated activities and rituals. Coming from those environments, patients don't know how to implement structure and instead run amuck in a life that lacks accountability and defined parameters. The structure-less life can be seen in many realms: self-care, time management, sleep and eating, stimulation, social and family contact, financial accountability, and financial responsibility. It is important that patients learn and absorb the therapist's regulating environment.

Another typical situation that unmoors the therapy is missed appointments. Patients will call at the last minute and cancel, or rearrange their session time, or miss a weekly session too often and lose the thread of why they are coming. One missed session leads to another and another. I have discussed this with professionals for years. A few misses and soon the patient terminates treatment. Their defenses have guided them out of the relationship, and they are back to living their lives as they did before they started. They have drifted off consciously or unconsciously, but nonetheless they have sabotaged their efforts and in that sense wasted their time and resources as well as the therapist's. Therapists are partly to blame for this situation as they avoid discussing the process of missing appointments promptly when it happens. Often patients will nonchalantly pass off the cancellation, and the therapist will go along with that rather than investigating why therapy was not a priority. Why is the patient's life overbooked or so filled with extraneous business that their self-care is cast aside?

From the moment of the referral, you guide the process from the very first phone call. At that time you define the way you work and see if there is compatibility with the patient.

Many a supervisee has complained that the patient decided to leave before much was accomplished. This can happen for a variety of reasons. Sometimes the patient leaves prematurely without fulfilling her own hopes of improvement because she did not really grasp how to be in therapy and what was required. The therapist may not have clarified the requirements of therapy from the beginning and periodically reinforced them along the way. The aspects of patient defenses and resistance need to be discussed in the first session, as they will factor into the relationship immediately. The patient's resistance and unique defensive structure must be illuminated right away, or these defenses can march the patient out of therapy quickly.

Like any good marriage, the two individuals live together within a container that is bigger than the sum of the parts. The container builds strength when the couple is working well together, and it holds them tightly through hair-raising times as well. The marriage container solidifies if the two people can function together with basic accountability, stability, and consistency. Trust is established over the long haul as you learn to rely on these factors. As two people learn to work together, their container becomes more and more durable.

The therapeutic relationship is founded on holding a consistent therapeutic frame (Masterson). Or, as Reich emphasized, the first task is to instruct the patient on the process of analysis. Establishing cooperation goes a long way in ensuring a successful therapy (Baker). We launch the therapy with our clear guidelines eliciting cooperation as we set up a collaborative environment.

We see whether the patient is willing to embrace the outlined path. Our job is to educate the patient on how to be in therapy through the guidelines presented and discussed.

Protocol for First Phone Contact

The first phone contact is a mutual interview. The patient calls because he is considering therapy. There are parameters of the relationship to consider. I usually start by asking how the person found me, as it is important to know whether it is through referral from another patient or through my network and/ or my marketing efforts. Then I find out what the problems are and whether I have the expertise to help. The patients may divulge prior therapies at this time. There may be certain situations where you as the therapist may feel you lack sufficient knowledge or experience for a particular issue. Better to refer him on, as our ethical mandate requires us to work within the scope of our expertise.

If you feel the patient's problems lie within your scope of knowledge and experience, you must determine if the other parameters are mutually compatible. If you take insurance, ask for that information so you know if you are on his particular panel or plan. If you do not take insurance of any kind or just take PPO plans, you need to be clear on that so you can either refer the patient or feel equipped to take their insurance and move forward. You then state clearly that your format for therapy is *weekly* 45-minute or 50-minute or 1-hour-plus sessions (depending on how you work) and explain that creating consistency in the treatment is critical. You state your rates as well, and that may preclude the patient from starting with you. A referral to a therapist that you know takes lower fees would be the next step. If you do long-term therapy, rather than a modality of 10 sessions or fewer, you state that as well and explain the rationale for longer-term treatment.

If you are compatible on these business issues, then pitch your immediate grasp of what you heard and help the person feel comfortable coming in. Set up the appointment in order to further determine the question of compatibility. Sometimes patients are dubious about starting, and we can help them get over the hump. It is to their benefit not to be caught in doubting and inaction. We must be willing to state the benefits of therapy. If they have revealed some significant issues, we can assure them that help is on the way.

Discuss your style up front. I say, "I am a direct therapist and I will be straightforward with you about what I observe and the conclusions I come to." I also explain the somatic component and how that form of treatment does not fit for everyone, adding that we can review that option after we work together for a period of time. Through each described segment of the framework you ask the patient if she feels she can invest in the process described.

If you both decide to set up an initial consultation, at this point I tell the patient about my cancellation policy. I explain that I have a week cancellation policy, so if he decides to cancel, please do so within that time limit. Of course, for the first session the cancellation policy may not apply if there is not a week in between your phone contact and consultation. But it is important to state your cancellation policy. The first phone contact should set the initial parameters of how you work—your expectation of consistent weekly sessions, the fee you charge per hour, your style or approach, and your cancellation policy—as well as establish a sense of his basic problems, giving you a view into his character structure.

The reason to set the stage from the initial contact is to create a container that holds and will help to defeat the inevitable discouragement, loss of momentum, and tenacious resistance to the process. Therapeutic work is not easy, and the investment necessitates sacrifices of time and resources. So dropping out is a tempting option that rears its head over and over again. Setting up a strong container allows the therapist to help the patient stay and achieve the best result. The patient's quality of life is at stake, and his hardships have wrought sometimes deep wounds that need healing. Or her life may have lost purpose and meaning, and a self needs to be uncovered so life can become worth living. Sometimes symptoms of anxiety, depression, eating disorders, sleep problems, or panic overshadow all else. Whatever the reason a patient enters therapy, we as therapists have to guide the ship so he can find his way to discovery and healing. The therapist has to create a clear path for the patient to help her not waver as she threads her way through the challenges and successes.

The therapeutic frame gives parameters to the patient and therapist that replicate the terms of other life realities. For those patients who have problems with commitments, boundaries, limits, and internal or external regulation and authority, the therapeutic structure may arouse defiance, rebellion, and lack of cooperativeness at points in the process. The therapist does not waver from the course set no matter how much the patient may rail at the limits. If the therapist is clearheaded, the container will hold the resistance.

Protocol for Initial Sessions

The first session/initial consultation is an important hour as the therapeutic relationship is defined in more depth, and the patient and the therapist determine if they will go forward together. I recommend a protocol for the first session.

I created a document, the Psychological History Form for Therapists (see the appendix in the web Online Resource Guide for this book), that organizes the therapist's process through the information-gathering phase of the first few sessions.

To begin, I recommend taking a thorough, methodical survey of any and all problems. Patients have a few in mind when they come into therapy. I request that patients tell me all the things that bother them whether small or large. I also ask probing questions to stimulate recognition of any areas they may not have considered. I will ask if they have reoccurring thoughts, feelings, images that disturb them. I will ask about their medical issues, injuries, prior medical issues, and medications. We can cover items such as sleep, diet, exercise, and body image issues. Relationship issues and work status should be addressed. I will ask for a review of psychological symptoms: depression, anxiety, negative self-talk, anger problems, fears, phobias, and social distress. The goal is that both of us see and understand, in detail, the entire picture of both positive attributes and those that reflect difficulties.

When I supervise other therapists, I notice that the problem assessment is often too thin, as the patient may launch into one specific problem and the therapist does not gather the complete picture. Once therapy begins it gets harder to get a grasp of all problem areas and the specific information that would be helpful in getting a larger contextual view.

Part of the problem picture may include a cursory overview of family of origin dynamics, so it is important that you get an in-depth picture of the basic family template with historic problem areas defined.

Also in your assessment of medical issues, find out whether the patient has had appropriate contact with medical professionals such as periodic blood tests and exams; if necessary advise him to get a physical from his primary care physician. Blood pressure, lipid profiles, triglyceride count, and other aspects of traditional medical exams should be encouraged and noted. If you have questions regarding *any* medical issues such as potential early onset dementia, sequela from prior head injuries, possible neurological issues, autoimmune symptoms and allergic reactivity, and so forth, ask your patient to get checked out with the appropriate medical professional. Note that personality or behavioral changes that have lasted for over six months can indicate an early stage of dementia or be an early indicator of Alzheimer's. The patient or family members might complain of changes in mood indicated by increased agitation or emotional sensitivity, changes in normal behavioral patterns, or changes in attitudes such as an appearance of unrealistic, grandiose beliefs. Often patients will avoid following up on problematic symptoms or medical issues. If the patient is not managing weight, alcohol, exercise, and other health issues, that becomes part of the treatment plan. Sexual functioning also needs to be on the table. You can ask a series of questions so that you understand how the patient is functioning in this area. Is she having consistent sex if she is in a long-standing relationship? Is he achieving satisfaction? Are there problem areas? Get specifics. This is often a difficult topic to discuss, so you want to normalize it in therapy so he feels permission to discuss all aspects of sexuality.

As the patient goes through this process I am assessing her character type and begin to get a picture of the dynamics at play. Midway through I may give her a summary of what I see, namely, her character bent, the origins of that from her history, and how her character approach factors into her symptom picture. This gives the patient an opportunity to experience how I work. I am direct and open about the dynamics of her defensive structure. I see if or how she integrates my direct approach and will titrate it if it causes discomfort and defensiveness. Character analysis begins right away, and the patient goes home with information she can think about. If the therapist is frank, the patient will know what to expect and gain confidence in the therapist. It is a critical balance between enrolling the patient in the therapeutic process by active questioning and listening while giving frank, direct observations or summaries at certain points. All the time, the meta-sense of patient confidence is beginning to form.

The next step is defining the frame, in more detail, educating the patient in how you work. I discuss the process of long-term therapy and what she can expect. I go over the importance of building and sustaining momentum that comes from weekly proximity and consistent concentration on issues of importance, including changing the dysfunctional aspects of her character stance. I go over the expectation of weekly therapy as ensuring the momentum. If the patient becomes inconsistent with her appointments, the therapy will suffer and lose the momentum. Sometimes a patient may be in crisis and distress, necessitating more frequent sessions, biweekly or three times per week. I go over the importance of consistency, not missing appointments, and capturing focus so issues can be addressed and changes made.

I touch on resistance—there will be times when the patient won't want to come; she may feel negative about me or the therapy; she may feel angry or disappointed and want to quit. I assure the patient that she will have those feelings more than once. At that time she must come in and tell me all about the resistant feelings so they don't derail her work. I make sure she understands the importance of resistance and that she will inevitably have her version of those conflicts. Resistance is critical to explore. Patients are resistant to life, to love, to change, to moving forward in ways that challenge them. Those resistances play out in their relationship to therapy. As therapists, we must not bypass the resistance and hope it goes away. We must go right to it, and let it amplify in the discussion so all of it is expressed and the patient can feel how he resists and the consequences of it. In resistance is negativity that needs to be unmasked. When it is revealed and discussed the patient can get back on track and not sabotage his life or the therapy. If the therapist tries to ignore it—as it is uncomfortable—the resistance goes underground, and when it emerges again it may pull the patient out of treatment.

A therapist described an encounter where her patient had come in and said he was thinking of wanting to quit. She bypassed that statement as they had jumped into an issue of importance. She admitted she hoped secretly that he would see the worth of her help as they discussed his issue. He ended up leaving therapy soon after. Need I say more?

An element of resistance is the patient's tendency to spread herself among multiple providers on a regular basis. Some patients unconsciously are afraid to invest in one person; this way she can have herself fortified by multiple dependency objects. Letting this continue creates conflicting advice and dilutes her relationship with you. Many patients consult with psychics, healers, astrologers, masseuses, coaches, and others, seeking advice and support. I suggest they would get more benefit if they settled down in therapy and stopped creating chaotic input from a myriad of professionals. It is a way patients soothe their anxiety or feelings of aloneness and fear. Yet, anxiety plays an important role in therapy. It means the homeostasis has been upset and change can happen. Or anxiety lets us know there are deeper issues and feelings that need exploration. The patient needs to tolerate anxiety, as it is a signal to respect. If the patient defends against anxiety and the deeper feelings of fear by running away, the contact with the feeling and the potential insight is denied.

The next step in the first session in the last quarter of the interview is to ask for the patient's honest reaction to the therapist. I state that honesty between us is critical to a healthy relationship, and I invite patients to tell me any concerns they might have in working with me as well as the structure of treatment. I ask for their input and encourage the honest feedback. After that, we decide if we will work together.

In the last portion of the first session I give them a package of my policies and procedures (see appendix file New Patient Package in the web Online Resource Guide for this book). This multipage document is a vehicle for signed informed consent. It defines the therapeutic process, what to expect, with full disclosure, so legally the therapist is covered and the patient understands the policies surrounding treatment. I recommend you meet with an attorney that specializes in psychological treatment to make sure your policies and procedures are thorough and represent your therapeutic guidelines. Your local mental health provider association provides templates as well. There are ethics classes that describe current changes in the laws that can help you design and stay up-to-date with your patient packages. I have separate documents, in multiple bright colors, to enhance the package—documents that define billing procedures, parking instructions, emergency phone numbers, missed session protocol, fee schedule, somatic disclosure page, arbitration agreement for signature, and consent to treatment. It is a comprehensive package that covers the therapist in the event of a disagreement as well as defines the parameters of therapy. There is a patient questionnaire that lists many symptoms with check boxes and space to describe further information. I ask them to take it with them and fill it out for our next session.

We go over briefly the billing system and I give them my medical biller's business card. Many therapists do their own patient billing with easy-to-use accounting software. I outline the payment options: pay each session, at the end of the month for all sessions, or receive a bill next month for the month prior and pay then with a small fee added. Then we schedule our next appointment and go over briefly the best times for them and my space limitations.

I have covered the first session in a detailed fashion, as the details are important. We are not trained in the business of therapy, and that aspect of practice is critical to the success of the treatment. When you create a tight frame, the relationship with the patient does not get muddled with compromises, negotiations, and adjustments unless it is therapeutically correct. The defined business contract and understanding creates and strengthens the therapeutic frame. Managing the business aspects demonstrates to the patient that she is entering into an organized system that has clear procedures to adhere to. You model competency as well.

The second session will follow up on what was laid out in the first. When the patient is settled in, I ask how he felt about our last session. I ask him to express any concerns, doubts, or other feelings that came up. It is a big deal to pick a therapist and start treatment, and I want the patient to get used to revealing his authentic feelings.

The patient should be coming in with his patient package completed. If not, ask him why he didn't complete it. Sometimes it warrants a discussion about not attending to or avoiding a task he deemed important. Or other mechanisms are at play and need to be defined during this session. Sometimes, the patient simply didn't bring it in and I leave it there. Then I look at how he filled it out. Many patients leave lots of blanks and barely add information. I discuss that with him and help him burrow deeper. Sometimes a patient is hiding symptoms or situations, perhaps violent thoughts or actions, substance use, or other aspects about which he is ashamed. Going over the patient questionnaire in detail will enable you to glean more information. Sometimes he has further questions about your policies or procedures, and that discussion brings you both into alignment about the frame. These discussions are grist for the mill if the business parameters bring up relational issues.

> Susan, age 50, contacted me for therapy referred by another patient. She had multiple prior therapies at various points in her life. After our first session and reading through my patient package, she took issue with a few items.
>
> She felt my cancellation policy was out of the norm and didn't feel like she wanted to comply with a one-week cancellation policy. I explained that if I could reschedule her I would try, but if I couldn't then she would have to pay for the session if it wasn't cancelled a week in advance. She felt I was rigid and too structured. She had never seen a patient package as thorough as mine and felt offended by it. She wanted a reduction in my fee as her last therapist charged less. She wanted special treatment and attempted to convince me to let her be an exception to my policies. I was firm and held the frame, and she still wanted to continue but not without wrangling and expressing discomfort. Therapy had begun in short order. What character type could Susan be?

The therapeutic frame can bring up important therapeutic issues. Many patients want what they think of as a supportive therapist that will not have limits and boundaries. Others become defiant and uncooperative around authority issues or rules or regulations or commitments. Other types feel controlled and want to be in the driver's seat. Others want special treatment and feel entitled to change appointments repeatedly to suit their own needs. Some patients want gratification and feel like the therapist should not have parameters, only the patient. And some patients believe that all rules should be suspended if the patient has a crisis. The policies can bring up disappointment and unconscious abandonment feelings as the therapist is not acting "touchy-feely." Some patients will project the mean therapist or the uncompromising parent and will be challenged by the therapist's frame. All are issues to be worked on characterlogically. The parameters you establish effectively bring these issues to the surface.

The patient questionnaire in the second session provides content to ask more specific questions on symptoms, current medications, and problem areas. I will take notes as I go over the questionnaire, and we discuss the items they checked or didn't check in greater detail. We both are getting a clearer picture as to what we think is important. This interview includes a thorough review of medications. For example, patients may be medicated for a variety of physical issues and complaints such as cardiovascular problems and might be on blood thinners, statins, and blood pressure medications for hypertension. Some of these have side effects that affect mood and other areas of functioning. You need to educate yourself on the side effects of your patient's medications. There are a variety of diseases that your patient may describe: diabetes, pulmonary disease, esophageal reflux, asthma, diverticulitis, and cancer, to name a few. Educate yourself on your patient's conditions and the side effects of his various medications so you can thoroughly understand what's what.

Patients may take prescribed psychotropic medications for a variety of symptoms such as anxiety and depression. These medications are frequently prescribed by primary care physicians, who are not sufficiently trained in the treatment of psychiatric disorders. We have expertise in the treatment of mental disorders and must evaluate effective treatments for our patients. Assess the length of time your patient has been on these medications, get the name of the prescribing physician, and discuss with the patient whether there has been improvement while on the medications. As you work with the patient you can assess whether the patient's medications are necessary and the best treatment option. Sometimes patients remain too long on medications that are no longer serving them or are on a cocktail of drugs. You can work with prescribing physicians (or the patient can) if you deem that the patient should titrate off her medications—as she integrates the benefits of psychotherapy, exercise, general regulation, and biophysical somatic interventions.

ADHD (attention deficit-hyperactivity disorder) is a commonly diagnosed disorder, codified as a neurobiological illness when in reality it is a syndrome dependent on subjectively defined evaluations of clinical traits and behaviors. ADHD is a legitimate diagnosis for some, but it is an overused diagnosis for many. Young children and teenagers are routinely diagnosed and put on medications. The diagnosis has been extended to toddlers as well as the elderly who are given stimulants rather than utilizing viable treatment alternatives to help regulate the family. Adults become dependent on a lifelong course of medications and identify as having attention problems and impulsivity rather than looking at the psychological reasons that drive their behavior (Silberman, 2016). Evaluate this diagnosis if your patient tells you he is taking ADHD medication. I have found that the majority of patients can titrate off these medications and incorporate self-regulating behaviors that work.

I also leave time in this session for discussion of current problems the patient wants to discuss. So the patient feels she is getting immediate assistance.

In the third session I begin a detailed history (see the appendix file Psychological History form in the web Online Resource Guide for this book). Although the best historical material comes with real feeling triggered in the present conversation, I want to know right at the beginning the historical contributors to the character problem. I do a methodical history taking, starting with each of the patient's parents and his parent's legacy. Getting cultural details, geographic placement, socioeconomic factors, educational information, socialization, deaths, and other crucial events is critical. History taking usually takes two to three sessions. I ask patients to describe their parents' early years of marriage when they were conceived. I track their lives from birth asking them to imagine their infancy and how they might have felt within the family context. Were they breast-fed? I want to envision the early critical attachment years as well as the dynamics up to age five. The latency period and socializing years of school are covered. Then I investigate the development of independence in the launch years of late teens. Did they leave home and go to college or a career path or did they get waylaid in terms of separation? By the time you have completed a thorough history you and your patients have an understanding about critical milestones and ruptures in healthy development.

As you go through their history, important defining aspects become clear to you, and you can summarize critical dynamics that formed their character. There is still much to learn but you have the broad strokes.

> Bill, a successful male in his early 40s, came into therapy wanting to change careers and find meaning. He had a wife and a child. His father left the home when he was young, and he was raised by his sisters and mom. Due to the circumstances of an absent father and full responsibilities falling on his mother, he felt the urgency to make money as his main priority. Finding success and security was the imperative, but he left behind the formation of a self and felt responsible to become "the man of the house" at an early age. His mom always kept a super positive outlook that denied the many other feelings that lurked beneath the surface. Now the patient was confused about his feelings, his direction, and he felt alienated from the life he had created. He relied on his controlling and dominating, hyperpositive, energetic style to cope, and that was off-putting in his marriage.
>
> I summarized his character style that was partly defensive in nature and helped him make sense out of where he found himself now and the historical roots. This condensation was helpful to him, and he felt I had a grasp of him quickly. There are many more critical points of discovery, yet when you can grasp a central dynamic, you can begin the work in an organized way that helps both the patient and the therapist establish clarity of focus.

The initial sessions are critical to set the stage for the rest of the therapy. The therapist sets out the therapeutic frame. The mechanics of therapy are clearly defined and agreed upon. When the patient finds herself rebellious or defiant regarding an agreement, that points to a therapeutic issue. If patient suggests missing sessions or cancels frequently, the frame guides you on how to deal with the breakdown of consistency and continuity. The therapist should not ignore these shifts and hope the behavior changes, but rather deal directly with the patient the moment her commitment begins to falter. If a patient is not paying his bill then that is a therapeutic issue, not one to be ignored and put aside. Not paying a bill calls up important aspects of the patient's handling of his life. These are examples of frame issues.

In the first three to four sessions the therapist has captured information that defines basic issues, character style, critical problems to manage, and the therapeutic relationship is launched in a steady direction with the patient on board and agreeing to the guidelines.

Sustaining the Frame-Business Aspects

How the therapist holds the frame or doesn't is apparent in the way the therapist manages various aspects of her business. Habits of extending session into overtime, lowering fees inappropriately, and other compromises reflect a loose frame and poor business skills. Learning the business aspects of practice is a helter-skelter proposition. Mastery of marketing in the relatively new and constantly changing web-based model is a steep learning curve. Therapists need to understand that they are in business and need to learn and develop a business model that allows them success in terms of sustaining a lucrative practice. A therapist who is struggling financially may make inappropriate clinical decisions due to the default need to retain patients.

When I supervise therapists I frequently witness that issue and its negative consequences. Decisions are made to avoid alienating the patient so the therapist will substitute inappropriate interventions that reflect pleasing, complying, ignoring negativity, and general soft-pedaling. How does a clinician do that? She might go overtime in session or communicate too much outside of session on the phone, through email, or texting. He might ignore the patient's acting out, not confront unhealthy attitudes or behaviors, or allow therapeutic frame violations so as to not rock the boat. Or she does not confront the character defenses in the room or outside and instead listens without limit to the patient's deflective style. These are not wise clinical decisions. It is better to organize one's practice to follow set guidelines no matter what. If you start negotiating the frame, you are in trouble. Have a business-like approach that brings you confidence and a successful practice so you do not feel desperate. I recommend that new therapists work part time at a clinic to supplement private practice so you are not dependent on your practice to survive.

Lowering your rates for the wrong reasons is questionable. It is acceptable to take a certain number of patients at lower fee. I have often reduced my fees for graduate students in psychology, as I want to support their capacity to be in therapy and study at the same time. Always assess if the fee is appropriate given your patient's income and situation; do not be afraid to ask for specific information on income and other financial variables that affect the patient's ability to pay for therapy. That information should be revisited yearly. As I mentioned, watch going overtime. Sometimes therapists extend the session. Rarely should you break the frame and go overtime. If it is critical to extend the session for a brief window, the therapist needs to announce to the patient that she is going overtime and get agreement that there will be an additional charge. Keeping to the session time limit established is not simply for financial reasons, but the patient may not want to be limited and will want to extend the session to get more from the therapist; that attitude and behavior needs to be discussed. Some patients feel they deserve more or will take more by not getting up to leave when their time is up. The frame helps the therapist keep to limits so she is not pressured or unconscious as to what is at play. If a therapist feels a lack of confidence, she might extend sessions to gratify the patient and rationalize that she is providing necessary support to the patient by going overtime.

All communications with patients fall under the therapeutic frame and the business model. That means all communications are billable time. Patient calls and emails are billed and prorated at session rate. There are no non-billable conversations. Therapists make this mistake. All conversations are therapeutic unless it is simply scheduling emails or conversations and those are at no charge.

I discourage therapists from texting. I feel this is an informal way to communicate and can be used, now and again, for quick scheduling changes or emergency notification of a need to talk. If there is content, do not use text. A more formal approach is email if the therapist can attend to an issue in writing. Our best mode is a phone conversation that acts as a short therapy session. Although texting is used frequently, the therapeutic relationship is a formal one and needs to be treated that way and not compromised.

Some patients have to be regulated or they will overuse these forms of communication outside of session. If a patient needs more proximity it is better to schedule the patient twice or three times a week. If there is a crisis, more time might be required. Patients, over time, develop skills from the therapy that hold them over between sessions. That is a goal of therapy: development of abilities to self-soothe, tolerate, and manage anxiety.

The business of therapy starts with clear management of the details: fees, time, and procedures are clearly accounted for in a businesslike manner. Vacations should be announced ahead of time with appropriate arrangements of backup professionals. The details need to be accounted for so that the business runs smoothly. Get as much help or technical expertise as you need so that you stay on top of your clinical practice and marketing for new patients. If your business runs smoothly you will feel competent and in charge and model that for your patients.

Lastly, account for time off. Many therapists don't take sufficient time off. I recommend at the beginning of each year to plan time off every season: maybe a week, 10 days, or longer. Some analysts traditionally take the whole month of August off—although that tradition is changing. It is important to take national holidays, too, so that you allow rest and recovery. Patients benefit from time off as well, as they get some time to digest and practice what they have learned.

9   The Therapeutic Relationship

Establishing Trust One Step at a Time

Any therapeutic relationship that sustains and succeeds is founded on trust—yet the relationship for much of the first half and at times, well into the second half, may accomplish only a modicum of actual trust. Real trust is established when both individuals have the capacity to grow strong, deep, abiding roots and links with each other that weather challenges and survive; yet many patients have arduous life stories that seriously compromise that capacity. At the start of treatment, the patient checks out the therapist, is tentatively respectful and senses that the therapist has his best interests in mind, and commits to the relationship initially. Although there will be periods of doubt, discouragement, and alienation, the foundational stability set up by the therapist and the enduring nature of the therapeutic relationship will help the patient weather his ambivalent feelings and lack of trust.

In the last chapter we discussed guidelines that reign in the unwieldy process of therapy so that the relationship proceeds within a strong therapeutic container. That container allows for trust to build slowly, stabilized by the mutual agreement to work together within the terms of that agreement. The therapist's therapeutic intention can be made clear—he is with the patient to help her explore, gain clarity and insight, make life changes, and do the work of character transformation so that her goals can ultimately be met—if she is industrious and responsible. This direct and forthright communication to the patient establishes preliminary trust as the patient knows where the therapist stands.

Authentic trust does not come quickly or easily in a therapeutic relationship and replicates trust challenges in the patient's other relationships and family history. Reich understood that truly positive feelings toward the therapist emerge after negativity is flushed out, and that can take a significant portion of the time spent in therapy. Baker felt true positive feeling for the therapist came toward the end of treatment. Masterson references the "therapeutic alliance" formed in the middle phase of treatment where trust in the relationship is settled sufficiently for the patient to engage his deepest feelings, often traumatic material, and can activate his own exploration and discovery without defenses.

Good feelings toward the therapist will wax and wane. The term *transfer-ence* refers to conscious or unconscious thoughts and feelings that originate in childhood relationships and experiences and are redirected to others. Sigmund Freud coined the term and defined it as a therapeutic vehicle for understand-ing the origins of patient conflicts originating in childhood. Transference illu-minates maladaptive relational issues that confound the patient, and through insight, the patient is helped to work them through—not always an easy task. As transference issues with the therapist are repeatedly aroused and explored, trust has a chance to build. I will say more on the types of transference later in this chapter.

Why do we have such a hard time trusting? No matter how wonderful you think your childhood was, circumstances and events may have shaken you more than once, making real trust challenging to achieve. Trusting another person fully is an evolved state that many of us have difficulty accomplish-ing in a lifetime. Our instincts for survival are primary and dominant. Many individuals are committed consciously or unconsciously to complete self-sufficiency so as to avoid counting on others in any significant way. Even if we don't think of ourselves as having to be self-sufficient and, in fact, con-sider ourselves as able to be dependent, there is still a sequestered place in our psyches where we do not trust our dependency partnerships completely. Our fears can be quite unconscious or nuanced because, on the surface, we live with others, rely on family and friends, and for the most part are buoyed by our established community. Yet, deep down for many of us, we are vigilant and careful about how deeply we depend on another. That deep-seeded survival instinct creates vigilance and enters the therapeutic relationship right from the start.

Reich thoroughly grasped that reality, and it is part of his masterful contri-bution to the field—the understanding that people do not trust easily even though a patient may appear positively inclined toward the therapist. His understanding of character developed from his experience of patients' consist-ent and tenacious defensive armor and enabled him to postulate that real trust and positive transference was an illusion at the beginning of treatment. This concept was revolutionary and still is. Underneath the pleasant and seemingly cooperative attitude lurk various strains of mistrust and negativity that the patient buries. Those attitudes and feelings contaminate his relationships—although that buried negativity may not be apparent on the surface. Reich labeled the complex aspects of relational life that emerge in the therapeutic relationship "transference neurosis," including distrust, disappointment when needs are not gratified, contempt, apparent feelings of love, suspicion, and more. Effective therapy brings various relational issues to the surface.

I encourage therapists not to assume that their patients are filled with enduring positive feelings about them and the therapy. Although it is easy to bask in feelings of being needed, appreciated, and valued and seen as special, powerful, and indispensable, those assumptions are not realistic nor are they therapeutically helpful. For the therapist, the patient's negative expressions toward her may be ego deflating, anxiety provoking, and uncomfortable. Yet the therapist does a disservice when she avoids negativity and perpetuates a false sense of trust simply to keep herself in her comfort zone.

Trusting another is a hard-won experience and takes time and patience. Trust and mistrust will be revisited over and over again in an authentic therapeutic relationship. It is up to the therapist to create space for and repeatedly invite the patient to always express negative feelings, anger, or disappointment with the therapist. The therapist must pick up those sometimes-illusive cues and call attention to them so that the patient can explore his feelings. As negative feelings are expressed and the relationship sustains and endures through it, better understanding is accomplished and real trust is built step by step.

The therapist may perpetuate an illusion of trust by not commenting on difficult aspects that might engender the patient's discomfort, anxiety, annoyance, or hostility. If the character style of the patient is one that is conflict avoidant, for example, as in the compliant, pleasing, cooperative patient, and the therapist does not point that out, the therapy will get stuck and stall out. The patient may want to feel taken care of, parented, and supported by the therapist and will demonstrate pleasing behaviors that ingratiate her with the therapist. This is a habitually stylistic trait of the patient to illicit gratification from others. The defensive maneuver of the patient does not build real trust as she knows she has bought good feeling from others by self-compromise. Nor is trust founded on a therapist who sets himself up as the one who is needed, the faux parent or the authority at all costs. In these instances, patient and therapist are in their defensive structure, ensuring that authentic trust will not develop.

If the therapist avoids tension with the patient and is always nice, accommodating, and gratifying, the patient gets the message that we park negativity outside and do not bring "those uncomfortable feelings about the therapist" into the office. "The nice therapist couldn't handle it," and the meta-message in the relationship is to act nice.

Ted told the supervision group how his many patients adore him and consistently feel safe and comfortable. He was an amicable gentleman, slightly pudgy and soft-spoken, and his demeanor could be described as a very nurturing, gentle type that would provoke an idealized father image. This was all well and good, except that who would want to upset that sweet apple cart with negative feelings? He had difficulty with my input as his professional presentation was so compatible with his own characterlogical need to please, protect, and be needed. He would not challenge himself to give this up and felt that his supportive and nurturing style was appropriate. I told him that patients have negativity, and their negative feelings can be a problematic factor in their lives. If those feelings are avoided by always being the gratifying therapist, patients won't face their abandonment rage and it is likely they will never fully mature. Ted didn't agree and was content to continue on in his own way.

The therapist needs to provide firmness and an edge that the patient can strongly push up against. The therapist has to challenge the patient, be serious and not smiling—many therapists smile most of the time unconsciously. If the therapist consistently smiles, she communicates, "I am a kind therapist, so you be nice, too, and we will both feel good." The therapist should not consistently present a soft comforting stance to relax into but rather offer some abrasion, an honest edge to work with. That edge may bring up patient anger or hostility as in "You are pushing me, and I resent that"; "You don't understand me"; "You are mean and don't give me the support I need"; or "I hate you." The therapist's character intervention may create tension that evokes honest, negative feelings from the patient toward the therapist.

At the clinic where I supervise interns, they are taught to be "very cautious" with their interventions; the patient is seen as "fragile" and not able to take feedback. What squeals of relief could be heard when I give them permission to comment on what they observe and be more authentic.

> A student described a patient who had been in analysis for many years. He knew the ins and outs of therapy, could analyze himself, speak the language of therapy, was well-read in self-help, and controlled the session from beginning to end, rejecting the therapist's comments. He never felt sadness, anger, or any other actual feelings, and underneath was quite hostile to the therapist but masked it with intellectualizing psychobabble. The therapist was trying to work with him cautiously, as she was instructed. She would say, "I feel so sad when I hear that." He, of course, was feeling nothing but impenetrability; so the intervention made her sound vulnerable and foolish. He, in turn, was running amok with his character defense of narcissistic dominance and contempt. If she doesn't confront his defenses, the therapy will be added to his list of therapeutic relationships that went nowhere except to reinforce his character defenses of control and domination. In reality, he was isolated, without friends and relationships, and he spent an inordinate amount of time at the gym lifting weights to look buff. The therapist could begin to point out his defenses of intellectualization and rationalization, his need to dominate and control, and his dismissal of the therapist. Then the room would heat up. If she pointed out his contemptuous attitude every time he acted smug and challenged her feedback, real work would begin and it wouldn't be easy.

As therapy proceeds and the outermost layers of defense are dismantled and the patient enters the middle phase of treatment with less resistance, the patient may touch experiences, memories, and painful feelings. At this time, the therapist holds those experiences with a softer style and creates safety for the patient to uncover and explore deeper experiences. The patient can access that depth because the character defenses have been dismantled. And even at this depth, distrusting layers emerge again.

Initially, the patient may feel relieved to find a therapist and may feel positive feelings as he unburdens long-standing worries and concerns. That sense of relief is appropriate—it is normal to feel supported as the patient settles in with the therapist. The patient begins with a sufficient acceptance of the style and expertise of the therapist to sign on. In mental health clinics, patients may be assigned to a therapist or intern and will go along with the assignation unless there is a disturbance. In private practice, the therapist establishes an initial level of safety with the patient. That doesn't mean you play it safe. In fact, it is better to confront the character defenses right away so the relationship gets off on a more authentic footing, without gratification that sets unrealistic and unhealthy expectations. The patient needs feedback as well as support. Character change and change of destructive behaviors is required. The therapist can make that clear: change is necessary in order to better one's life. The therapist is not there to support for the sake of an idea that therapy should be supportive. Then you have a situation where the patient is supported by the therapist, in her unhealthy attitudes and habits. I advocate starting off from the beginning in an authentic way so that the patient knows what is required. Then trust will form over time due to the many trials that are worked through within the relationship.

Therapeutic Neutrality

Therapeutic neutrality is a staple of the Mastersonian approach and a skill to master. Neutrality supports the development of patient trust as well as therapist confidence. What does this term mean? A neutral position is one without strong bias and prejudice but rather a position of discrimination and clarity. As the therapist sits with patients, she is met with a variety of patient attitudes, behaviors, and events that could provoke her to judge harshly or be intimidated. Neutrality does not mean we don't have feelings or opinions, but we are able to suspend those in order to view and hold the patient as he is. We understand his character and why he may be predisposed to act the way he acts or to think the way he thinks. That neutral approach stops the therapist from reacting personally and emotionally, allowing objectivity that is imparted to the patient.

Therapy is a process where both therapist and patient learn and develop a deeper understanding of the patient. If the therapist speaks with reactivity from a biased, emotional position neither person in the room feels safe. There is an absence of neutrality when the therapist is triggered and reacts defensively—resulting in an absence of interventions that could be effective. The therapist might say something strongly for effect, to create a dramatic moment, but that is a conscious choice on the part of the therapist. The therapist has many tools to utilize in the hopes of ensuring the most effective response—including using a dramatic confrontation or humor and banter to make a point. But that choice of intervention does not originate in reactivity that the therapist cannot control. Now and again the therapist may choose to state her personal feelings if she deems that intervention to be helpful.

Neutrality is the ability to speak without personal investment, bias, and judgment. Instead you speak with knowledge, compassion, tolerance, and clarity about the situation. Neutrality is not a defensive posture but rather an open, clear stance of stating or confronting what is observed in a neutral way. Aspects of neutrality are engagement, attentiveness, composure, and discriminating clarity in order to state the best possible response that results in illumination and awareness. Many times, the therapist's intervention may be off—slightly or quite a bit—and the patient reacts. That happens and a discussion might ensue that deepens the authentic relationship. But if the patient senses a therapist's hidden negative feeling, it may cause defensiveness and distrust in the patient.

Neutrality is not coldness, distance, or an analytic blank-screen posturing. In fact, a neutral stance can be warm, lively, and contactful. The therapist is a real human being and responds that way. Another word to describe the neutral sensibility is equanimity. The therapist is relaxed and settled as she listens carefully, with an open heart when appropriate. The therapist feels balanced within, collected and composed and therefore is not reactive.

Therapist neutrality creates safety for the patient to say and feel issues that have been unspoken and unexplored. The patient does not have to worry about the therapist's judgmental response. He often will wonder inside, "What is she thinking? Is she judging my behavior?" The patient may state that he feels criticized or has anxiety about revealing, yet again, that he screwed up. His anticipation can be discussed, cleared, and further trust is built. Over time the patient experiences the therapist holding the neutrality consistently and trust is confirmed. Reich's concept of contact adds an element—the therapist is energetically available, present, and unarmored. The patient feels the contact without the burden of carrying inappropriate feelings that belong to the therapist. This is another reason therapists need good therapy themselves.

The boundary between patient and therapist is flexible and depends on many variables that the therapist has to assess: the patient's character type, clarity about the type of transference (does the patient see you as whole or do projections still unravel the relationship?), length of time working together, and level of trust established. The therapist needs to be clear and conscious of the boundary at any given moment. At times the boundary is more open if you are tracking dreams and utilizing deep resonance and intuition—usually with a long-term patient in the middle phase of treatment. It depends on the stage of therapy and the type of patient and that topic will be covered in another chapter. But if a patient does not view you clearly, then the boundary should remain firm so the patient can work through difficult projections.

> Another therapist told me about a patient, Sara, who challenges her. The therapist repeatedly loses her neutrality. Sara is a borderline who is highly reactive with exaggerated provocative responses. A typical scenario goes like this: The session seems to be going well with Sara gaining insights, and then toward the end of session, she erupts into complaints like, "The work is not helpful. I want to stop coming in or cut back on therapy." The professional, rather than lean back in her chair and state simply, "This is a topic to be discussed at the next session," enters into the fray and the end

of the session unravels and the therapist feels awful. She knows that she loses it but this particular patient makes her very anxious as she worries about Sara being a suicide risk and her fear compels her to jump in rather than hold her neutrality and firm boundaries.

Therapeutic Stance

Masterson also relays the importance of the *therapeutic stance* as part of sustaining a clear therapeutic frame. The stance refers to the expectation that an adult is in the room (unless you are working with a child or teen), and the therapist speaks consistently to the mature part of the patient, the Self that is trying to be birthed. The stance holds that the patient is expected to produce material and take responsibility in the session and in his life, keep the agreements defined at the outset, and in general act in his own best interest. Many patients do not live their lives in a responsible manner, but if the therapist relates to them with a healthy expectation, it sets a responsible context. The therapist intervenes when the patient is not acting responsibly. If the patient stops keeping agreements, uses acting-out behaviors, and utilizes defenses that sabotage, the therapist intervenes. The therapist confronts the attitudes, feelings, and behaviors that are destructive, immature, or nonadaptive. Reich had a similar stance of expecting mature behavior and would confront the patient on regressive, paranoid, or immature approaches to life. Again, it is done neutrally, not judgmentally, but the message is always clear even if the patient struggles to think, feel, or behave maturely and change old habits.

The stance embodies one of realism. This therapeutic attitude is essential when the patient cannot find his own sense of reality, as distortions cover a realistic sense of what is going on. When emotions are coloring a clear perspective, it is the therapist who needs to hold the clearest objective view possible. When the patient is not clear on reality and is self-destructive as a defense against facing into real pain and seeing situations as they are, the therapist works with those defenses to dismantle them. Point out the repetitive character defenses that stop appropriate adaptation. That is our job. The therapist becomes the true ally of the real self that is able to function in reality.

To maintain therapeutic neutrality and a therapeutic stance, therapists have to guard against overly gratifying the patient with too much advice, becoming a surrogate parent, and in general engaging in caretaking behaviors. If the therapist is passively engaged in listening to content without a clear focus, then the stance is lost. The therapist must see and work the defenses consistently that are in the way of maturation. If you are overly caretaking, you keep the patient regressed (as Ted did). Be alert to therapist boundary violations such as going overtime, wavering on policies and procedures, accepting inappropriate rates, and engaging in extended email or texting exchanges. If you are overly worried about a patient, speak to a colleague or a supervisor to renew your equanimity and get underneath your concerns to investigate what the patient triggers *in you*. If you are not confronting the defenses in a thorough manner, explore what is holding you back. These are signs you have lost your stance.

> A therapist, Suzanne, was seeing a couple. The female, Donna, had terminated individual therapy with Suzanne and was coming only to couples' sessions with her boyfriend, John. Suzanne had lost track of the character traits of Donna, who we designated a paranoid schizophrenic type due to her distrusting nature, withdrawal from contact, spiritual bypass, and brittle defensiveness. Donna had been focusing intently on John's problems, sidestepping her own contributions to the relationship failure. Suzanne identified with Donna's point of view and lost track of Donna's therapeutic issues. When we went over character diagnosis, it made sense that Suzanne had lost the thread of Donna's negative projections and withdrawal. The therapist had lost her therapeutic stance and had gone along with Donna stopping individual sessions when she needed individual therapy desperately. Many therapists believe that one should not do individual sessions if you see the couple. I prefer to see the individuals and also see them together in couple's therapy, as I understand each person's character issues and how they interface. Although challenging, I find I can hold the neutrality and look at each separately and together. If there is extreme paranoia in one or the other, or serious splitting, then it would be better if they were seen by someone else for couple's therapy.

Types of Transference: Patient Negativity

Our discussion of transference and resistance is of paramount importance in establishing and keeping your bearings as a therapist. Reich's quintessential teaching is on resistance. The therapeutic relationship is the laboratory for relational dynamics. The therapist becomes both parents, husband and wife, sibling, most wished for gratifying object, most hated and loathed person, and at times a scapegoat for all that goes wrong. If allowed, patients can bash the therapist relentlessly and dump mounds of negativity, hostility, contempt and ridicule on the therapist and walk out relieved. The latter is certainly not helpful as it supports the patient to be his worst abusive self. It can also make the therapist feel sick and battered. Transference reactions must be understood and worked with consistently.

There are a few types of transference to note: basic neurotic transference, latent negative transference, transference acting out, and transference psychosis. I mentioned neurotic transference early in this chapter. That is your generic projection of parental figures on to the therapist that may trigger certain emotions in the patient that need to be worked through. We are discussing the neurotic patient who has whole object relations—remember that concept from a previous chapter? The neurotic can see the therapist and himself as whole. So the patient may get triggered and view the therapist as a father figure, arousing past disagreeable feelings, but is able to clarify that the therapist is not his father. He then works through, over a number of sessions, the remaining impasses on that topic. Neurotics do not lose sight of the therapist as a person with strengths and weaknesses and accept the therapist's features as is, even if at times the patient is quite challenged to view the therapist in this manner.

Reich discussed latent negative transference as a critical element of treatment. I referenced examples of latent negative transference in the first section of this chapter on trust. Latent negative transference is the underground negativity within the patient that gets directed toward the therapist. Patients may notice characteristics of the therapist and feel disdain, disgust, hostility, jealousy, judgment, and competitiveness. The patient hides this from the therapist much as he hides his negativity in his life, if he does. So the negativity lurks silently in the room or comes out with a sneer, an aside, a dismissal, repudiation, a lack of cooperativeness, an undercutting, sabotage, or sarcasm directed at the therapist. Usually the therapist is aware of most of these behaviors and may disregard them or shy away from commenting on them, as they are not trained to do so. Reich insisted, and it is the hallmark of his theory, that the therapist immediately comment on negative responses, no matter how subtle. That no treatment can go forward without first excavating the latent negative transference. The patient protects himself with his negativity so the therapist cannot impact him. Why? If the therapist makes an inroad, he might feel pain and vulnerability and make contact with the realities of his life. Better to hole up, sneering inside at the therapist or others and make it the therapist's problem rather than his own.

Latent negative transference will be audible and visible in some form or another. It is your job to catch it and send the missive back to the patient to consider. Without working this negativity, the therapist perpetuates an illusion that the patient is blissfully content with the therapist and only positive appreciation resides in the room. That is a naive position as the character defenses are in the room with all the attendant stylistic points of resistance to the therapist and the treatment.

Transference acting out, as I described previously, is enacting maladaptive behaviors rather than experiencing and feeling difficult emotions in a responsible manner. So a patient clings to a destructive relationship and plays out a highly dramatic yelling match with the boyfriend, calling and texting desperately, rather than feel the deep pain of loss and the anxiety that it provokes. The patient does a version of that with the therapist. He may cancel appointments at the last minute to play out his narcissistic preoccupation with his importance in order to minimize his feelings of inadequacy. Or she may not pay her bill as a way to express hostility toward the therapist. Or a patient may terminate therapy abruptly to either avoid confronting the therapist with angry or disappointed feelings or run from inner pain. These are examples of acting out in therapy. Patients may do behaviors such as continuing substance abuse, violent temper tantrums, lying, cancelling sessions, confounding the relationship by seeing other professionals, quitting prematurely, and in general sabotaging their path of health. If the therapist does not recognize these signs right away, the patient will abort, terminate, and all is lost. We can't always prevent self-destructive acts, but the sooner we call this out, the better the chance the therapist has to help the patient investigate and understand the consequences of her behaviors and stop the acting out.

Transference psychosis is a form of transference that occurs with paranoid types, schizophrenics, and Disorders of the Self personality disorders such as borderline, narcissist, and schizoid with serious perception difficulties and splitting. These patients do not realistically see the therapist as a whole and real person. Rather they see the therapist in their projection screen as a replica of a bad person, and they react accordingly. A patient may see the therapist as destructive toward her, as not having her best interests in mind, as out to compete with her, be better than her, or control, hurt, or destroy her. The projection screen is so tarnished that the therapist exists in his mind exclusively as a threat, and he can't be reasonable. These projections on the therapist create a serious conundrum, and the therapist has to interrupt this distortion and stabilize the relationship. In time, the patient understands his propensity to distort and learns to consciously make adjustments until he develops more wholeness in his psyche.

Transference dynamics are a necessary part of treatment and illuminate unresolved templates that contort a patient's ability to cope and adapt. As transference feelings become clarified, the patient faces into pain and trauma that have been repressed. Less material gets projected onto the therapist, and instead the patient is able to look inward and gain insight from contacting the deepest layers of remembrances and feelings.

Resistance

Resistance to treatment winds its way into the process on a regular basis, and the therapist needs to be on the lookout for signs and symptoms. What is resistance?

Naturally we resist looking honestly at our lives, especially when we might feel regret, guilt, pain of loss, an absence of a meaningful life, and disappointment in ourselves. These can be excruciatingly painful realizations, and it is quite challenging to face them. The adaptive human, consciously and unconsciously, moves away from pain and toward pleasure. Psychologically that mechanism is not always helpful because if we block off painful awareness, we become housed in our defensive structures and ignore reality, therefore perpetuating our mistakes. So resistance is a natural impulse to shield us from bitter truths, realizations, regrets, guilt, and deep loss and grief. Therapy is a process that facilitates uncovering the ingredients of a life and with it comes many wonderful and also disagreeable or extremely painful recollections. Resistance comes with therapy as there is a natural reticence to delve into painful issues. Resistance is the basis for all acting-out behaviors.

I suggest in the first session to warn the patient about resistance and explain it in depth so at the first sign of those feelings, the patient may remember what the therapist explained. As the therapist notices resistant behaviors and expressions, those need to be commented on and discussed so resistance doesn't take over. Periodically I recommend that the therapist ask the patient how she felt about coming to session today. Soon the patient will volunteer that she felt resistance as she was driving to the office. These discussions minimize the resistance as well as shed light on a specific issue that may be causing the current resistance. This way resistance can be understood by the patient and doesn't take over in a way that is destructive to her continued growth in therapy.

Therapists describe some patients as difficult. That usually means the patient is stuck in resistance and her defenses obstruct exploration and deep insight. Therapists have to work tenaciously to dismantle chronic defenses that the patient puts up to fight therapy. Reich believed that when therapy is stuck in the mud it is the therapist, not the patient, that has lost his directional cues. Therapists may focus on the patient as the problem, but I suggest first looking at how the therapist may have lost his way with a specific patient and situation and why.

Georgina, age 40, is a difficult patient and a therapist. She came into therapy with hostility issues, with problems in her relationship, and to learn more about Orgonomy. When provoked she would become indignant and devalue the therapist. She was a phallic narcissist who was quite enamored with her abilities to control those around her. She felt, for the most part, "on top of her game." She hated to feel vulnerable and lose her competitive edge. When confronted she would usually devalue the therapist. At times she would sink into honest self-reflection, but would rebound back into her ego-dominant position and her hostility won out. She resisted surrendering to the process with her female therapist, as she hated her overly indulgent mother and had contempt for women. Her resistance to the process was never conquered before she ended up quitting. It is likely the therapist fell prey to her narcissistic glow and colluded with her stance of superiority.

The therapist learns to work with resistance in order to move it aside. Resistance shows up in session in the character style and how each patient tries to divert the therapist from the real work. Patients are masters at this, as they have learned this survival mechanism early on. For every character type, there is a different diversionary tactic. Resistance can look like overtalking about something other than what is important. Or a patient will go numb and silent, not activating material, or will try being the comedian to distract, or will divert to talking about the therapist, or will control the therapist— these are all forms of resistance. Resistance will rear its head at many junctures in the process. Maybe the patient is finally ready to leave a destructive relationship or activate a long-feared goal or become more independent, and she will resist that movement by missing a session, getting sick, ignoring the therapist, or overeating or binge drinking. As Reich states, we are terrified of movement and will resist it in tricky ways. The therapist has to understand that mechanism and help the patient get out of her own way.

It is well worth the therapist's time to read Reich's *Character Analysis* (1972) for his extensive treatment on resistance. He provides diverse examples and guidance to further your understanding on the critical topic of working with resistance.

10 The Therapist's Reactions

Sustaining Our Clarity: Context of Treatment

The prior chapter establishes the importance of maintaining a therapeutic stance and therapeutic neutrality. These concepts are guiding therapeutic principles that help contain unruly emotional tides that may flood the relationship with feelings and reactions on either side of the couch. As the patient fluctuates from intense feelings of hopelessness, desperation, and despair, to attitudes of defiance and stubbornness, to playing out dramatic scenes, to settling down to exploration of deep feelings through dream analysis, followed by renewal of destructive behavior—the therapist's clarity holds the course. If the therapist loses her clear perspective, both partners in the relationship can plummet, ending up in tatters that can, in the worst-case scenario, destroy the therapeutic relationship.

If we maintain our therapeutic stance of neutrality and consistently embody our therapeutic position in the relationship, we are less likely to falter and get lost in the myriad of detours available in any given session. What is our role and what are we trying to accomplish? At a minimum, the patient has sought our help because he is distressed and has a specific issue to discuss with "an expert." Or the patient has had lifelong disturbances with debilitating symptoms and is seeking further resolution of her suffering. Symptoms and issues may fall somewhere in between. As we sit with the patient, we always hold the assumption that the patient can access within—at some point—a guiding, mature self-direction. Our operating assumption is that patient responsibility is required for the endeavor, and we create that abiding context. We intervene to challenge the character style, to dismantle defenses, acting-out behaviors, and inauthentic daydreams, as those chronic response patterns are maladaptive. Our role is to hold the preceding assumptions and context at all times as we voice a realistic perspective so the patient can mature from living in a fantasy to clear contact and adaptation in reality. Clear contact creates the opportunity for a clear perspective. The therapist's role is to create a working environment and guidelines that structure the therapy so that the therapist can actively engage defensive, unhealthy attitudes and behaviors that stand in the way of health, no matter the patient's starting point.

With our best efforts, we accomplish what the patient is capable of accomplishing. We set the stage, and demand a level of responsibility that creates tension as the patient pushes himself forward. We create space for the patient to explore freely; we allow him the time he needs—except when he is dillydallying. Then we might ask for more responsibility. The patient sets his goals as the process moves along. The goal posts may be moved as he knows himself better. The therapist keeps her eye on the patient's goals while maintaining a rich sensibility of what the real self may be communicating. The patient's desires and the real-self communiqués may differ. The therapist helps translate deeper psychic messages that come through dreams.

The therapist starts by comprehensively assessing the patient's situation and obtains a picture of the patient's character style and pathological defensive patterns. He assesses if the patient is high or low functioning, which determines critical pieces of the game plan. As the therapist determines the character type and the larger symptom picture, the issues begin to make sense. The therapist determines a direction as she works the character defenses to gain access to the layers underneath. If crisis and symptom amelioration are necessary at the outset, then more case management might be required along with character analysis. I will discuss case management in the next chapter.

As the therapist sits with the patient, his overriding assumption is that the patient has a central core, a potential real self that can be realized. We understand that not every patient can achieve this realization. For many, becoming adaptive and able to stop addictions, self-regulate, maintain healthy relationships, and be self-sufficient are worthy goals that the patient can feel proud to achieve. If the patient can become autonomous and actualize more of her potential, resulting in meaning and fulfillment (what Jung called *individuation*), those ambitions are wonderful benchmarks to achieve. It is difficult for many patients to realize a state of individuation, particularly when one grew up without good role models and likely faced challenging adversity. Even if a patient thinks his childhood was "close to perfect," the real self may have been ignored, denied, or quashed, resulting in the development of a false self and faulty character structure that has hampered his potential for a meaningful life. Regardless of whether a patient was relentlessly criticized, neglected, or overindulged, there are ramifications to his life that need to be understood and resolved sufficiently to permit contentment and peace of mind.

Coloring Outside the Lines of the Therapist's Role

The therapist has many faces, depending on the patient's therapeutic needs. We can have a multitude of approaches within the basic role and assumptions that guide us. Some patients may require a softer approach at different stages of treatment. Others may require more crisis management and more therapeutic direction. Certainly, younger folks in late teens and early 20s may benefit from directive therapy. For some, sitting back and letting the patient direct her activated exploration is the best seat. We can be a voice of silence, attentiveness, sensitivity, empathy, curiosity, compassion, tolerance, and responsiveness; a voice that expresses questioning, incredulity, doubt, or potent confrontation.

What do I mean by *coloring outside the lines of the therapist's role*? For many therapists the lines or boundaries blur; many times the therapist doesn't realize that boundaries have been crossed. It is a complex relationship—intimate in that the patient confides exclusive, confidential, personal information, laden with complicated emotions. The intimate relationship can last for years. Therapists can feel emotionally drawn in, consciously or unconsciously. "If the patient is sharing, she must feel trust and feel close to me." Or a therapist might say, "I feel so protective of Marilyn. She is so fragile that I worry about her a lot." Or "Julie's stories are fascinating; the hour goes quickly." The therapist is oblivious to the fact that she has lost her therapeutic position and has become personally involved, overextended, and captivated.

Patients are barraged throughout their lives by relationships fraught with baggage. They learned to kowtow to a destructive parent who intimidated them into submission. Or maybe they felt a duty to take care of a needy parent who co-opted them by various emotional manipulations if they tried to separate. Or if they became autonomous, they felt guilty that they weren't sacrificing. Relationships are often filled with trade-offs, conflicting allegiances, bargains, deals, and confusion. The patient comes into treatment with those conflicts still intact and may be as exquisitely tuned into the therapist as he has been to his family relationships, current spouse, or siblings. He needs a pristine environment to sort himself out. So the therapist has to stay out of the way and not violate the relationship with unconscious needs, personal issues, and wanting the patient to somehow sacrifice her autonomy to assuage the therapist.

Allen, age 42, entered therapy with martial problems. He and his wife have a three-year-old daughter. The wife was in therapy with a female therapist. Allen described his wife as highly anxious and she complained of feeling constantly overwhelmed with her life and parenting tasks that resulted in angry outbursts at the daughter. She often left to go on retreats for days at a time. Finally, Allen asked to see her therapist as the wife had declined to go into couple's therapy. The therapist stated that she "loved his wife and found her to be amazing!" The wife had often stated that her therapist told her she was protective of her. I am not inferring that the therapist was "in love" with the patient but rather she had crossed a boundary in feeling and saying "I love this patient" and that she "feels protective." To be overly enamored by a patient creates a biased lens, and the therapist is blinded to the obvious dysfunctional feelings and behaviors that are right in front of her. If the therapist then projects fragility and feels a need to protect the patient, this may be a projection of the therapist's own feelings of fragility and need to be protected while disregarding the patient's problems that need to be addressed. The therapist seemed surprised to hear Allen's input as if she hadn't realized many aspects of her patient's maladaptive functioning. Of course, as therapists we have to be careful not to become biased when we hear only one side of the story.

Both newly minted and more mature therapists may get personal fulfill-ment from the intimacy of the therapeutic relationship and therefore foster a nurturing bond or feeling of togetherness that goes on too long and keeps the patient in stasis. If a therapist is hungry for attachments to others, he may foster needy attachment in the patient. Or if the therapist was rejected or neglected early in her life, she might compensate by giving to the patient what she always yearned for from family and friends.

The therapist is not the patient's personal friend. We may have fond and warm feelings for our patients. We are human in our role and have warm-hearted feelings for most that we work with. But we must not co-opt or seduce the patient into feeling a fantasy that we are or will be personal friends. It is because we are not personal friends that the patient is free to be fully herself and have a myriad of complicated feelings toward us. The patient has the freedom to be unencumbered by our feelings, even though due to their character they may want to protect us, take care of us, or devalue us, depending on the type. They require space around them that is not sticky with enmeshment—with the therapist acting as a friend, parent, sister, or brother. Also we want them to activate in the world and create intimate friendships and connections that are enduring and find intimate love relationships with relational fulfillment.

As Mastersonian therapist Dr. Barbara Short discusses in *Ownership of Mind: Separation in the Counter-transference*, many problems are created by therapists who do not have clear boundaries. She advises therapists to be careful of creat-ing false expectations: The patient should not be seduced by the expectation of receiving love. If the therapist has created this expectation through gratify-ing the patient inappropriately, then the therapist has created a false expecta-tion that the patient can make up for all the losses in her life with the therapist now. This blocks the patient's contact with unresolved abandonment grief that needs to be reexperienced and resolved. It does not mean that healing does not take place around loss and grief currently with the therapist; but the expectation that the therapist is the all-loving individual that will make the grief and abandonment feelings go away is fraudulent. That is a cruel hoax and one that gratifies the therapist's need to be needed or administer all the love she did not get in her past, or fulfill unmet needs in her current life. This inappropriate expectation may also retraumatize the patient as she is betrayed again by the narcissistic needs of the therapist (Masterson, 2015, 85).

The therapist is not a parent or imbued with the omnipotence a toddler experiences as she looks up and sees her larger-than-life parent. We are not an all-knowing person with magical powers to predict the future, make magi-cal pronouncements to woo the patient, or take on personal powers that are not realistic. Therapists have to watch the inflation that comes with the role of therapist. It is an instant status that is very seductive. We feel respected, wanted, and empowered—all dangerous poisons for the ego. We may go by the title of doctor, and that title gives more status and power. Some therapists thrive on those ego inflators that come with the territory. We have to constantly practice our "not-knowing" and humility in the face of our patients' life complexities. That is a hedge against the inflation that comes from our position. We don't necessarily know the right answers nor can we know what is truly best for our patients, as they need to discover answers from within. We can help guide them to make those discoveries.

> Murray is a therapist who practices without obvious boundaries. He will talk on the phone to patients in a familiar way for extended periods of time, making himself available almost 24/7. He seems to cultivate the attention from his patients and slurps up the syrup of being wanted and makes himself available for all calls. Murray lacks a personally compelling life, so he uses his work relationships to buoy him. He varies his therapeutic identities as friend, intimate, and parent while cultivating patient dependency.

This example is extreme, but therapists can fall into these unhealthy and unprofessional modes unconsciously. The patient wants to depend and be gratified and not stand autonomously. Granted that developing autonomy can be a lengthy process, but the therapist must not create an illusion that the relationship will satisfy all that was lost. The relationship, with the building of trust, can help the patient set up new inner psychic structures that enable him to grow into a stronger more self-sufficient person. The purpose is not to sustain dependency so the patient never feels her abandonment feelings. Rather, as the therapist maintains an appropriate position, the patient, at that phase of treatment, will deepen into her early experiences of loss of love and losing her real self. She can feel into the innermost layers of grief and loss. If the therapist has porous boundaries it may prevent the patient from deepening into her necessary grief that must be felt rather than acted out with others or with the therapist.

If the therapist engages in a sexual seduction or relationship with a patient, he has seriously crossed a line. It is both unethical and illegal to engage in a sexual relationship with a patient. The therapist will lose his license to practice. Laws vary between states but the point is the same. Don't do it. There are many other ways to seduce a patient without having sex. Therapists need to watch those lines. It can happen that opposite sex or same sex therapists and patients may feel affectionate or even attracted to each other. If this happens it is informative for both members of the dyad. If there is attraction, that can be discussed, can inform the relationship, and the therapist can use that feeling to help the patient transfer erotic feelings to the right person. Or it may be informative in other ways including that the patient may be seducing the therapist as a form of resistance that blocks her feelings of loneliness and emptiness. Some patients are talented at seduction and use it to gain power over others and a naive therapist can be caught in the web. Or therapists may use their good looks or charm to seduce patients and gain power and adoration. Be aware if you are having these feelings and seek supervision and guidance. As a therapist you do not want to be caught off guard with erotic feelings run amok.

Therapists can cross boundaries without noticing that the relationship becomes too informal. If the therapist is on email after hours, it might suggest that the therapist is overly available; if texting becomes habitual, then communications are occurring outside the therapeutic frame. Sharing information that is outside of the therapy context is another problematic area. Trading services is also a slippery slope. Then the therapist is both a therapist and a recipient of the patient's wares or services. That is quite complicated to navigate, and I do not recommend it. Asking a patient for a favor or an introduction to someone, or using the patient's business position is dangerous as the therapist is using the patient for his own personal gain. The therapeutic relationship must remain therapeutic and be held within the frame and not be diluted, compromised, or tarnished by other purposes.

Even habitual hugging at the end of session can cross a boundary. If it is an appropriate gesture for a long-term patient and both feel this established ritual makes sense, then that is a conscious therapeutic choice. If you hug a patient habitually for no good therapeutic reason, it is a questionable act. Sometimes patients may feel upset with you or distant and alienated and hugging them causes them to deny their negative feelings or camouflage them. Be aware of habitual actions with patients that are not founded on a conscious decision-making process.

I am not suggesting an overly strict and rigid model that annihilates the therapist's aliveness, spontaneity, and humanness. The best interventions emanate from the therapist's willingness to be authentic, utilizing responses that flow easily such as humor, banter, indignation, and other ways of interacting that break the ice or create a fresh way of relating. A good therapist is freely creative and enjoys the aliveness that she brings into the room. The boundaries must stay clear for both parties. In the chapter "The Therapist Tool Chest" I will discuss various types of effective interventions.

Counter-transference is the term used to describe the feelings that the therapist has in relation to the patient. Feelings inside the therapist are normal. We have a variety of simple and complex feelings, attitudes, and cognitive stances within any relationship. As therapists we must stay continuously conscious of all those feelings and cognitions that change with each patient.

The therapist can express many feelings toward the patient—he can be inquisitive, curious, challenging, understanding, helpful, compassionate, empathetic, incredulous, and confrontational. Those are some of the expressions that are part of the therapist's tool chest. All of those and more are appropriate and heartfelt reactions to the patient.

Counter-transference Reactions: Fear, Anger, Inadequacy, Envy, Boredom

Fear

Intimidation is a typical feeling that many therapists complain about. There are a few types of patients that provoke the counter-transference reaction of intimidation. Patients that are highly successful in the world and have high earning capacity and wield power can intimidate the therapist who does not feel successful. Phallic narcissists fit this bill. These qualities in the patient may evoke envy in the therapist who feels he doesn't measure up in the world. The therapist who feels less-than is not capable of matching the energy level of this type of patient. The therapist can feel fearful and intimidated by a patient whom he deems intellectually superior or embodying other traits that the therapist emulates.

> A female professional described a CEO of a large successful company who entered therapy with marital problems. He had an exaggerated, confident style and treated the therapist as he treated his wife: arrogantly, in charge, and ready for any debate that he would inevitably win. The therapist felt she couldn't influence him and ended up rather desperately giving advice in a rationalized way that did not impact him. She was not able to point out what he needed to hear in terms of his character approach of domination and one-upping. He was hungry for adoration from others, particularly women, and that was a problem for his wife. His compulsive need for adoration should have been discussed and unpacked. The therapist was frozen as he controlled the therapy.

The pervasive feeling of fear can be common in therapists, and there are many inciting elements that contribute to this feeling. First, there is the concern that the therapist may lose the patient. Particularly with new therapists who are starting a practice and are unfortunately dependent on their patients for income, that situation can breed fear that the patient will leave. Thus the therapist's hands are tied; he might not make adventurous, effective interventions but instead play it safe and not risk riling the patient. Being economically dependent on each of your patients is never a good situation, but mature therapists also find themselves in that situation. I always recommend working part time in the field or creating other sources of income as a way to offset economic dependency on patients.

Another element that provokes fearfulness is the risk of potential rejection. Therapists may feel that if a patient is dissatisfied or leaves treatment, it signifies a personal rejection or failure. It is important to review with a supervisor what has occurred to gather information about each situation that resulted in premature departure; but taking it personally is not helpful. Rejection feelings or inadequacy issues are likely part of the therapist's history, and therefore the therapist is vulnerable to fears of rejection. That fear may result in reluctance to push for patient negativity and resistance that if worked through might have stopped the patient from leaving prematurely. Just being the nice therapist to avoid conflict, rejection, or loss dilutes the therapy or results in the treatment stalling out entirely. The patient leaves out of boredom, as she feels the therapy is ineffective.

Yet another contributing factor in fear reactions is the concern about licensing board complaints. These complaints may necessitate involving an attorney, may affect the therapist's liability insurance, and can result in litigation.

Just the thought of those events can make therapists shiver and quake. No therapist wants to endure that process. Therapists can be disciplined by their professional boards and/or lose their license to practice if they are found to be unethical or if they have committed illegal acts. Those therapists deserve the reprimand or worse if they have violated ethics and laws of health-care professionals. Most therapists will not transgress to that extent, but a litigious patient can provoke fear even in decent therapists. This type of patient might enjoy wielding power or acting out anger or revenge by punishing the therapist with scare tactics.

Therapists are quite fearful of situations where a patient might be at risk of endangering themselves or others. In California and several other states there is a legal mandate to disclose and report if the therapist has probable cause to be concerned. Those risk factors can add another layer of strain to the equation. If a patient makes threats or the therapist feels that he may do harm to a family member or engage in random acts of violence, this becomes a grave concern and makes any therapist extremely alarmed and hypervigilant. Therapists need to be hypervigilant in this circumstance. If the therapist feels a patient is a suicide risk either due to prior attempts; severe, unrelenting depression with a potential thought-out plan; or other indices of suicidal risk then the therapist can feel highly anxious and fearful for the patient as well as the weight of responsibility inherent in the professional role.

Suicidal gestures and self-destructive actions create crises in therapy and can generate intense fear in the therapist. I mentioned a case earlier in this book of the therapist who colluded with the patient's clinging to a boyfriend in a dysfunctional relationship. When we got to the bottom of why the therapist was not more confrontational with the patient's clinging defense, she admitted fear that the patient would harm herself as she had done before. This patient had also been accident- and injury-prone as a way she played out her dependency needs.

As noted in the character type section, individuals with borderline personality disorder are prone to dramatic gestures that demonstrate their despair or helpless, hopeless feelings. The therapist has to keep clear boundaries regarding these displays and confront the consequences of these behaviors. These displays can be defensive in nature and not true expressions of deep feelings. They are a more surface level of protest or identification with hopelessness or helplessness. This helps keep the patient from facing responsibility for her life. The therapist needs to be aware of these maneuvers and act accordingly rather than get caught up in a personal fear reaction.

Therapists' fear that patients will harm themselves is, of course, an occupational hazard. Therapists have to strike a balance between clear perception and concern of real threat along with appropriate distance from the ebb and flow of patient distress and despair. Patients may feel awful and their desperateness can seem overwhelming at times; we listen, support, or confront during hard times. Yet it is a counter-transference reaction if we identify with that part of the patient's psyche and stop holding the Self as capable of transmuting the darkest pain into the will to live and flourish. I encourage all therapists to have a No Self-Harm document that the patient signs when he or she begins therapy. It is a record of the agreement signed to help prevent suicidal behavior from occurring. Obviously, if a patient is determined to end her life, she will. One hopes the patient can be hospitalized before this happens so she is contained in a hospital setting and benefits from the necessary 24/7 attention.

Another element that may provoke a therapist's fear and anxiety is a patient's disrespect, criticism, or devaluation. If a patient excels at being judgmental of the therapist, the therapist may feel cowed by the attacks and feel fear or intimidation rather than remain clear about what is transpiring with the patient. The therapist can be caught off guard and react internally, becoming anxious and therefore ineffective. At those times it is better to say nothing until you regain your footing.

A patient's critical, attacking, and judgmental style is a defense that takes the burden off of him to face his own problems. It is easier to attack the therapist, just as he attacks others in his life. To keep the spotlight off his own inadequacies, he bludgeons the therapist, seeking revenge and releasing tension by discharging onto the therapist.

> Sam came into therapy in a bad mood. He began to criticize the office conditions—"The noise down the hall is annoying"—and went on from there. "You think you know so much, but I see you fumbling the ball with me." "Therapy is not helping; I am the same as when I first came to see you." "Do you really think people can change? You are wasting your time." "You sit here listening to my garbage so you can collect your hourly fee." "You are like a toll-taker, just here to collect your big fees." You, you, you—spoken with an acidic, bitter tone filled with contempt and disgust. Sam would dump his vitriol onto the newly minted therapist and leave with a sense of relief that he got his poisonous feelings off his chest. Did it help him? No! The therapist let Sam reinforce his defensive attack mode. Internally he continued his simultaneous self-denigration in the background. The therapist was afraid and too intimidated to confront the patient and stop his disrespectful behaviors that might necessitate kicking him out of the office if he didn't stop.

Anger

Therapists do feel angry with patients. At times, patients can be extremely provocative and are looking to pick a fight. They are angry, resentful, belligerent, hostile, and seek revenge for their perception of being victimized or treated unfairly. The best target of all those feelings can be their therapist. If allowed, hostility can run rampant in the office. The therapist can be drawn into a dog fight. The therapist may not know why she is feeling angry; is it the patient's anger inciting her own feelings of anger? Is she feeling the way the patient felt with his father? Is the patient projecting his rage into to her and provoking her to feel it, too? Or is she having a bad day as she had a fight last night with her husband and didn't sleep well? All of these may be options.

Patients can provoke the therapist's reactions in a myriad of ways. The patient may continue destructive behaviors that have been discussed repeatedly and the therapist feels frustrated and ultimately angry that the patient keeps repeating without recognizing the consequences. Or the patient is disrespectful and cancels the sessions repeatedly, or acts out entitlement in demanding appointment time changes, and the therapist feels annoyed. Or the patient dominates the therapist, and the therapist feels abused and ultimately furious. Or the patient criticizes the therapist repeatedly and resentment builds in the therapist. Or the patient talks badly about the therapist to another patient she knows, and the therapist feels that the feedback is unjustified. Or the patient chronically blames the therapist for various things that happen in the patient's life. There are many issues that might incite the therapist yet more than not, the therapist is provoked by her own unresolved personal material. The therapist may have had a dominating narcissistic mother or father. The therapist might have had a bully for a sister or brother. The therapist's history can make her more vulnerable and reactive.

Inadequacy

The therapist tries hard to meet a standard of excellence. Still, feelings of inadequacy may plague the therapist. She may not feel she has command over her interventions and finds herself giving rational advice over and over again that does not impact the patient. The therapist is trying too hard—overtalking, overworking, convincing, rationalizing, giving advice to the patient—and all the words of wisdom do not result in a breakthrough. The therapist is in a consultation group, and the other therapists seem more successful, have bustling practices, and their interventions sound more astute. Or the therapist has not gotten a new referral in quite a while. Other therapists she knows have full practices. What is wrong with her?

These feelings of inadequacy can plague the therapist if he has deep-seated insecurity and lacks confidence. Then the therapist may overcompensate by going over time, being overly available, or coloring outside the lines in other ways to make up for imagined or real deficiencies.

The therapist may feel disappointed in the patient as a displacement of her own feelings of disappointment in herself. The patient has his own pace and trajectory of development, and it is not on our schedule. The patient is not there to succeed so we can feel proficient.

We can also join our patient in feeling helpless and hopeless. We have tried our best bag of tricks and the patient is still feeling hopeless. What can we do now? A feeling of hopelessness sets in; feelings of despair and discouragement can and do provoke the therapist to identify with the patient and feel immobilized.

If we overwork and don't recharge, we can become depressed and immobilized along with patients. It is imperative to recharge, enjoy life, relax, and retreat to invigorate ourselves and feel the pleasures life affords us.

Envy

The therapist may envy a patient's wealth, success, inheritance, and ease of life. If a therapist is prone to loss of self and looks outside to others and compares, then the therapist is vulnerable to envy. The therapist may witness a happy marriage, or a relationship filled with love and sexuality, and feel envious if those qualities are lacking in his life. If the therapist is feeling deficient internally then he may lose himself in the patient. Similarly, if the patient has activated a certain level of accomplishment and success externally, the therapist may feel he hasn't achieved enough; envy, jealousy, and self-disparagement can be provoked in these cases.

A therapist may envy the appearance of a patient. We may see a strikingly glamorous patient and feel jealous of her good looks, athletic body, or sumptuous hair. If a therapist is not feeling attractive, has weight issues, or is not keeping fit, she or he may be prone to envious thoughts toward patients who are maximizing their appearance. These visual aspects may overwhelm our character analytic viewpoint that needs to be front and center. Rather than examining the patient's preoccupation with external appearance, we are immobilized by our own insecurity and don't comment on the obvious.

A therapist might have a lifelong desire to be creative, to write poetry, paint, cook creatively, or study a musical instrument. If that yearning remains unfulfilled and a patient is living that dream, that can cause a conflict within the therapist. To the extent that the therapist is unfulfilled, there are empty pockets within that are stimulated by patients who are living aspects that the therapist has not claimed. This disparity needs to be made conscious through personal therapy or in supervision.

Therapists need to steer clear of judgments about themselves or their patients and maintain a clear perspective, keep to their purpose, and color inside the lines. Bias, prejudice, and critical judgments will contaminate the relationship, destroy our attempts at neutrality, and be destructive to the patient. This is a difficult task unless you work inside a framework that holds true. Getting good supervision helps. The supervisor can help the therapist unpack what is going on with a patient, track the interventions and the outcomes and the counter-transference reactivity. Personal triggers and reactions enter awareness and can be dealt with effectively. I can't emphasize enough the importance of ongoing challenging therapy and supervision for the therapist.

Boredom

Boredom is a form of contactlessness. It means there is little if any energy exchange, engagement, or interest in a subject or person. Therapists may experience boredom in a session when they are tired, overworked, preoccupied with other matters, have not exercised, or have not taken care of basic self-maintenance requirements sufficiently, such as adequate sleep, eating healthy food at regular intervals, relaxation, and sufficient personal stimulation.

If the therapist is not fatigued, then it may be due to the patient's own listlessness or contactlessness. At times, therapists can feel the deadness in the room, particularly with schizophrenic or schizoid patients who are out of contact. These patient types may be in a state of withdrawal and therefore they are hard to find, much less engage with. Their eyes may be partially closed and they might mumble so the therapist can barely hear them. Or they may be silent in session and need lots of time to find themselves. And they may state repeatedly, "I don't know" when asked what they feel as they struggle to gain access to thoughts or feelings.

The patient may have not slept much as often patients are unregulated with their sleep and may be up into the night playing video games, surfing the net, or streaming series. He comes to session exhausted and disinterested and the therapist feels like she has to pull for material to discuss, as the patient is not activating his own. Always check out what might be exacerbating the patient's seeming tiredness or disinterest. Was he drinking or smoking the night before—or on his devices into the night?

If the patient is evasive and spacey, we can point that out and help her come into better contact in the room with her eyes, suggest sitting up and not slouching, and ask the patient to raise her voice level. We can speak about his evasive style or his spacey quality as a character analytic point of inquiry.

If the patient is barely able to connect to herself, it is challenging for the therapist to stay engaged. Yet, the therapist, in understanding pregenital schizophrenics, recognizes they integrate slowly and carefully, taking in interventions in small bites or what Hyman Spotnitz (1908–2008) called verbal feedings, limited to two to five per session. The important developmental rupture for this type of patient is before the development of language, necessitating deeper nonverbal exchange of feeling states through the therapist. The patient needs to test reality cautiously and carefully (Masterson and Klein, 1989, 121). The therapist must remain in good contact internally in order to help the patient sustain an adaptive framework grounded in reality while holding the patient where he is. Therapists must practice patience with types that have difficulty engaging, activating material, and connecting to their feelings, sensations, and perceptions.

When a patient is silent much of the session and not forthcoming, it is best to sit with him without urgency and not demand more. We can point out the long spaces between and investigate, or we can sit in resonance with the patient, allowing silence in the room for longer spells than we are naturally comfortable with. If we try too hard by talking (also a form of entertainment), we may lose connection to the patient and the patient may feel engulfed.

Be careful not to be overly detached or mechanical as a way to cope with the situation. Also watch out for your own aversion to the patient's pull that reflects his fusion or symbiotic transference.

Boredom is a deadening feeling, and we must be attentive to sustaining our own aliveness by living a fulfilled and happy life.

The Challenge of Objectivity

When we sit with a patient we are in a relationship, and both parties are affected in conscious and unconscious ways. We strive for neutrality and objectivity, yet we are human and have a steady stream of subjective feelings in session. The intersubjective and interpersonal schools of therapy emphasize that both therapist and patient are influenced by each other and that countertransference is ever present and in fact a necessary condition of therapy. Both therapist and patient exist in the intersubjective field and therefore will inevitably be impacted. This school rejects the notion that objectivity or neutrality is even possible.

I agree with this concept up to a point. We need to stay aware of the everpresent intersubjective field as we are immersed in it. Yet, we must also remain conscious and aware of our steady stream of subjective experience with each and every patient. Our feelings are quite informative and give us constant and valuable information. We must be aware of how we are impacting the patient. Our intuitive feel for the interactional climate informs us and stimulates potent on-target character interventions. When we can comment on how a patient affects us in the moment, there is potency in that present-centered, subjective response that brings the therapeutic relationship into the here and now. Reich would give catalytic present-centered feedback to the patient about his feelings with the patient and memorable exchanges occurred.

I will say more on therapist self-disclosure in another chapter. Here it is important to acknowledge that our neutrality is always challenged. Our subjective feelings are informative and often lead to potent interventions. After all, it is a relationship endowed with the complexities of any relationship and therein lies the learning. We need to stay aware of how we are affecting the patient moment by moment and comment on what we notice. The patient may expect the therapist to act in certain ways that are unrealistic, and the therapist may present a challenge to her viewpoint. Here the therapist does not resonate with the patient's subjective feelings—he instead comments on the patient expectation. With patient projections strongly at play it is important to maintain sufficient clarity to not collude with the patient's projections or distortions and to not be coerced into acting a certain way. Neutrality allows us to stand outside the distortions, projections, and pulls from the patient. Or the therapist may be pulled to view himself in a certain way as defined by the patient. If we are aware of this pull, we can articulate that to the patient and he gains awareness as to how he engages the therapist and why. The therapist must constantly monitor his subjective experiences through observation and awareness using them responsibly and in the patient's best interest.

To ensure the most objectivity, we have to track the flow of the session. Stay aware of the conscious and unconscious influences. We must be willing to search for confirming data in the patient's reaction to interventions. Acknowledge the possibility that you may misunderstand the patient, and pay attention to your own reactions. The therapist's honest acknowledgment can unlock a logjam.

Responding out of our humanness is the essential ingredient. We are not play-acting a role; we are in our chair as real human beings. The elements of our humanness and heart-felt integrity will ensure that we are acting in good faith.

As Jung states,

> The relation between doctor and patient remains a personal one within the framework of professional treatment. By no device can the treatment be anything but the product of mutual influence, in which the whole being of the doctor as well as that of the patient plays its part.
>
> (Jung, 2014, 163)

Part V

Therapeutic Basics

11 The Therapist Tool Chest

Patient Outer Adaptation: Case Management

Therapy is a varied and multilayered process: unraveling difficult historic wounds; supporting during times of upheaval; clarifying goals, intentions, and meaning in a patient's life; and analyzing conflicting feelings, relationship issues, and family problems. The therapist makes interpretations, and the patient gains insight leading to change. With character analysis we do all that and more as we challenge chronic patterns of being and behavior that often result in the symptoms and circumstances we hear about. Therapeutic interventions should attend to both outer adaptation and inner exploration. The therapist needs to open two fronts: He keeps his eye on how the patient functions in the real world, and he helps the patient deepen into his unconscious psyche to excavate the buried treasures of memory and feeling simultaneously. In burrowing into the depths of his psyche, the patient discovers the guidance of the Self. Working the two fronts consistently, without losing sight of critical elements, is a tall order.

> Loren, age 40, an intelligent, overweight woman, was in therapy many years as she had serious difficulty activating structure, responsibility, and consistency in critical areas: career, financial security, regulation of eating and sleeping. She spent inordinate amounts of time in bed—reading, watching TV, and eating—as her life fell apart around her. Even after many years of treatment there remained hidden pockets of self-neglect: unpaid bills, procrastination, and avoidance of important action items resulting in serious consequences, jags of overeating, and weight gain and loss—a stop-start process of exercise and attempts/failures at constructing a consistent personal structure.
>
> I was often caught off guard when she would reveal, long after the fact, that she had been gorging on sweets for three weeks but did not bring the problem up in her weekly session, and I neglected to track the obvious. Her hiding out lasted for years until she discovered the importance of accountability and dependability. As she developed more trust in me, she had less fear and resistance, but arriving there took much confrontation.

I once told her how frustrating it was for me that she chronically hid her self-destructiveness from therapy and I had to hunt for it; that seemed to make a difference. She ultimately discovered the rewards of leading a responsible life, but it took many years of resistance, anger, and feeling pushed, and rounds of successes and failures. Over the long haul the functional trajectory of her life stabilized as she battled to stay on target. Now, she manages her own commitments and is less evasive if she has a slip.

I am not suggesting our job is "cop on the block," yet our role is to observe and confront lifestyles that are not attuned to reality in a functional way and that tend toward self-sabotage. All the analysis of painful historic material and current stories will not net a healthy life if our patients are not responsible and functional in the external world. Patients hide from their fears and inadequacies by utilizing defenses of avoidance, procrastination, dissociation, obsessive behaviors, and multiple gratifying diversions that contribute to their avoidance of challenging pursuits.

As we observe a patient's style we understand how all those symptoms relate to character structure. We utilize our understanding of the various types to give us direction. Our patient Loren was diagnosed a schizophrenic character as her indolence came from a state of heightened, lifelong fear precipitated by any initiation of movement out of her comfort zone. She was prone to lethargy and stasis, so I diagnosed her a catatonic schizophrenic, according to Reich's typology. That type is reluctant to create movement as it scares them. Reich understood the "terror of living," the deepest fear of surrender to the movement of life. Catatonic schizophrenics have inordinate amounts of fear that inhibit their capacity to expand and function. There are clear historic roots that contributed to Loren's ongoing state of fear and propensity for immobilization. She was raised in a chaotic, "unregulated" household where structure was nonexistent; this type of patient had no inner healthy models. The parental neglect led to nonexistent bedtime schedules and rare regular healthy meals, and she was not helped to structure time and activities. Many homes are a free-for-all of chaos where each member of the family fends for herself.

Many catatonics function better if they learn to self-regulate with a structure that overrides their basic fears and helps them establish confidence, as they diminish their helplessness—an inevitable outcome of their chaotic lifestyle. Loren has now stabilized with a workable structure that covers every area of her life. Implementing a structure—such as an eating plan, sleep schedule, and career and social structure—has reinforced her growing confidence in her ability to function well coupled with healthy physical routines that keep her moving daily and experiencing increased energy.

Alongside the structural component, Loren has delved deeply into her historic pain and has made significant progress. She was able to feel her angry feelings, and over time those feelings evolved into healthy neutral aggression that powered her activation and fulfillment of goals. Patients need to cultivate healthy aggression and assertiveness that comes with freeing anger and rage. Those feelings are an antidote to chronic fear as the patient experiences empowerment rather than helplessness and intimidation.

We cannot overlook how our patients function in their daily lives. Patients do not see the correlation between their moods, state of anxiety, and depression, and how they function in their lives. Are they up late, lost in their electronic world of stimulation, sleeping too little, jittery from sleep deprivation, which all results in feelings of falling apart accompanied by appetite loss, anxious depression, and feelings of self-loathing?

> I unraveled a case with this symptom picture with my patient Sorren, an intelligent, highly educated narcissistic female immigrant, who started her own business. She was highly competitive, fraught with feelings of failure and worthlessness, as she felt she was not measuring up to her perfectionist standards. On social media, often late at night, she would "follow" other women in her particular marketplace and be ravaged by jealousy and feelings of defeat and despair. This complex had accelerated to the point of panic attacks and feelings of loss of control. It was time to set up serious guidelines regarding her habits so they didn't unravel her further, requiring more serious measures. A rule was set up that devices were not allowed in her bedroom at night, nor were her husband's phone and iPad allowed. I advised over-the-counter sleep aids to catch her up on sleep.
>
> We explored her narcissistic inflated expectations, how she hated herself when she didn't match up to her perfect ideals; confronting that process offered her relief. We worked on both her cognitive and emotional inner mandates and the historic backdrop of her family and her status as an immigrant, while making drastic changes to her lifestyle to allow more spaciousness within and without. She was encouraged to take time to sit quietly, listening internally, so she could find an inner voice to substitute for her external mandates. She had immediate relief from the crisis.

We must be vigilant about what the patient might be hiding even from himself. Patients are embarrassed and ashamed of their habits. I had a patient who woke up nightly and raided the refrigerator to soothe himself. Another patient plays video games when he should be working and plays excessively daily. An adult patient watches sports and other shows during the day, losing vital hours of productivity, vegging out like a lost teenager. Or the adult female patient who avoids paying bills, has delinquent notices from the court regarding traffic violations, and has not filed her taxes in years, as she depends on her parents for money. Or the patient with obsessive-compulsive traits that lacks a social life as he is too busy with his tasks and controlling rituals. There is the caffeine addict who is downing caffeinated soda drinks and excessive coffee as a substitute for real stimulation. What a surprise to discover a patient was drinking 15 sodas a day! Daily compulsive masturbation or porn watching is another addictive habit that ends in long bouts of lethargy and depression. And there is the intelligent and creative patient who mitigates his anxiety by smoking pot on a daily basis, resulting in limited artistic production. The list goes on of the ways patients live a defensive lifestyle that blocks healthy adaptation to reality.

We must ferret out those behaviors, spotlight them, and allow the patient to explore why he lives the way he does. We can see destructive behaviors in the lethargic patient who won't focus his attention as he is too fearful and would rather regress into sleepiness. Or there is the patient in session with almost-closed eyes who avoids contact. We have to ask ourselves: What is going on? We observe a highly driven patient who can't calm down to look inward. These are signs and clues that show us how patients live their lives. We investigate the how and why of habits appearing in the picture before us. We can help with "case management," figuring out and then instituting healthier ways of coping so the person can escape his swamp. If patients are acting out through dysfunctional behaviors they cannot get to the next level where they can stabilize, put foundations in place, and pursue the deeper emotional work of putting their puzzle pieces together. If a patient acts out, he is not feeling but rather instituting defensive behaviors as a distraction from facing himself.

Hillary, age 45, was an educated mom and wife with a successful career. She was plagued with fear, anxiety, and acted out dependency with her husband. She feared driving and establishing her own pursuits and friendships, and revolved her life around her spouse and children. She ignored serious health issues, and would binge eat sweets to soothe herself. She often hid her binge eating from her therapist. As she worked through these acting-out behaviors she began to realize how her dependency on her husband and his need to keep her regressed due to his own dependency needs was becoming very dangerous for her. She was regressing more and more and losing contact with her stronger more confident self. The more she regressed, the more her fear increased and her anxiety became debilitating, resulting in panic attacks. The therapist helped her to see these dynamics and understand them as a cause of her anxiety and fear. She can work with her feelings of abandonment and depression that cause her to cling to her husband, and the loss of self that goes with it. As she establishes her natural aggression she will feel stronger, more confident, and less afraid.

I treated a highly functioning wealthy business owner who created messiness and external chaos in his wake. He needed to have everything visible around him or he felt anxious. This compulsion resulted in an unsightly, chaotic accumulation of papers both in family dining areas and in his office. He was very resistant to viewing this as a problem. One session we spoke about it and he started to cry realizing "that if I couldn't see it I would lose it, or it would be taken away."

Then there was Jim, an intelligent entrepreneur who overworked and rarely spent time with his family. He tended toward irritability with friends, family, and work associates. He was prone to moodiness and temper tantrums as he reached frequent fever pitches of extreme overwork, driving himself forward against all odds. His need to succeed and his arrogance and contempt for others belied feelings of inadequacy that he did not face; instead he kept driving himself, maintaining a manic high. He was heading for a crash landing.

Substance abuse and addictions are paramount ways patients act out. These types may have impulsivity that must be addressed. If substance use is not consistently discussed, limited, or stopped, the therapist is in a sinking ship with the patient. Patients use alcohol, pot, opioid pain medications, and other drugs as a way of camouflaging their inner pain, yet inevitably it will lead to a downward spiral. Many addicted patients need rehabilitation in residential treatment centers before they begin therapy. They are not ready. First they have to gain sobriety, commit to Alcoholics Anonymous or similar programs, and maintain a sober lifestyle. Then they are ready to begin the serious work of therapy. We, as therapists, must assess the condition of our patients so we can direct them to take the appropriate first steps.

Often primary care physicians prescribe opioid pain relief medications without considering the long-term effect on the patient or that he or she has a history of substance abuse. Individuals with a hankering for pain medications can easily manipulate their doctors for prescriptions. Further, these patients may hide their ongoing opioid use from their therapist, and you will need to pick up on cues or ask directly what they are taking if they have symptoms of chronic pain.

There has been a dramatic increase in the mortality rate of white middle-income Americans since 1999, attributed to suicidal overdoses and alcohol and drug poisonings. Physician prescriptions of opioid painkillers like Oxycontin and the extended-release form of Oxycodone contribute to the increasing rate of drug overdose in this population. Since the 1990s there has been a significant increase in the use of these medications by physicians who once limited these to treatment of pain for terminal cancer or post-op recovery. Currently, the trend has been to prescribe these addictive drugs for a whole range of problems from low-back pain and musculoskeletal problems to general symptoms of pain. Fortunately there has been a backlash within the medical and health-care community, and there are now regulatory stipulations that make overprescribing these types of medications more difficult, but addiction is still rampant.

Over-the-counter anti-inflammatories are shown to be both safe and as effective for pain relief as these dangerously addictive medications. There is weak evidence supporting opioid use for long-term nonmalignant pain in terms of safety and effectiveness. The patient habituates to the medication with resulting side effects of anxiety and depression. As therapists we must first find out if a patient is using pain medications beyond a short duration prescribed for post-surgery or for an acute injury. If a patient has had cancer surgery or is receiving chemo and/or radiation with attendant pain, we need to monitor and suggest she consult her oncologist as to when she can reduce or eliminate these drugs. We need to educate the patient on the dangers of habitual use of opioids and if need be, discuss the problem with her physician (Friedman, 2015).

Impulsivity can be an aspect of certain personality types: substance abusers, manic-depressive types, borderlines, phallic narcissistic personalities, and psychopaths. Impulsive individuals make rushed, inflated decisions; often pursue foolish financial schemes; ignore realistic limitations; and make important decisions impulsively only to regret their faulty decision making later—if they notice at all. Observe this pattern and call it out. Sometimes patients present this in a way that does not send up a red flag; look beneath the excited, optimistic, and grandiose presentation of their latest idea to ask questions and explore it in more depth—point out their propensity for impulsivity and inflated ideas.

> A young man in his 30s, who was earning a decent living, impulsively invested his little savings in a new restaurant started by a friend. He had little to no experience in the restaurant business, had no money to spare for an investment, and lost all his money in short order. He had impulsively bought into the investment in part from pressure from the friend. He did not discuss this with his therapist ahead of time. This style of hiding important decisions from the therapist must be confronted.

Having secrets from the therapist is often the case when impulsivity comes a calling. "Do it first and evaluate later" is their motto; then reap the disaster sooner than later. We must not be naive to these shenanigans. We must help patients realize they have impulsive traits with grandiose thinking. The false inflation makes patients feel they can do anything, that they are bigger than life and can conquer all—and they lose everything quickly.

To succeed in the task of examining the patient's life in its entirety, you need an element of cooperation. Patients must be amenable to exploration and have the capacity to entertain suggestions for change—albeit with inevitable resistance. To begin therapy, patients need a minimum level of contact to benefit from weekly sessions. They also need a sufficient level of responsibility to keep their agreements within the therapeutic context. Without cooperation, the therapist swims upstream to be defeated in the end. Cooperation means you can point out a problem, and the patient will consider it even if he decides not to comply with your suggestions—yet. He agrees to the conditions of treatment.

Some patients come into treatment because another has encouraged therapy. Charles Konia, MD, an Orgonomist, discusses character types in relation to level of responsibility. He cites the hysteric who is suggestible; she enters therapy because her good friend is seeing you but has little depth or real interest in the process. Her life has been "on the run" and why should she stop now? On the surface she may be charming and pleasing, but you must confront her character traits and warn against her resistance/avoidance, running away to diversions that keep her superficial, hopping from lily pad to lily pad (Konia, 1978).

The phallic narcissist may come in when facing upheaval in his life: loss of a job, a wife, or partner, or another crisis that provokes feelings of inadequacy. He will leave when the crisis passes. Map out the larger issues so the patient can settle into a bigger context of therapy and have awareness of his patterns. This is part of case management, defining the character, the resistance, and educating the patient as to his specific acting-out behaviors that are defensive and will lead to repetitive problems. If you get that established, the therapy can be contained. Then when the patient initiates these questionable behaviors, he might be more likely to let you know, and you can help him manage his behavior.

Patients avoid the deeper work by keeping multiple balls in the air that distract them from themselves. They can avoid family and relational problems, anxiety, depression, loss, and despair with constant busyness. They may choose to avoid responsibility and make poor decisions over and over. Thus their lives never get beyond survival issues. They don't find meaning, purpose, or their unique creative path. They may never experience independence, autonomy, and individuation.

Affairs, betrayals, and sexual acting out have multiple defensive elements. The patient may be running from loneliness and emptiness by chasing after stimulation, adoration, or sexual gratification. Commitments are broken, families destroyed, and personal ethics eroded with much collateral damage. Cheap thrills cover the emptiness the patient feels within. Sexual acting out can be addictive. The preoccupation with the latest prey can create excitement topped off with sexual gratification that becomes habitual. Helping patients stop their runaway train is part of our case management job. Only when acting-out behaviors are contained can real therapy proceed.

Affairs can be symptomatic of serious marital relational issues that demand attention. Unhappiness abounds in couples. Out of the disenchanted relationship, affairs can happen. Couple issues need to be sorted out without the distraction of affairs. But individuals who have repetitive affairs, an ongoing string of relationships, and sexual acting out are likely in avoidance of facing difficult aspects within. This is a case management issue at the start and later the work deepens if the acting out is stopped.

> Jerry not only lied to his wife but he habitually lied in business, lied to friends, lied to his therapist, and justified cheating on his income tax—income paid "under the table." His lifestyle was based on many deceitful acts. As therapists, we do not sit on the board of ethical conduct, but a style of lying, deceit, and slipperiness shows a lack of integrity that does not bode well. Jerry's style conveyed defiance, a "looking to get away with something" attitude and pull the wool over the next person's eyes. He gloried in these deceitful accomplishments with a smirking grin. He felt he could do what he wanted when he wanted and no one should stop him. Jerry had a slick quality about him; underneath he suffered from feelings of inadequacy and worthlessness that were hidden behind his defiant

bravado. Inadequacy feelings result in compensatory behaviors and attitudes as the patient feels he has to cheat to succeed; to find a way out of societal mandates and expectations—if you can't measure up to what is required, change the rules. Therapists need to weigh in on these dysfunctional approaches to life as Jerry will never feel he is a decent, respectable person until he cleans up his integrity problem.

Preoccupation with others is another element to manage and is a lifelong avoidance technique. Patients can spend inordinate amounts of time caretaking others or preoccupied with others, be it friends, lovers, work associates, or family. Their lives are on the shelf because it is rationalized that caretaking another is of critical importance. One's life is denied through preoccupation with others, and one's life is never lived. Patients may want to discuss others and tell stories about friends, family members, or even celebrities. This is a distraction and investigating that propensity is important. This is a case management issue as you can see your patient living defensively through others. Sometimes adult children become preoccupied with caretaking their parents, acting out chronic dependency, and the parents are dependent, too. In this case enmeshment remains throughout adulthood in a variety of ways that inhibit both parties from maturing. Clinging to kids, clinging to adult kids and grandkids, clinging to parents, clinging to bad relationships, clinging to unchallenging jobs, the list goes on—defensive lifestyles that thwart adaptation to reality. As therapists, we must be clear on the larger contextual issues and not be distracted by the crisis du jour.

> Susan, age 50, was trained as a health technician and worked for a number of years; then she unraveled and lost her job. Her mother set up Susan as her live-in caretaker. They argued nonstop, and Susan's depression and hopelessness escalated and she felt trapped with her mother. Both had fallen into an enmeshed and unhealthy symbiosis.

Patients avoid challenges and responsibilities in a variety of areas, including finances, educational goals, career obligations, family responsibilities, and household duties. Patients avoid relationships, including friendship, love, and sexuality. Patients avoid independence, self-sufficiency, and autonomy. They may never seek a meaningful life and forfeit their creative potential. Life becomes a constant distraction from authentic growth; a life of fantasy not geared to reality. If the patient gets realistic, she might feel painful feelings, so avoidance is maintained instead. Drama takes the place of dogged tenacity. Flight substitutes for discipline, laziness replaces industriousness, cheating replaces personal ethics. As therapists we examine the feelings, habits, and attitudes that are expressed in nonadaptive behaviors visible throughout the patient's life. With knowledge of these habits, we can help the patient break down defenses so he has a chance to deepen into himself and make appropriate changes.

Inner Exploration: Phases of Therapy

With the structure of therapy in place, the patient is settled in, cooperative, and responsible regarding his therapeutic work except for periods of active resistance that are normal occurrences in the process. The initial testing phase of therapy is over and the patient understands how to get the most out of therapy—more or less. The patient's swings of negativity toward the therapist are out in the open. The patient and therapist are in an established relationship that allows the patient to enter a more inwardly active phase of work—what Masterson called "the working through phase." Masterson named this the "middle phase" of treatment defined by an established working alliance with the therapist. The patient's self-initiated inner work takes over as the patient unravels deeper historic material that more clearly illuminates key major conflicts and resulting issues. Profound emotional expressions and insights define this period.

What I am calling inner work is less plagued with defensive diversions and acting-out behaviors discussed earlier that divert from the deepening process that unfolds. In this phase of treatment there is a flow of recognitions as the defenses are conscious and the patient has the ability to disarm them. The patient will have access to painful memories accompanied by a myriad of feelings: sorrow, grief, anger, hatred, disappointment, loss, and disgust, along with a sense of accomplishment that many lifelong conflicts and confusions are now making sense. Each insight stimulates deepening awareness, fuller feelings, and at times a sense of resolve that comes from these understandings.

The therapist is less proactive in this middle phase; as Reich stated the patient knows how to be analyzed. The therapist works only to dismantle defenses. The patient comes in with material and we sit back as she explores, activates in session, and looks to us mainly to act as a witness to her exploration. We help in a variety of ways using various tools I will discuss in this chapter. I am accentuating an important shift in our level of activity; it is imperative that the patient is allowed to direct the sessions and mobilize explorations with us in a secondary position. If the session is not productive, then something else is going on that the therapist needs to determine.

If the patient is in somatic work, the intensity increases as emotions are directly expressed without the therapist interfering except to guide. Rage and grief are expressed loudly with an open voice and release of feelings gives the patient deep relief. Biophysical work helps deepen and release all emotions and allows the body armor to melt such that energy moves throughout the body and the patient can experience aliveness maybe for the first time. While doing the inner work, biophysical interventions facilitate a noncognitive connection through body memories, sensations, and the felt sense of physical pain and what that pain communicates. I will discuss the Orgonomic biophysical treatment approach in a later chapter.

Ally entered therapy 10 years ago suffering from a frozen numbness that constricted her life in all areas. She succeeded in graduating from college and establishing a career in business but was plagued with severe anxiety, obsessive-compulsive habits and rituals, feelings of emptiness, and depression. She had a mechanical robotic quality as she fulfilled her "duties," looking outside to others for direction. Inside she barely existed in her empty shell. Dismantling some of the more obvious defenses was the first line of business. Her numbness and absence of feelings were difficult to penetrate. On top of the numbness was her pleasing, "nice girl," smiling, frozen demeanor, which she had set up to avoid conflicts.

She was a serious patient and wanted help desperately but could barely access feeling or sensation. She had suffered much loss in her life, losing her father at a young age and experiencing amnesia of early memories. Her dominating narcissistic mother was difficult and insensitive. She had two brothers, who ran free as her driven mother overworked; her brothers took over the home with parties, alcohol, and pot use. Ally was submerged by this chaotic family and suffered from debilitating anxiety bound up in her obsessive-compulsive disorder and covered by numbness that plagued her all her life. In addition, she was forced to manage her perfectionist mother who expected Ally to embody her values and fit into her social swirl. Ally became a shell of a self—empty and forlorn inside.

In the middle phase of her therapy she grieved the profound loss of her father she barely remembered but knew was a special man from all she had heard. It took many years before she could experience anger and rage at her mother and brothers. The loss of self was her deepest grief. This period of therapy uncovered deep wounding, memories, and pain as the numbness dissolved. Her hard-won awareness resulted in a new life course that fit her. She continues to grow and express herself.

During the middle phase of treatment with Ally my job was to challenge defenses, if they emerged, such as artificial pleasing behaviors with friends and in relationships. The obsessive-compulsive behaviors created a false sense of order and security but denied her spontaneous life energy. Other than calling out these defenses, the patient initiated her own work, emanating from the awareness she had cultivated. She was no longer a mechanical robot filled with emptiness but rather a deeply feeling and aware individual who could chart her work in therapy as issues emerged.

During this phase in treatment, dream analysis makes an important contribution. As dreams plumb the depths of the unconscious they evoke the part of the psyche that illuminates intuitive information at times emanating from the Self. This material bypasses the rational intellectualizing parts of the brain and encompasses subtle insights outside of our normal time-space continuum. In the online resources connected to this book I have an entire chapter devoted to Carl Jung and dream analysis, as work with dreams is critical to deepening the therapy in middle phase.

As the patient deepens into difficult material, there will be "flights of health" as the patient may feel exhausted by the depths of the inner work.

Patients may want to scramble out of therapy with a hope that they can quit now. At times leaving therapy is appropriate during this phase if healthy life circumstances call them forward. For others, they may be resisting challenging activations and shirking responsibilities that they would rather avoid. Healthy decisions may be required but are extremely difficult: ending an unhealthy marriage, quitting a job that is toxic, seeking a new career, separating from unhealthy family members, activating relationship and friendship. Depending on the character structure these may be challenging next steps that the patient may want to avoid and terminating therapy prematurely is an easy way out.

The therapist holds the container and helps the patient move forward while keeping her connected to her deepest yearnings and longings. These yearnings, if she stays connected, light the way forward and will guide her if she stays with herself. When the patient has achieved stability within, and many difficult symptoms have subsided, along with an achievement of insights and awareness that allow her to maintain her psychic health, termination of therapy can be instituted. Each patient is different; thus the readiness to terminate varies. We do not want to encourage dependency that steals the patient's capacity to become a thriving independent person. Some patients may choose to be in therapy much of their lives as they continue to be inspired by the transformative process; or their wounds may be so serious as to necessitate long-term therapy and the stabilizing container allows them their best chance of happiness.

The therapeutic process is not an end in itself, and should not be used as a defense against living life. The challenge of finding and living one's true and authentic life is a critical goal. Not just talking about it but actually embarking on challenges. We must help the patient move along to autonomy and independence in all areas of their life. We need to encourage patients to eliminate chronic dependency that keeps them regressed. Not all patients will achieve all potential goals; each patient is unique, with different trajectories, none better than the other. For some, therapy brings stability and more functional behavior; for others, it brings relief from debilitating symptoms. For some, awareness and mindfulness are worthy goals—movement from unconsciousness to consciousness of self.

Inner and outer work includes the events that come along that were unaccounted for: a serious diagnosis, a spouse's diagnosis, an economic downturn, problems with children, and aging parents. There are many events that deepen the therapy as we help the patient realize that arduous and frightening challenges become an initiation rite requiring a new level of maturity. Facing into an abyss of fear and distress, the patient and therapist find a way through it. The alchemy of challenging pain can turn blackness into gold. These situations invite us to face the most difficult moments of suffering and yet realize possibly different, more spiritual values that help us accept and continue on. These are transformational opportunities as we see through the illusion of superficial disparateness to a universal core of connectedness that brings an experience of faith, grace, and compassion. These events bring awareness to a most profound level, and the therapist has to develop those capacities within to guide.

The inner work develops out of confronting the obvious unhealthy attitudes, behaviors, and feelings and exploring more obscure connections that contributed. At any time during the middle phase of treatment, unhealthy behaviors may reemerge. We keep our eyes on acting-out behaviors such as chronic dependency, externalization onto others, and behavioral acting out like drugs, alcohol, caffeine addiction, overeating, sugar and junk food addictions, gambling, Internet addiction, Facebook preoccupation, porn, TV and gaming addictions, debt accumulation, and more. We watch for loss of personal self-care structure including dental, hygiene, diet, exercise, and appearance. We look for reoccurrences of chaotic lifestyle such as unpaid tickets, tax evasion, and unpaid bills. We look at parenting styles and where the patient is losing connection or good instincts with children or spouse. Or we see compulsive focus on details as a substitute for creativity and a meaningful life. We watch for the patient's avoidance of creativity, meaning, and soulfulness that creates chronic emptiness. As the patient is working deeply, these patterns may return and need to be worked through again and again so the patient can sustain his deeper intention.

When you confront external issues the character defenses will be provoked. Even as you settle into the middle phase of treatment these character defenses will emerge again as they are lifelong patterns. The goal is to expose the character style and behavioral and cognitive propensities to be analyzed and then altered so the inner work keeps deepening. You must consistently question if something feels off in what the patient is saying. Use your intuition if a comment or subject smells fishy. That has netted me some real gems. Something the patient may be hiding or is ashamed of is keeping the therapy stuck. Notice everything. Explore everything you sense; don't wait and simply move on with a lame discussion that has no bite to it. If you notice something that perks your attention, explore it. Don't miss an opportunity; it is those unexpected junctures that deepen the therapy and allow for important issues to be revealed.

Inner and outer focus will alternate and vacillate. You will be analyzing historic material with deep feelings emerging, lots of quiet in the sessions, and then the focus may shift because the patient can't stand the depth and the pain. He might act out and divert to safer waters by externally creating drama or defensive maneuvers so the therapist needs to attend to that. The inner and outer focus teaches the patient to self-regulate his deep feelings and to not be overreactive to external circumstances. It is a critical balance to titrate one's inner life depth with outer functionality. The therapist models this stable regulating function.

The Arc of a Session

Sessions are most effective when there is a sustained focal point, a tension, an overall arc, and a finish line. Therapists fall prey to listening with what I call an undisciplined mind. The patient takes off with a piece of content, a story about what happened that didn't go well, and difficult feelings associated and may drift off into more associated content or random additions. The patient may feel some relief from communicating all that was on his mind, but may not have been challenged to assess more deeply what has transpired and why. The session ends without moving the dial of the patient's more important character problems forward, and the patient will leave and do it all over again.

I recommend that therapists think about each patient before he or she arrives: review your character diagnosis, isolate in your mind the current and critical problem you may want to work on, and focus your mind on what is important for this specific patient in terms of his trajectory in treatment. That focus does not mean you are planning the entire session ahead of time, but you have your eyes on what is most important. Usually, the patient will enter the treatment room and bring up something quite relevant to their larger issues, and you are primed. There are often consistent defensive or nonadaptive threads across multiple sessions and situations; make sure you sustain focus on those elements. That focus allows the patient to become increasingly aware and conscious of what needs to change. This thoughtfulness by the therapist prevents random unproductive forays into irrelevant chitchat. You are ready, rather than lazily greeting the patient and then tuning in: "Hmm, oh, here is Sam, let's see how he guides the session." During the middle phase, patient initiation and ownership of the session may be appropriate if she is working in an activated and nondefensive way.

A session can be described as a flow with the patient bringing up material (we hope) and the therapist responding selectively, helping to crystalize critical elements that connect the character difficulties to the specifics of what has been brought up. The therapist pulls out for examination a repetitive piece of behavior, feeling, or attitude that thwarts the patient. Having too many pieces on the game board can dissipate the energy, so focusing on one area creates more clarity. Then the work can deepen into necessary explorations that illuminate those repetitive reactions or behavioral patterns.

Remember, you are working more on process than content. Don't get overly trapped in content but rather work with the patient's process—how he does what he does, the way he is relating to it and to you.

If in a prior session, the patient made a comment right at the end of session and that comment needs to be picked up or if you realized afterward that the patient had said something provocative that you missed, introduce those items early in the session. Therapists are reluctant to bring up something that might be controversial, but that is where the aliveness is for that particular session. Maybe a patient revealed a clue that you need to follow up on, so you may initiate that topic. A patient may have quipped, "Gee, had I known he would foot the bill, I would have purchased many more items." You didn't comment on that at the time but afterward thought that attitude reflected her closet narcissistic immaturity, entitlement, and willingness to take advantage. Bring it up the next session, make the point, and explore. Pick up on off-the-cuff comments—they spontaneously reveal inherent attitudes. The male of a couple went to sit down in the chair next to mine (after I had motioned him toward it) and said, "Oh, yours is the more comfortable chair." How would you as the therapist respond to that?

With some patients you may be working on behavioral changes, or specific items they are trying to complete, or specific attitudinal changes; keep consistent with those and help the patient to be accountable. This approach works for certain phases of therapy when patients are having difficulty breaking bad habits or not following through to manifest their intentions and goals. Again, we are not taskmasters, and it is the patients' responsibility to follow through, but they have problems doing that. Sessions for a period can be helpful if the therapist keeps the thread of accountability and brings up the content if patients don't. Also work their resistance to following through with their lives. Confront their lack of responsibility.

If a topic emerges that links to a patient's critical problem area, then stay on it throughout the session. You can approach it in a myriad of ways and directions. Discipline your mind to keep to what is important. Sustain a tension in the session with a challenging discussion. Reach an apex and allow for a conclusion that drives the session's learning home. Sessions can produce a theme, and the therapist has to be disciplined enough to listen carefully, capture what is important, and hold the focus. Drifting from topic to topic or feeling to feeling is not as helpful and can create chaos in the session. The therapist can listen and still keep a sense of how what is said fits into this patient's general character style, the themes he repeats, and what he needs to work on to break the pattern. Keep that in mind so the session can focus on those aspects and bring that theme to the finish line.

I have watched demo sessions where a critical theme started the session and the therapist lost it and the session floundered with less relevant material. Rather than sustain the most important point, the session floated away and an opportunity was lost. More importantly, the session lacked aliveness and contact that makes therapeutic insight stick.

The therapist learns to draw together various linkages through *summary statements* that tie things together. The therapist can weave the patient's historical material with the current stylistic propensities and tie it to the presenting problem of the session. Keep a grasp on the focus, don't stray; keep a tension and allow pinpointed feedback and bring it home. To make each session count, the therapist needs to stay on track because patients get lost. They are driven by feelings or defensive maneuvers or are distracted or are mentally filled with extraneous thoughts and ideas. The therapist must hold the thread in a disciplined way.

Often supervisees say, "I am not sure where to go. We seem stuck and the sessions lack momentum." or "I am not sure what we are doing." That problem often comes from a lack of preparation, a lack of thoughtfulness about the patient, his character diagnosis, and the important themes necessary to visit. The therapist who has many patients may be unmotivated to do the preparatory work, to think ahead about the patient. When you get more mentally precise through experience, you can capture more readily the critical points of focus with each patient and initiate them with ease. But our minds can be undisciplined and then we as therapists are in the back seat and the patient is rumbling down the unpaved road going hither and yon.

Specific Tools: Attunement, Resonance, and Regulation

Shuttling between the patient's interior and outer life and behaviors requires the therapist to be abundantly flexible with her approach. It helps to have a tool box of instruments applicable to each and every situation. At times the therapist has to wield the sword confronting regression with straight talk; at other times she mobilizes a deep resonance with the subtlest of feelings, sometimes sharing a personal moment or joining the patient with what he feels. The therapist needs to be therapeutically effective, and that demands flexibility and an ability to master various tools of intervention. There may be laughter and humor, or a battle of wills, or mutual disappointment and hopelessness, or long, quiet silence, or at times warm feelings of exchanged tenderness.

Therapeutic work is like painting. The therapist may move through various shadings and brush strokes in a session. At times the therapist co-creates with the patient in a spontaneous fashion as both are engaging their intuition. At other times the therapist utilizes bold strokes of black paint to make a point. The relationship, or as Jung calls it "the encounter," includes magical elements within the dyadic exchange that transcend the rational mind. At times the patient and therapist co-create the painting, each adding a stroke and playing off what the other adds. The intersubjective field of shared consciousness is at play. There is the third force in the room that influences both—the synergy of the relational mix. There are many forces at play, some are not yet revealed fully and we need to be patient. How can we really know a patient's unique destiny, what James Hillman calls the "soul's code." He states, "What is lost in so many lives, and what must be recovered: a sense of the personal calling, that there is a reason I am alive" (Hillman, 1996, 4). We must sit with our various brushes at the ready as the painting reveals itself.

The inner work demands that the therapist stay deeply engaged. Intuitive interventions are called for. You enter a space with the patient where you need to be in resonance with her deeper feeling connections. If you are one step above the feeling, the patient may notice that you are unable to resonate with her and she will meet you at a more rationalized plane as an unconscious defense. Pulling the patient out of feeling or deep connection with her material and up to her head into a rationalized, intellectualizing defensive level is not helpful.

In a training session role-play I observed how the resonance was missing. There was a feeling of disconnect between the dyad. It is very subtle, but you know because the feeling didn't deepen for the person working; instead his communication would drift to the rationalized level more than deepening into feeling and insight, the "aha moment." It can be a matter of one degree off and the exploration will not deepen, the full connection is not made internally or between therapist and patient. The therapist was not able to go into herself to capture the conflict he was feeling so she stayed one layer above and so did he. Again, this is quite nuanced, but if you watch a therapeutic interaction you can observe when the therapist, with few words, can effectively state the image or dynamic in a way that the patient breaks through in that moment to real emotions and realizations not emanating from rational thought.

If true resonance is missing, there may be substitute contact. I notice this when I watch demonstrations or listen to session recordings. There is a tendency to try and express empathy by creating an unnatural cooing voice. The therapist loses her neutral voice, becomes barely audible, and coos in a contrived manner. The voice does not resonate with what is discussed, and it demonstrates the therapist is lost and not reflecting a solid state. Watch for an overly soft and cloying voice; keep your voice audible and differentiated from the patient. If the patient is quietly emotional you can drop your volume to meet him, but your tone and style should not be overly syrupy.

This tool is called attunement. In the middle phase of treatment, the character facade has been confronted and is increasingly dropping. The patient understands his character defenses and his initial resistance has diminished. The patient comes into session to work and brings up material including dreams. As the patient talks the therapist realizes the patient is operating with less defense. The therapist tunes in and the patient can drop into unexplored conflicts, early remembrances, and possibly traumatic memories and emotions. The therapist holds the space, holds the patient metaphorically as he travels downward on the steep pathway of inner memory and feeling. The therapist holds the emotions so the patient can enter the depths knowing the therapist is there as a guard rail on the path if needed. Venturing into altered states of feeling is treacherous unless you have the therapeutic relationship that buoys the patient, and he knows he is not alone in the room and in the experience. When he leaves the office with the experience he knows you have been there with him. Jung called the therapeutic relationship "the container" that holds the heat of the alchemical activity so the individual can transform over time. In object relations terms, the therapist helps "regulate" the emotions, meaning that there is form and structure around the flooding pain of memory and experience so the patient doesn't feel he will float away and drown.

Attunement has a life of its own as the session unravels mysteriously into spontaneous interaction. I will quote a story about Jung from the book *Jung's Last Years*, which speaks to the attuned and spontaneous interactions possible in a session.

> Once a simple young girl was shown into his consulting room, a school teacher from a village. . . . A doctor, personally unknown to Jung, had sent her to him. She suffered from almost total insomnia and was one of those people who agonize over having done nothing properly and not

having met satisfactorily the demands of daily life. What she needed was relaxing. Jung tried to explain this to her and told her that he himself found relaxation by sailing on the lake, letting himself go with the wind. But he could see from her eyes that she didn't understand. This saddened him, because he wanted to help her, and there was only this single consultation to do it in.

"Then," said Jung, "as I talked of sailing and of the wind, I heard the voice of my mother singing a lullaby to my little sister as she used to do when I was eight or nine, a story of a little girl in a little boat, on the Rhine, with little fishes. And I began, almost without doing it on purpose, to hum what I was telling her about the wind, the waves, the sailing and relaxation to the tune of the little lullaby. I hummed those sensations, and I could see that she was enchanted."

The consultation came to an end, and Jung had to send the girl away. Two years later he met the doctor who had sent her. [He] pressed Jung to tell him what kind of therapy he had used, because, he said, the insomnia had completely disappeared and never came back—naturally Jung was rather embarrassed. "How was I to explain to him that I had simply listened to something within myself? I had been quite at sea. How was I to tell him that I sung her a lullaby with my mother's voice? Enchantment like that is the oldest form of medicine."

(Dunne, 2000, 94–95)

There is a solid body of psychological research on the healing potential of relational exchange. As I discussed in an earlier chapter, the very earliest attachment years affect brain development and emotional self-regulation, and that regulation is an integral function of the therapeutic relationship. The healing therapeutic dyad helps ameliorate early ruptures in attachment as it functions to reorganize the disturbances by the very existence of a contactful, safe relationship with the therapist.

Reich understood that resonance biologically impacts the autonomic nervous system running amok in stress reactions of fight, flight, or freezing and rebalances it so that relaxation has an equal place. The very nature of a stable regulating relationship in maturity helps heal the earlier trauma of an unsafe or unregulated attachment history. The therapist in the regulatory role influences the patient's unconscious models and permeates the patient's entire psychophysiological adaptive functioning. When I discuss the biophysical component later in the book, those techniques make a further contribution to this aspect.

Attunement is a right-brain to right-brain conversation co-created by the patient and therapist similar to the earlier attachment maternal or paternal function described by Alan Schore, PhD. Schore describes the studies on empathic processes between the attuned mother and infant that create "affective synchronicity" and "disruption and repair" cycles that regulate the infant's "affective-bodily states" through the intuitive, nonverbal resonance established. Similarly, the attuned therapist fulfills a regulating function for the patient's changing physiological and affective states. Schore says,

> For a working alliance to be constructed the therapist must be experienced being in a state of vitalizing attunement to the patient; that is, the crescendos and decrescendos of the therapist's affective state must be in resonance with similar states of crescendos and decrescendos of the patient.

> (Schore, 2006, 7)

Jung's resonant approach is an example of the therapist acting as regulator of the patient's psychobiological state by intuitively tuning into what the patient needed in the realm of the unconscious; both the therapist and the patient were navigating the unconscious together.

Spontaneity, capturing appropriate metaphors, creative intuitive instincts are tools needed to enter and grasp key items in the maze of the patient's psyche. To enter the unconscious we tread lightly and delicately, utilizing our nonrational imagery; we enter a dream state with our patient, and we must lose our rational grasp, giving up, for a time, our dependence on our rational mind.

Interpretation and Mirroring

Interpretation is a valuable staple in the therapist's pantry. However, it is overused and becomes fodder for defensive intellectualization if emotional connection is missing. Psychoanalysis has relied on interpretation as its major technique. The therapist should use interpretation only when a patient's expression of feelings matches the interpretation. Avoid interpretation if the patient has not accessed a deep feeling state. If you provide interpretation without first getting access to feelings, there can be too much reliance on intellectual ideas. Do not interpret out of order in terms of the layers of defense and historic material. Stay tuned into the patient so the interpretation matches the patient's felt awareness and feeling so as to ensure impact.

Anita discussed an event at work when she felt criticized by her boss. She was incredulous that he chided her about an item she had completed—as she tried so hard to please him. She had not yet deepened into the felt historic pain in connection to her dominant, critical brother. She was a pleaser, and this defensive layer was still operative. If the therapist had interpreted her painful feelings surrounding her relationship to her brother she might acknowledge that issue but have no feeling attached to her acknowledgement of the therapist's comment. In fact, she would be pleasing the therapist to agree with the connection to her brother and would store it as an intellectual concept.

At appropriate times, the therapist can interpret from known historic material a certain behavior or attitude of the patient that is present and alive in the room. That creates intensity in the moment as the patient gleans insight as he explores the interpretation. He examines how his present style relates to elements about which he may have not been conscious. Interpretation can make a difference if it connects disparate elements into a more consciously understood insight that is felt emotionally. Your brilliance as a therapist comes from your intuitive and precise grasp of dynamics that interrelate. You perceive the gestalt. The patient is moved and sincerely helped by your precise grasp of the situation.

With narcissists who are quite vulnerable to feeling criticized, Masterson Institute clinicians suggest a mirroring interpretation. The therapist mirrors the pain of vulnerability when the patient feels criticized, even if the patient is not completely aware of feeling injured. The therapist notes what happened and guides the patient through mirroring to feel his sensitivity to being hurt. Narcissists have sensitivity to being criticized and viewed as not good enough. That is why narcissistic types command and control, because they cannot tolerate vulnerability as that is where their pain lives. If the patient does not feel understood, he can get defensively angry and self-righteous and will attack or control the session. In this case it is helpful to address what happened, go over the transaction slowly and carefully, and guide him by mirroring the pain inside and help him define how he felt injured. "When I questioned your response to your wife, you seemed to get upset. What happened? Did you feel misunderstood? Did that bring up a painful feeling?"

When the patient resists with anger or attacks you, meet the resistance head-on and take control neutrally so the patient doesn't experience you as intimidated or sense that he can control you. Then you can mirror the pain underneath: "Did you notice when you felt misunderstood, you reacted with indignation while underneath you felt hurt that I didn't understand you?" If she is less aggressive, she might retreat and not let you know she is upset and annoyed with you, but you will feel the tension in the room. Go over what occurred and mirror her disappointment with you and your inability to understand her. Ferret out her feeling of being criticized.

Narcissistic character types utilize an inflated defensive posture to ward off vulnerability. They avoid and deny realities that do not resonate with their invincible defensive stance. So this type can do better with mirroring interpretation than confrontation. I find that many narcissists can receive confrontations. As you meet their high energy with your energy, they will respect you. You can confront their character style and they will take it, except when they don't. Either way you are energetically meeting them and your observations will be received sooner or later if they stay in therapy. They need to respect you and feel you can help them even as you are knocking out their grandiose defense. If they are lower-functioning types, they will need more mirroring and less confrontation, as they are very sensitive to feeling unseen, unacknowledged, or misunderstood. Narcissists need adoration and acknowledgment, and they need to understand their pain underneath that drives their demands for attention.

Mirroring is an insightful intervention that expresses clear perception of the patient's experience. It engenders less defensiveness because it does not challenge but rather highlights your understanding.

Joining

The term *joining*, coined by Dr. Hyman Spotnitz (1908–2008), an American psychoanalyst who worked with schizophrenics, describes a technique of psychological reflection that expresses complete resonance and agreement on multiple levels. Spotniz observes, "*Motionless silence* communicates the message: I do not want to disturb you in any way" (Masterson and Klein, 1989, 120). Joining communications are made on a feeling level rather than cognitive and are often wordless. When you join a patient, you are with her where she is. You are offering no resistance to what she says, meeting her and receiving what she is saying with agreement and like-mindedness (Masterson and Klein, 1989, 119–121).

This intervention is particularly good with pregenital schizophrenics as they can be porous and diffuse and they need elements of a symbiotic relationship. As schizophrenic characters have an impasse at the earlier developmental phase of symbiosis, the therapist may need to start at that level. Meet them where they are and they can begin to grow to the next level of differentiation.

Silence is the deepest way to join your patient, as there is no interference in the resonance. There is no disturbance, only the wordless joining in quiet reverie. For types that fear engulfment, restraining your input is helpful, as larger energetic interventions might be perceived as overwhelming and threatening. As schizophrenic types can be quite sensitive, they need titrated responses. Know the character type with whom you are working and match your interventions; it is not a one-size-fits-all model.

Mirroring is an expression of the therapist's understanding of the patient taken a step further and fed back to the patient so it is not as undifferentiated as joining. With joining there is no light between you and the patient; therefore it is quite safe for those types that need merger and are threatened by co-option or engulfment.

You can utilize joining with any type when it fits. If patients are working through trauma with exquisitely painful material, your joining with them in silence sustains a regulating environment. At any point in treatment if the patient has a serious illness, joining can stabilize the patient where she is.

In different stages of therapy and depending on the type, differences with the therapist can be tolerated. As the intrapsychic structure develops, minimal merger with the therapist is needed. The interventions with a schizophrenic or other fragile types with weaker egos can graduate as the patient's ego develops. Interpretation, here-and-now observations, and confrontation become appropriate tools as this type of patient gets stronger.

Humor

Humor is quite therapeutic as it is expansive in nature, releases stress and anxiety, and teaches the patient a potential lightness of being. The seriousness of therapy is broken up by laughter and an experience of joining between patient and therapist. It communicates that we don't have to take ourselves so seriously; we can still laugh out loud together. Chronic self-absorption is a maladaptive style. Therapists need to encourage patients who are habitually lost in preoccupation with their problems to allow distance from constant self-rumination. At times humor can break up this chronic, negative self-focus. The therapist can use humor to counter the negative cognitions and obsessive preoccupation. Tell the patient she can let go, for the moment, of her preoccupation with her weaknesses and failures. Problems weigh down patients and therapists as we take them seriously; yet we must keep our humor and lightness-of-being intact. We must also not overdo mirroring our patient's distresses. Our humor gives the message of a balanced attitude: "You can take things less seriously," and "Let's enjoy laughing together about this or that," or "Smile and relax; even with your difficulties, you are still OK." As patients get healthier, they become less complex; life takes on a simplicity, freshness, and ease. They learn to laugh at themselves. As Reich states, armoring creates complexity; health is simple and straight-forward.

Humor is a way to join the patient in her life and yours, lighten up the heaviness, and take a slow, deep breath. It soothes the fatigue of the work and creates a release; the relationship sings for the moment. Cultivate your own style of humor and spontaneity. Allow it to burst forward and the patient will be grateful.

Bantering

Bantering is a "go with the resistance technique" stated in a light but provocative way. This is an effective intervention and breaks through stasis. Feel free to tease your patient, but make sure the relationship is solid and this intervention is compatible with the character type.

You can highlight the patient's habits, "Keep checking your phone and Facebook; you don't want to miss anything!" "Oy, the whining and complaining. You will make lots of new friends with that approach." "I think you need to do less so you don't exhaust yourself." These twists of the problem, where you exaggerate or reinforce their unhealthy patterns, loosens the control of their defenses and creates less identification with their habits. This intervention can be utilized with neurotics and some high-functioning borderlines.

This technique is known as "paradoxical intervention"; the clinician uses the symptom that troubles the patient: "Make sure you procrastinate on that assignment." You create some frustration in the patient, and it brings forward their resistance that can then be processed. You are acting on the unconscious rather than the rational mind that is having difficulty changing. Watch sarcastic or devaluing delivery. Bantering necessitates a high level of trust to be effective. This approach mixes things up a bit and breaks stultifying patterns in the therapeutic relationship. Anytime you disrupt the stasis and status quo it is a good thing.

Importance of Confrontation

Confrontation is the mainstay of character analysis. As we analyze the character defenses of our patients, our approach goes right to commenting on what we observe that thwarts the patient's healthy adaptation. Confrontation can be seen as commenting neutrally on defensive structure. The patient's defensive structure does not allow her access to her authentic Self and blocks important information, feeling, and awareness. The confrontation can be, more or less, dramatically expressed. If the defense is quite problematic and the patient is acting out self destructively, then our confrontation must have teeth. If we are observing a defensive habit like chronic smiling or repeatedly looking down, we may confront the defense in a lighter fashion. As the therapist confronts the style, he is putting a wedge between the patient's habitual modes of defense and the layers underneath that reflect its origins. The Masterson Group has written extensively and eloquently on this essential intervention technique (Masterson and Klein, 1989, 215–224).

> A couple, each in their 40s, entered therapy after many years of back-and-forth regarding commitment. Both were successful in business and financially well off.
>
> The gentleman, a phallic narcissist, was calling the all shots, dominating, controlling, and dismissive. His partner was clearly distraught over years of his compromising behaviors with other women and lack of commitment as demonstrated by those behaviors. She, a closet narcissist, was emotionally broken down and lost in him, without sufficient anchors in her own life. My job was to confront both of their defensive structures that were in the way of a healthy relationship. I told him about his controlling, dominating, dismissive style and how he appears to listen well, but it is strategic rather than sincere. I told her about her obsessive preoccupation with him that leads to a lack of self and increased feelings of weakness and despair that feeds his dominance.

Starting out with confronting the individual character structures allows the therapist to discuss the family dynamic at play with these two styles. The work begins at the first session with these confrontations.

When I teach students, they express fears about using confrontation as they worry about alienating and losing the patient. "Have they built-up enough trust yet?" "Will the patient be offended?" "Is it too fast to point defenses out?" "Maybe the patient will get angry and leave?" "How about a less invasive approach?" I hear these concerns over and over again. Patients want help and want the therapist to give clear, helpful messages rather than let the session succumb to a repetition of their story again and again with a new sympathetic listener who doesn't add much to the equation. Patients, for the most part, can handle realistic and well-thought-out interventions that engage the problem rather than sidestep what is in the room.

Good confrontation highlights the therapist's ability to observe and see through each patient. This understanding is obvious if the therapist is seeing clearly and expressing accurately what she observes. Her observations are founded on an understanding of development, character structure, and defensive postures as they relate to character. So when she intervenes with a confrontation it is informed. For the most part, patients recognize themselves and are relieved that the therapist can see them as they are, even if it is not pretty. So the interventions emanate from your observation of their defensive patterns and how best to confront those.

The intervention is always neutral and not oppositional. Confrontation should not express the therapist's frustration with a patient or her own felt weakness. Therapists have to monitor their inner climate to make sure they are clear about their stance. It is not to say therapists will never feel frustration, because we will. It is what we do with it. We can utilize our feelings as information and respond with a specific intervention. We might use humor to quell our frustration or make a confrontation that is applicable to the patient's provocative style. We can utilize self-disclosure of our feeling of frustration, if strategic, to make a point.

What exactly do we confront? Patients may want to feel better but do not want to change. We confront a patient's regressive behaviors, his willingness to avoid his own responsibility and blame others. We confront patients who are bullies and treat others with distain and contempt. We confront addictions. We confront abusive anger and outbursts that are disrespectful. We confront patient inflation, grandiosity, and self-centeredness. We confront patient withdrawal and sulking. We confront a patient who is mean, unforgiving, and punitive. We confront contactlessness. We confront chronic whining and complaining. We confront passivity and buried hostility. The list goes on. These are not healthy behaviors and act as defenses that create a barricade to real feelings, vulnerability, and expression. The Self lies underneath the barricade and *does* want to come out. Yet the patient has not understood how to express his real self and therefore lives out of his defenses and perpetuates unhappiness. Confrontation actually strengthens the ego structure as it works the muscle of facing reality and feeling the relief of coming out of hiding.

Confrontation builds a therapeutic alliance founded on reality, not perpetuation of false relationships. If a patient is a chronic caretaker that hides behind those she cares for, that will be confronted as she attempts to do that with the therapist. If the patient is not responsible for his life but asks others to take care of him, that will be exposed and confronted. Substance abuse is confronted so that therapeutic alliance is founded on healthy parameters rather than the therapist colluding with the patient's continued maladaptive behaviors. The therapeutic relationship will demand the patient change and will not support them "feeling better" because they found a caretaking therapist who supports regression.

The therapist always confronts resistance. Patients will resist life, both its pleasurable aspects and its pain. They will resist therapy, the therapist, responsibility, challenges, and risks. Our job is to confront resistance in all its forms. Resistance is normal but can destroy the therapeutic relationship and the patient's progress. We need to ferret out resistance in its many forms: missed appointments, diluting therapy to alternate weeks, flights to health (feeling one no longer needs therapy because for the moment the patient feels better), flights to other professionals, negative talk about the therapist to others, and many more.

We ferret them out and confront them specifically. Comments like "I am thinking of taking a break from therapy," "I didn't want to come today" (Excellent! she brought it up!), "Therapy isn't helping," or "I had an important meeting so I had to miss" are examined and open up a conversation that reveals hidden negativity and fear.

Confrontations will disrupt defensive maneuvers: her reliance on parents to take care of her, clinging to a destructive relationship that feels good in the "reunion" phase before the next assault. These are defensive, self-destructive patterns that will continue unless confronted and dismantled. The patient will then experience anxiety, conflict, confusion, loneliness, pain, loss, and depression. They are feeling what the acting-out behaviors have been covering. We want patients to be able to feel these feelings rather than avoid contact through self-destructive behaviors. Blaming others, yelling, demanding, cajoling, and controlling others defers the inner pain while making others miserable and a dumping ground for unmetabolized feelings.

We teach patients to contain their torrent of unmetabolized feelings. They must contain them in any way they can. Leave the room, sit quietly, take a walk, journal, or cry and yell on their own—but not at another. We confront and demand a different approach to life. Our confrontations set limits and provide a view of reality that is chronically denied. We confront distortions of reality rather than be an accomplice to the distortions. We set limits on inappropriate behaviors inside and outside the office.

As we confront we see how the confrontation is integrated. If it is fended off we explore that defense as well. Through questioning, the patient can examine his response in session and examine his behaviors out of the session. We expect self-examination and exploration (Masterson and Klein, 1989, 221–224).

Reich was a master of confrontation. He was willing to provoke the patient and said provoking was a necessary part of the process. Why? Reich wanted to unveil the patient's negativity and the negative feelings toward the therapist. He knew that patient negativity was in the way of a healthy life as it is often expressed toward others, toward self, and in self-destructive behaviors. The negativity plays out in resistance. I am not saying that he purposely provoked, but if he needed to confront a defense, he would, and if it brought up negativity that was fine. He was not afraid of hostility. If hostility is not exposed, the patient is likely to leave therapy, pushed out by his own hostility, and will forfeit a chance to get well. Reich was creative in his approach; he would imitate a patient, get in his face, and at times his confrontations were quite dramatic. This is an art to be mastered.

Confrontation in a neutral and precise way builds trust, as the patient trusts you to be honest and authentic. You will need to be creative. If a patient is comatose, raise your voice, change your style to make the point. When you are confrontational a patient may accuse you of being uncaring or critical. One patient, who came from a "nurturing therapist," would accuse me of being too tough on her. Later, she was grateful for my approach because it helped her control her destructive emotionally abusive style of relating. You have to keep very clear regarding negative attributions from patients.

If the therapist feels insecure that he is not seen as caring and empathetic, then he will waffle and be caught up in patient projections and there will be a lack of integration and consistency of input. Frequently therapists feel insecure and fearful of the patient viewing her as uncaring. These insecurities will weaken and dismantle the appropriate interventions. Rather than backing up and off, confront the distortions: "When I mention the negative consequences of your actions, you get indignant and feel criticized. I am doing my job."

After many confrontations of character, the patient sees clearly her own unhealthy patterns and learns to confront herself both in and out of session.

Therapist Self-Disclosure

I keep personal self-disclosure to a minimum. Patients have enough to contend with, and staying in their own skin can be a challenge in the best of circumstances. Many patients are fascinated with their therapist and spend time thinking about possible scenarios of the therapist's life, spinning fantasies about the therapist. Patients who are prone to lose themselves in others will try to do that with their therapist. They will bounce off comments and ask the therapist personal questions or get engaged in arguments or dialogue about the therapist as a defense against staying with their own business. So self-disclosure is only recommended when it might be appropriate for a given patient at a given stage of therapy.

In the middle stage or termination stage of therapy, when the testing phase is over and the patient has hunkered down to business, there might be times that a simple disclosure to make a point could be meaningful to the patient. It can be a form of joining with the patient and affirms the trust that has been created. It models vulnerability and humanness. The personal item you share should not be for your own needs ever, but rather because it has usefulness for a particular patient. It may highlight a struggle she is having and the fact that you have had that struggle too. The patient doesn't feel so separate and alone with her challenge. For patients who are isolated, therapist self-disclosure creates an access point that creates connectedness when needed.

Self-disclosure of items that will not overly engage the patient with you and not be a boundary crossing may be relevant. The meta-message is, "I respect the patient enough to share an aspect of my self and my life."

If a patient is paranoid, envious, and jealous and projects negatively on the therapist, it is best to keep the boundaries absolutely clear. Projections can run rampant so no further confusion should be created. A patient with projections that you are unkind, malevolent, mean, critical, needing power—whatever it may be—necessitate clear boundaries so he can work through those projections over and over again. If a patient inflates you with idealization or sees you as a caretaker, clear boundaries are a priority. Patients may feel co-opted by their therapist and self-disclosure can muddy the waters. If the therapist is expressing his own needs through the sharing, patients will pick that up as they are exquisitely tuned to the therapist's every move. If the patient feels he has an inside track on the therapist, that impression can create a blurring of the patient-therapist boundary and cause the patient untoward conflict.,

Do not create an inappropriate opening because of your need to share or to get something off your chest, or possibly your personal need to connect, or wanting to impress the patient, or needing information, help, or a contact that the patient could facilitate. There are any number of inappropriate reasons that lead to an impulse to share. Those impulses have to be strictly monitored, and they can emerge due to the seeming intimacy of the relationship. We are not in the room to use the patient for our personal needs, and we need to stay conscious, at all times, of our mental state.

Self-disclosure is a tool in the tool chest and it can be momentarily rewarding for the patient to feel a kindred spirit with his therapist. It can be a cherished moment that moves the patient along in his journey.

12 Challenging Junctures and Difficult Patient Interludes

Therapeutic Standstills

At any phase of treatment, progress may come to a standstill for a single session or for weeks at a time. The patient and/or the therapist may feel at an impasse. How is a standstill experienced? The therapist may sense a lack of momentum; the sessions are experienced as missing a relational energy, aliveness, and vitality. The conversations lack depth and authenticity as the patient is not feeling deeply nor expressing overt resistance. Rather there is a pervasive sense of boredom in the room; the work is not "going anywhere" and it has a repetitive, lifeless quality. The therapist senses gridlock; the patient is not engaged or exploring his life and significant problems. He is talking, telling stories, but there is no real point to the conversation. The sessions seem to lack an arc of deepening and stay on a surface level. There is an absence of completion, noted by realizations, decisions made about a topic, and a felt sense that the work has been productive.

The patient may complain: "I didn't feel like coming to session today," or he is late as he was talking to an "important" client on the phone, or he left without accounting for sufficient time to get to session—as he was preoccupied with other matters. He isn't sure anymore why he is coming to session. Maybe he is thinking, "I don't need it anymore; I have learned what I can at this point."

The patient may demonstrate disinterest in therapy by stopping his internal exploration and filling time with aimless chatter. The therapist senses the patient is cut off from the process and does not activate his own exploration but rather exhibits passivity regarding his issues. He is no longer taking treatment seriously. The patient mentions evasively that he is considering spreading out sessions to alternate weeks, stopping sessions altogether, or taking a break.

On a weekly basis a normal therapy practice will include sessions that seem to have gone off the rails, sessions where the therapist feels she went in the wrong direction and missed critical interventions. The patient may be annoyed with therapy, discouraged, or feel debilitating anxiety or depression. Therapists take all of this seriously and the ebb and flow creates stress, as the therapist analyzes each situation and figures out the best direction with each patient.

Private practice is both rewarding and demanding, as the therapist needs to keep track of the treatment progression of each patient in a satisfactory way.

Therapeutic work can flow at times, without needing to watch it intently from the outside but letting it proceed from the inside out. If the therapeutic relationship is set up properly and the therapist has gathered sufficient information throughout the duration of the treatment, been accurately summarizing to the patient the dynamic at play, kept the arc of the session sustained by sufficient focus and tension, and managed acting-out behaviors, then the work will deepen on its own. The therapist can get out of the way as the patient unravels his material and shares more and more. That is all well and good except when the patient gets stuck and the progression or movement stops; then both therapist and patient land in a ditch. With every therapy, stasis points *will inevitably* occur.

When therapy is at a standstill, the therapist senses something is amiss and can feel confused, frustrated, discouraged, and incompetent. Therapists will notice a sense of malaise that comes over the therapeutic relationship. Both therapist and patient feel bored with what is happening. That means mutual contactfulness is at a minimum. Therapists will say, "I feel something is missing." "The therapy with Sal is flat. I think he will leave"; or "I am not sure what is happening, but we are at a standstill"; or "I don't look forward to sessions with her"; or "I notice after 20 minutes in, I feel sleepy."

When therapy devolves into a repetitive, storytelling, content-oriented exercise, or when the patient has little to contribute or the dialogue lacks excitement, depth, meaningful contact, or a spark—those are signs the work is losing steam. Maybe the patient has detoured, and the therapist has followed the patient into her safer zone and is likely not challenging her. There may be too much discussion of content rather than process; too much advice, "reasonableness," or intellectualization. Defenses are up and the therapy is in stasis. This can happen in any phase of treatment.

Loss of energy can happen within a single session as well. When I listen to sessions I note the places where the contact and energy drops too low. Possibly a missed resonance that doesn't deepen the feeling or intellectualization and rationalization are occurring and the topic remains at that level. The patient is engaged in his defensive structure, and the therapist is not noticing nor challenging that. Sessions require an "edge," a tension, a focal point that challenges, and a focus in each session that is sustained—rather than meandering into the weeds with noticeable dissipation of energy. Creating the arc of each session must be the rule not the exception. If the therapist can readily pick up that the arc has been lost and the session is off track and make an intervention that reinstates contact, authentic interaction, and reengages poignant feeling then the therapy stays alive and productive. If too many off-trail junctures occur and the therapist is not attending to them regularly, the therapy may lapse into general stasis.

Always be conscious and register stasis both in a particular period within a session and in a phase of treatment. It is most important that the therapist sense stasis as quickly as possible so the relationship fire doesn't burn out completely. Once you are aware that there is no juice in the room, no fire, no edge, no movement, it is wise to bring it up. "I notice you seem less interested in exploring difficulties; in fact, you seem bored with the process." "You are not bringing up material and seem to be waiting for me to initiate." "What is in the way these days?" "Are you having negative feelings about me?" "How are you feeling about therapy?" These statements and questions will encourage authenticity and usually clarify a current block before it takes over. After cleaning out areas of resistance, negative feeling, or situational difficulties or concerns, the therapy usually picks up steam again and the relationship depth increases.

Let's start with the first phase of therapy and look at a critical juncture that can lead to an impasse if not handled properly. The first phase sets up the relationship; the Masterson Group calls this the testing phase. Treatment can have a standstill right at the beginning.

> Sandra, age 49, came into therapy having had prior therapeutic relationships. She still suffered from bouts of depression, abused alcohol, exhibited impulsive behaviors, and reported volatile emotions including explosive anger in her dealings with others. In the first few sessions I summarized her problems and character defenses. Sandra did not like to be confronted about her alcoholism and acting-out behaviors and became petulant in session as she criticized me for not being "supportive." She was accustomed to a more accommodating therapist. By the second month she was still annoyed with me and spent most of the session blaming me for her upset feelings and expressing contempt. I continued containing her volatile expressions, as well as confronted her impulsive behaviors out of the office. By the third month she understood that I was not going to tolerate her angry outbursts and blame—the way she had treated other therapists in the past. She began to see that her treatment of others was rude and manipulative. She at times would focus internally, facing into her overwhelming anxiety yet continued to feel disappointment with me that I wouldn't simply absorb and "support" her unruly behavior. She vacillated between a developing respect for me and negative feelings that I was "rigid and insensitive to her needs." Her vacillation between viewing me as good and then bad went on for years, but the initial phase of clear and consistent containment kept her from bolting.

Reich succinctly describes this critical juncture in the early phase of treatment. If the therapist is able to grasp this conceptual understanding he is prepared for this turn of events and can avoid disaster during the first phase of treatment. In *Character Analysis*, Reich states,

> In the initial stages of the analysis, we are always dealing with narcissistic attitudes, i.e. an infantile need for protection. In view of the fact that the reaction of disappointment is stronger than the positive object-relationship, this narcissistic dependence can readily change into hate.
>
> (Reich, *Character Analysis*, 1972, 18)

In another excerpt:

> When anxiety subsides at the beginning of treatment, this merely attests
> to the fact that the patient has channeled a portion of his libido into the
> transference—the negative transference also—not that he has resolved
> anxiety. To make analytic work possible, the analyst may, by some form of
> reassurance, have to relieve anxieties that are too acute. Apart from this,
> however, it must be made clear to the patient that he can be cured only by
> mobilizing the greatest possible quantity of aggression and anxiety.
>
> (Reich, *Character Analysis*, 1972, 18–19)

What does this mean to our therapist? The patient initially comes into therapy wanting protection and relief from anxiety. Those needs are legitimate at
the entry level. We set up the therapeutic frame, settle the patient into the therapeutic structure, and the relationship provides reassurance. These initial conversations relieve anxiety, but do not resolve it. At that point, the patient feels
hopeful and protected by the therapist. Some patients would just as soon maintain that position of feeling protected and gratified for the duration of therapy.

The next step, which can be initiated almost simultaneously during the
first few sessions, presents the first challenge point for some—you describe
the character defenses that you have observed throughout the sessions and in
information gathering. That first challenge of defensive structure can erode
the initial idyllic feeling of protection and the work begins. As Reich warns us,
the patient may soon enough feel consciously or unconsciously disappointed
in the therapist, and negative feelings will begin to emerge.

This is the first challenging juncture for patient and therapist. Does the
therapist settle for a comfort zone that does not challenge the patient nor
help them solve their long-term problems, or does the therapist move forward with dissolving maladaptive attitudes, behaviors, and style that keeps the
patient from accessing what is underneath these defensive behaviors. If too
many defenses stay intact initially, the work of introspection and insight will
not begin. Defenses function to hide memories, conflicts, and psychic pain.

Soon enough if the therapist notes the character defenses and acting-out
behaviors, the patient may feel negative feelings, as the sessions are not as
comfortable and cozy as she had hoped. As I have stated, patients don't necessarily want to change; just feel better. But that comfort is not sufficient for the
therapy to be effective. If therapy stays gratifying, stasis will set in.

If the therapist does her job with describing and challenging maladaptive
attitudes and behaviors right from the start, the patient may feel uncomfortable and at odds with the therapist. She may question her choice of therapist.
"This therapist is not as nice as my prior therapist." "Hmm, Dr. Smith is so
expensive; maybe I should go back to the lower fee therapist." "I don't like his
serious style." "She is stopping me when I want to tell her my upsetting stories.
I don't appreciate that." "My therapist challenges me and it is difficult." "She
is so strict with her rules, I am not sure this works for me."

All of these considerations need to be discussed and worked out as part of treatment launch. The patient expresses her ambivalence about treatment, her concern and conflicts with your style, doubts, and disappointments. As this is worked through the patient can settle in further, and the first phase of treatment is well on its way. The patient has tested the therapist. "Is there wiggle room?" "Is the therapist going to maintain the frame or not?" "Is the therapist going to get distracted and not really listen and understand me?" "Can she accept my embarrassing and shameful behaviors if I tell her?" "Will she cave if I challenge her?" "Can I control this lady?" These questions and many more are entertained by the patient initially and need to be taken on a test drive with the therapist. As the patient openly works out his ambivalence, his anxiety is titrated and he relaxes with the therapist. He can commit to the therapeutic relationship and the challenges it offers.

The therapist needs to be clear that the patient can learn to tolerate his anxiety and allow his aggressive feelings to emerge in the therapeutic relationship. Only then can the healing effects of treatment take hold. In inviting the patient's negativity and aggression, the therapist needs to be ready to take it on. You discourage the polite patient from hiding behind his facade and encourage him to express more honestly his reservations about you. The patient who is gratified by idealizing you and hoping you will take care of her is helped to develop a more realistic view that may provoke disappointment and discomfort. You are not fulfilling the role of the protector. The therapist has to cope with the disappointments and even the hatred Reich mentions, and those patient feelings may be uncomfortable for the therapist until she grows accustomed to engaging each and every feeling the patient has about her. If these phase-specific variables are not dealt with then a standstill may ensue.

Why? Because both therapist and patient are bypassing the uncomfortable testing issues, bypassing patient doubts and concerns and overriding those doubts with pacifying "supportive" messages. All the concerns and negativity go underground and what surfaces is superficiality; a relationship founded on the false self or facade activated in both therapist and patient and resulting in artificiality and deadness in the relationship. Instead, we want to teach the patient to be honest in relationships, to communicate her true feelings more openly so the authentic self can grow. This authenticity may have been impossible in childhood and beyond and has to be learned in the therapeutic relationship.

Why do patients need to tolerate their anxiety and aggression? Patients bind up their anxiety in physical and mental symptoms, as anxiety is hard to tolerate. Patient character structures are coping strategies to manage anxiety so the patient can minimize his exposure to his own anxious thoughts and feelings. For example, the borderline with high anxiety may act abusively to another, blaming and attacking rather than feel her insecurity and flood of anxiety. When the therapist stops those behaviors, the patient feels her anxiety and is less comfortable, as chronic unhealthy patterns are curtailed. If you ask a hysteric to stop talking so much, she might feel anxiety emerge when she is advised to stop chattering.

A patient may have chronic physical symptoms and complaints due to the binding of anxiety in somatic symptoms: irritable bowel syndrome, stiff necks and tight backs, constant colds, chronic headaches, constipation, asthma, skin flare-ups, bouts of fatigue, and other disorders. These physical complaints can be a result of relentless anxiety and stress flooding the autonomic nervous system and resulting in physical symptoms.

A narcissistic patient may dominate and demand rather than feel his own inadequacy and his attendant anxiety. A schizoid may avoid contact, retreat, and withdraw rather than express his aggression to a close other and will have headaches and stomach problems as well. When patients learn to tolerate their anxiety and aggression, their issues become conscious rather than masked in symptoms.

Obsessive-compulsive symptoms—rituals, hyper-busyness, preoccupation with order, control, and cleanliness—are ways that patients try to override their fear and anxiety by overmanaging their world. This patient ends up with other problems due to his preoccupation with controlling his environment and the folks that share it. These symptoms are an unconscious attempt at binding anxiety in the hopes of gaining mastery. Habits such as tightly controlled food restrictions with multiple instructions and requests played out at restaurants or at other people's houses drive friends and family crazy. Fear of germs and fear of getting sick are a way of fending off deeper fears of loss of control by instating a false sense of control. If patients understand that they can survive their anxiety, if they learn to live with it rather than acting-out defensive avoidance, they will be better off. Then the deeper issues related to their anxieties can be sorted out. In extreme cases, medication may be indicated to get serious obsessive compulsive disorder rituals under control before the therapy can be effective

Understand that patients do not want to face and feel the psychic and physical pain associated with their anxiety and will fight you all the way. This can happen right at the beginning if you call out their defensive behaviors and not gratify them in the way they expect. They may criticize you, judge you, and demand that you fulfill their expectations

I suggest you not cooperate with those demands but rather conduct the therapy in a way that directs them to look honestly at themselves. Clarify their expectations of you and work through them so patients understand the nature of the work. We are willing to catalyze strong feelings that move the therapy along. In the first phase of treatment you are highlighting the defensive structure, looking at what their symptoms describe about the patient, and summarizing for the patient his long-term character problems as you see them. This is the first difficult juncture and many therapists never get this far through an entire course of treatment.

I have painted a challenging picture of this phase yet I can assure you that my average patient feels relieved by an honest portrayal of his problem and readily gets down to the business of making changes. We begin with honesty in the room that holds both our feet to the fire. That makes for a lively process.

If the patient disagrees with your portrayal, that is fine, as their understanding of themselves is important. We don't have all the answers, but we are engaged in an authentic exploration together.

If you have not confronted defenses openly, the therapy may end up flat; the patient is bored and feels it is ineffective. Have you avoided confronting the patient, moving from the "protective role" to the challenging role? Have you summarized, in an honest, forthright way, the patient's problems, even if it is not a comfortable portrayal? If not, the therapy becomes like a flat tire lacking air; it lacks energy and movement. Is the therapy stimulating for you and the patient or are you listening to stories and lots of "blah, blah . . ." that is defensive in nature?

We need to assess the character type accurately as some with fragile egos cannot tolerate excessive anxiety, and the therapy needs to be conducted in a slower, more delicate fashion. But make sure you are not taking that tack out of your own fear and insecurity. Low-functioning patients can thrive with challenges too. Challenge grows their ego strength and perception that you believe they can face their problems head on.

Life circumstances may redirect the treatment at any time; if the patient is in a crisis, that needs to be sorted. Crisis does not determine an absence of character work, but it does mandate help figuring out current difficulties and challenges. The patient needs you to be on board with their real problems.

If therapy is at a standstill there are interventions that can free up the log-jam. First and most important, admit to yourself that therapeutic progress has stopped. Discuss it with the patient. That observation can stimulate an interesting conversation and may immediately clarify the stasis. Secondly, look at the patient's defensive structure; what defenses are apparent in your interactions lately? Those are likely stopping his progress. Is the patient muting the process with numbness and disconnection as an avoidance or denial of difficult feelings? Is the patient overtalking to avoid anxious feelings? Is she vague about details lately? Is he lying about recent events? Whatever the patient is displaying, these defenses are in the way of an authentic, energetic process; examine those with the patient. These defenses keep the patient in stasis outside of therapy as well, as they inhibit his forward movement. If she is acting that way with you, she is approaching her life in the same fashion. Confront the resistance, discuss it in depth, and see what is stimulating this new round of resistance. It could be the patient hasn't told you a negative feeling he has been having about you. Or his wife is communicating her upsets about his therapy. Or she is more dependent on a destructive relationship and hasn't wanted to tell you. Or he is overeating again. She has been drinking and hiding it. The patient may be acting out an increase of obsessive-compulsive rituals and not keeping you in the loop. All these behaviors may cause the patient shame and will contribute to resistance. Find out.

If the patient is in covert resistance that has not been exposed, the stand-still will continue. There are other ways resistance plays out, along with many I have described. The patient may be on a silent sit-down strike, as he is thwarting you and you sense you cannot get to him. A patient is escaping from difficult conversations about difficult things and is diluting the therapy by discussing less meaningful items meant to distract while the therapist continues to cruise along beside him. The patient is evading sincere effort and becoming passive in his approach; maybe he is behaving with you like he acted with his mother. Is he feeling resentful that he has to work in therapy and not rely on the therapist to generate all? This can be a way the patient feels loved: if he gets the therapist to generate the work in session, "taking care of him" as he acts out his passivity. The patient wants the therapist to figure everything out for him. "What should I talk about today?" "What do you think is my problem?" "Do you feel I am getting better?" Or there is silence and an absence of patient material, rather waiting for you to begin the session and dig for material. Check out the passivity as resistance in the room, yours or theirs. Resistance, negative transference, defensive structure left intact, and contactlessness are the major causes of stasis.

Are you colluding with the patient in stasis? Maybe you are going along with her because it is easier for you. Sometimes therapists will not alter an "easy relationship" with a patient that is comfortably on autopilot. We, too, look for an easy way out. Why kick up dust? Because if we don't, the therapeutic momentum will stop and stasis sets in.

If stasis continues, the patient will get restless (rightly so) and believe that therapy is unproductive. She may bring up the financial cost and other things she would rather spend money on. Or conflicts in scheduling emerge; therapy is no longer a vibrant priority but relegated to an obligation to be avoided. The therapy is derailed at this point and getting it back on track is challenging. All these elements need to be discussed and tracked so the patient realizes what has happened. But first the therapist needs to have a handle on the derailment. Remember, the patient may seem difficult but it is really that the therapist has not realized there is stasis and figured out how to reinstate movement early enough. If stasis continues for too long, the therapy will inevitably be defeated and you won't be able to revive it. The patient is determined to leave, and he will not cooperate with further discussion.

If you can intervene before that point, explain to the patient that she has already devoted significant time and energy to her therapy. To give up before you both determine that sufficient gains have been made would be an unfortunate outcome. If she leaves, she will inevitably start therapy with someone else down the road, and a chaotic history of multiple therapists ensues. If a patient can stay with one therapist and do productive work, that is the best scenario. But roaming from therapist to therapist can create a feeling of disillusionment over time. "Here I am again, starting over with a new therapist." "I have to tell my story all over again." It is better to encourage sticking with the current relationship—through thick and thin. I am not suggesting that patients stay if therapy is truly unproductive, and they need to assess that honestly. But often it is due to a failing on either or both sides of the dyad, and if the failings can be discussed, the relationship may get back on track and be better for it. If the therapeutic relationship weathers the hurdles, it becomes tried and true. Encourage patients to stick with you and work to resolve stasis points with good supervision.

As Reich instructs, "resist artificially positive approaches" as a way to cajole the patient out of stasis (Reich, *Character Analysis*, 1972, 18). Only the cleansing work of discussing defensiveness, resistance, negativity, and contactlessness will bring the patient back to an authentic relationship with herself and you. If you work methodically through these aspects without distraction, you will break up the logjam. Stasis can occur at any time during the treatment; beginning, middle, and even with a strong therapeutic alliance, in the termination phase. Always stay tuned in to your experience in the room. Notice if you feel bored, sleepy, disinterested, and resistant to a particular patient and feel stuck on how to proceed. These are indications of stasis; get ready to immediately kick up some dirt.

A Challenging Defensive Style: The Devaluing Narcissistic Defense

Devaluing narcissist defense mechanisms are particularly difficult to work with and plague the therapist. Keep in mind that the devaluing defense can be utilized by many of the other character types at one time or another. Either the devaluing defense is a habitual overlay on another type, or now and again emerges simply as a defense. For example, hysterics or borderlines who had devaluing narcissistic fathers may have this type of overlay on top of their primary structure and will exhibit this defense in addition. Schizoids can utilize this defense as they may have an internalized sadistic object inside. Paranoid schizophrenics can exhibit narcissistic character traits with devaluing defenses. Understanding this defensive style and behavior can help you in a variety of situations.

Our discussion will include the Disorders of the Self (DOS) narcissist, and the DOS devaluing narcissist as devaluing is its principle defense and the phallic narcissist who may resort to this defense on occasion. What causes the devaluing is the presence of splitting in the intrapsychic structure (review Part III). The DOS types have major splitting and view themselves and others through the lens of bad or good. The neurotic has a more balanced perspective and perceives wholeness in himself and the therapist. He can be captured by momentarily strong projections but can recalibrate his awareness and withdraw the projections from the other.

As discussed in a prior chapter, the DOS narcissist has a split that either sees the therapist as omnipotent and self as a grandiose extension of the therapist or sees the therapist or others as malevolent and self as inadequate. Masterson delineates the intrapsychic "units" that vacillate causing serious projections onto the therapist and others as well as entrenched self-inflation and self-loathing. These patients literally get lost in their split psyche with its attendant projections and distort reality—creating a dismal relational world.

The DOS devaluing narcissist is a lower-functioning type, who developmentally did not have an idealized fusion with the parent, and therefore did not develop a grandiose self and idealized other, as did the DOS narcissist. Devaluing narcissists have more internal emptiness and fragmentation. They became paranoid due to isolation, neglect, and often a violent family life. Their fractured intrapsychic condition is a reflection of a contorted life experience, possibly chronic abuse from parental figures with extreme suffering; we must never lose our compassion even if they present as extremely unlikeable. These individuals are less likely to seek treatment, as their capacity to trust is minimal.

Devaluing means the patient attacks or criticizes the worth of something or someone. When he harshly devalues, he seeks to damage the other as well as destroy and annihilate. The function of this defense is to shore up the devaluing person who then feels powerful and in charge. When the patient acts this way in therapy, he tries to dominate the therapist. He chronically blames the therapist and others for his problems. If a patient was verbally or physically abused by his parent, he may in turn take that sadistic parental role and force that projection into the therapist (Masterson and Klein, 1989, 313–318). The patient becomes the aggressor and the therapist becomes the victim, similar to what the patient went through in his life.

The therapist feels disparaged, helpless, and may experience an unconscious draining of power. The patient feels empowered with feelings of revenge and relief as he dumps his negativity onto the therapist. This acting out allows the patient to disown his depression and his inadequate feelings and gain mastery over his fantasy enemy, the therapist. As the patient displays his aggression, he is caught up in his empty bravado. He seeks revenge against those that hurt him early on, although it is unconsciously played out in the present. The patient is no longer vulnerable to past hurts and has removed himself from his vulnerable feelings.

As we look at the devaluing defense according to character type, we can see some distinguishing features. For the schizoid their narcissism and potential devaluing serves their need to maintain safe distance from everyone. They control the space so as not to risk hurt. The self-sufficiency may look like a one-up defense but its function is maintenance of a safe distance. They do not use devaluing as a way to annihilate the other as their aggressive feelings are more muted and their aggression more repressed.

Borderlines devalue as a way of forestalling responsibility by attacking the therapist as nonsupportive. Rather than activate with autonomy, they devalue the other for expecting responsible behaviors. They see the therapist as the problem rather than their own desire to regress and be taken care of. They often identify as helpless victims and project the attacker onto the other. When they feel abandoned and alone they can mobilize devaluing rage at the abandoner. Borderlines devalue themselves as well and cut off their own legs rather than risk abandonment by being strong. Then with their legs cut off they feel awful, depressed, inadequate, and worthless and may lash out at others.

Devaluing the therapist is a transference acting out that creates major challenges for any therapist. Phallic narcissists have access to plentiful aggression and can be arrogant, inflated, grandiose, and highly competitive, so their devaluations can be quite vicious and unrelenting. They are excellent manipulators, and this style creates a dilemma for the therapist. The DOS patient type feels all-powerful and particularly enjoys sadistic domination. The more power he wields over another, the more sadistic he can become. He relishes his attacking prowess; the more he diminishes the other, the better he feels. Making others squirm is enjoyable to the devaluing narcissist.

The patient is unconsciously driven to project his own inadequacy and self-loathing so that he does not have to face those feelings within. As we experience attacks, we can lose contact with our self and collapse into insecurity and immobilization. Or we become defensive and lose track of the patient as we defend our actions against the blame that is coming at us. We might try to reason with them, refute their allegations, disagree with the content, and fight them in the ring. If so we have lost the process and are cajoled into the content. Fighting content is a mistake, as the devaluing narcissist will enjoy the debate and is determined to win. We may want to put them down in return and use punishing interventions. Or we might withdraw and create a chasm.

When the patient turns against the therapist, neutrality is seriously challenged. The narcissist—being sensitive to criticism—can respond with cold rage if you threaten his grandiose, inflated self. This defense is quite demanding on the therapist, to say the least, as it feels abusive. Therapists must not collapse into weakness as that provokes contempt in the patient. However, no therapist should tolerate abuse under any circumstances. If the patient cannot be contained with multiple attempts over a few months, then the therapy needs to be terminated.

Devaluing can also be observed in a quieter tone: relentless criticism of everything and anything—office environment, procedures, your appearance, what you say, what you do—and the patient may pull in other justifications like Internet comments about you, gossip from other patients, anything she observes is fodder for devaluation. Or the style can be overt, loud, agitated, angry attacks on your character, your expertise, and your competency—pushing you into a corner and getting in a few more punches. Either way, attacks can debilitate the therapist, hopefully momentarily, as they can provoke extreme anxiety and fear in the moment.

How do we remain in our own skin and able to literally defend ourselves from the onslaught? How can we match their energy enough not to be annihilated? Neutrality is difficult but we must remain both the observer and the experiencer at the same time. We cannot buy in to the criticism and the patient's contempt. We have to see it for what it is, a destructiveness that is destroying the patient. Abusiveness cannot be allowed. Tell the patient if she continues the attack she will need to leave the office immediately unless she can control herself. Ask her to turn her attention inward, off of you, and observe what triggered and threatened her. If she can readjust her behavior, you can insert a probe inside her for further investigation. If not, tell her clearly that others may take this outlandish behavior but you will not.

It is a challenge to not identify with the projection of the worthless child who was sadistically punished. We may respond with retaliatory moves that can incite the patient further, or we may distance and that provokes the patient as well. We will have to meet the patient energetically, and that is challenging. We cannot avoid him, so do not freeze up. If you feel like a failure, then he has co-opted you and you are in the quicksand of your own counter-transference. Therapy is at a standstill. He is numb to his own issues and fortified by acting out his dump. Confront and stop the behaviors quickly. Try not to get pulled into a debate, as it is nothing but an irrational dialogue.

We contain sadistic aggression a few ways: First, we must not let ourselves be abused and must set limits on outrageous hostility. Always put a stop to bombardments of personal attack. You can tell the patient, "Your attack of me will not help you get better. This habit of critical attack on others is a way out of your own pain and feelings of defectiveness. I will not tolerate it. So contain yourself first of all." The patient is seeking revenge against his own life of humiliation at the hands of sadistic persecuting others.

Next we need to get the patient to focus inward. He is not in the room to focus on the therapist, and we must tell him that. "Focusing on me is an avoidance of looking at your problems and pain." Confront his defensive style in an aggressive but neutral way. Ask him to look at his need to be superior. Ask him to look underneath his attacking mode. If he has settled down, see if you can insert a simple interpretation. If that doesn't work, go back to confronting the character. If you get a break there you can mirror his pain and see if he can allow vulnerability. Discuss thoroughly his contemptuous style and his criticisms of you. In time he will face into his contempt as a defense against his own inadequacy feelings and fear of fragmentation.

If the patient needs to return to idealizing you for a brief time to reestablish the alliance, so be it. That can be handled later.

Members in a couple can have this defense in spades. Your office can shake with hostile rage attacks, blame, and power struggles of who can annihilate whom first. The same limit-setting applies with couples as with devaluing narcissistic defenses. The intensity can be double-fold, so get ready to raise your voice and control the session so it is not permeated with attacks, blame, and devaluing. If one member of the couple dominates, disarm that individual and teach the partner to stand up and set limits. Work with his defenses of passivity, numbness, dissociation, or collapse in the presence of an attack.

We may experience anger at the devaluing patient and that is acceptable as it is an authentic response and helps us to mobilize our healthy aggression. We should not become her dartboard. We must resist our fear and anxiety and come back strong. This type of patient acting out can provoke our own feelings of helplessness, worthlessness, incompetence, and general vulnerability depending on our own historical material and current life situation. If we have suffered a critical parent or dominating siblings and currently have a belligerent spouse, we may have less bandwidth for this type of patient.

Their need for mirroring and adoration is quite unnerving for the therapist. The therapist can resent that the patient pushes this need constantly. "You don't understand my feelings and you should." "I don't feel you respect my opinion; you are failing to hear what I am saying." "You missed my point." "Can't you hear what is really important to me?" These are demanding patients who want to be seen and crave respect although their behaviors undermine that possibility.

If we keep our seat, we can help them—if they truly want to be helped.

Other Challenging Interludes

The manic-depressive phallic type, or character types that also have this tendency, can be a handful. They have periods of instability and create chaos in their lives. They have the phallic aggressive controlling quality, but it is housed within a more volatile, unstable reality ego. Their self-centeredness and inflation run rampant in a chaotic style that calls for close management. Due to her manic impulses, this patient will thwart your caution and control with self-righteous proclamations about what she is planning. This patient needs to be contained and defenses confronted so she can get underneath her inflated schemes to feel her hidden depression. Manic-depressive hyperactivity is an over expansiveness that is a defense against depression. This patient can vacillate between the two. She has to understand and work with her vacillating expansiveness and contractedness. Helping her find a middle ground in thought, action, and emotional displays is helpful while systemic regulation is instituted. Regular sleep, regulation of caffeine and substances, regular meals, and vigorous exercise and yoga, and stopping overstimulation with media, devices, and gaming is helpful. When someone is more depressed, exercise and yoga, limited alcohol, better sleep, and continuing healthy habits curtails the depression along with implementation of a structure of activation.

Paranoid phallic characters or patients with paranoid traits have abundant and chronic devaluing defenses as discussed earlier. This patient feels suspicious at every twist and turn in therapy. Even after many years of work with a paranoid, this individual can still be suspicious and accusatory if she feels threatened in anyway. This patient hears things you say and feels you are against her, or you misread her, or you are undercutting her power, or you are jealous of her strengths, or you don't want her to succeed, or you are singling her out and are against her, or you are going to abscond with her ideas. Due to their lack of clear perception, these patients can be difficult to contain as they react to their distorted perceptions with their inherent aggressive capacity to attack.

The therapist needs to stand up to their misperceptions so they can accept that they have paranoid features and how their paranoia undermines their relationship with you. During their lucid moments, discuss their chronic trust issue and how it unravels and makes them feel alienated and undermined as they see you in the shadows of their paranoia. This type needs to see his under-lying fear, terror, and the historical roots of his ocular block that contorts and distorts reality.

Patients with paranoia and splitting will still succumb to these fears often and attack the therapist in ways that can be frustrating for the therapist. As the therapist, you feel your intentions to help are not being received and are distorted. Once you understand how paranoia works you can accept it and call it out. I always tell a patient when she is having paranoid thoughts that they are not an accurate reflection of reality. See if the patient can relax and move under the paranoid feeling. Then discuss the paranoia and how it works. Go over the dialogue to see what provoked the response so the patient can see what triggered her. Always let the patient know he has paranoid tenden-cies as that helps the patient learn to mediate his paranoid process. It should be quite out in the open. When patients with splitting (can be narcissists, borderlines, schizoids, schizophrenics, or paranoids) perceive you at times as the bad object—out to get them, sabotage them, undermine their best inten-tions, control them—slow the process down and figure out what provoked the threatened feelings.

Hysterical patients can be frustrating to work with at times as they defend against their constant state of intense anxiety. This patient may maintain silence or be overly talkative, always covering their deeper feelings. As they tend toward superficiality, they are hard to pin down and can run from treat-ment in complete denial of what they are doing. The therapist may have a month or two of productive work with them, and suddenly they suggest a yoga retreat or take a trip to India to study with a guru or go off with a new boyfriend. It is not that these ideas in and of themselves are not interesting, healthy pursuits, but for the hysteric, diversions are a way of life, and depth and maturity are avoided for the next thrill. The therapist gets frustrated by these lapses in the process and has to rein the patient in rather than allow the running defenses to take over. They are also prone to multiple relationships and affairs to create superficial stimulation and avoid the mature tasks of find-ing meaning.

Compulsive types can be difficult as they are quite controlling in the ses-sion. They resist movement, change, and spontaneity. Their doubting and caution can frustrate the therapist as they will rein in the therapist's energy. If the therapist is making a point too strongly, the patient may tell the therapist to back off and let the patient do it his way. The compulsive types can act passive-aggressively as their aggression is submerged in a passive style. They appear unthreatening in their speech and behavior but underneath they are angry, resentful, and seething. It is important to get underneath and explore their anger, as they are not comfortable with rage. Other types with narcissis-tic overlays can be very angry and controlling on the surface and demand what they want from partners and the therapist. The narcissistic element of self-centeredness plus the controlling aspects of compulsivity and the obsessive focus on detail makes for challenging interludes. Understanding those elements allows you to approach the narcissism in one way while also confronting the anal traits of control, obsessiveness, and self-doubt. These types manage everything there is to manage with a fine-tooth comb: details in your office, germ concerns, placement of objects, details regarding appointments, duration of sessions, and so on. They can be hyperverbal as they delineate their obsessive mental processes from start to finish. Watch getting caught up in obsessive dialogues with these types. They like to describe every aspect of a situation and go over the details of their thought process, as they go back and forth trying to figure something out. Spontaneous actions are hard for them as everything needs to be thought out and then the waffling of doubting begins. Often meaningful life pursuits and pleasures are forfeited as well as success in relationship.

Catatonic schizophrenics are challenging as often they have difficulty sensing, perceiving, and feeling. They fear any kind of movement and feelings create movement. They are terrified of change, spontaneity, and expansion of their organism—opting for stasis instead. Fear is their middle name, and their primary focus both consciously and unconsciously is to reduce any experience of fear. They utilize trance states, spacing out for long periods, dissociation, busyness, lethargy, or anything else that numbs their constant fear. They can be numb yet controlling much of the time and can shut down with little or no access to emotions. Sessions can be dull and laborious with lots of "I don't know" responses. What are you thinking? "I don't know." What are you feeling right now? "I don't know." Is something upsetting you? "I am not sure." What happened when you went to the party?" "Hmm . . . [shrug] . . . I had an OK time." End of story. This type of patient needs you to be patient. If you want to be entertained, this character type will not accomplish that for you. Rather you will have to tune in deeply to the subtle nuances of activity and feeling, always realizing this patient is quite afraid even if she is not aware of it. She is coming because she wants contact and is suffering, but her feelings are muted. These patients need us to help them access their feelings and be patient with their process. Due to their anal traits, they are trapped in doubting and obsessive-compulsive tendencies, which further immobilizes them and protects them from change and movement. Most decisions are labored to the point of immobilization. Help them to tolerate more movement in all areas of their lives. Biophysical interventions may be helpful to increase their capacity to move, feel, and tolerate anxiety.

In summary, get supervision, tolerate your imperfections and flaws, and respect your good intentions—as we do have the patient's best interest in mind. Watch and alter your counter-transference feelings. Over time you will gain expertise that will give you great strength in the face of patient pathology. Be compassionate as patients suffer terribly and are trying to be better even if it doesn't look that way. Patients have had difficult lives and are products of those lives; we must feel for them and support their best efforts, without getting lost in the morass of their challenging worlds.

13 The Business of Therapy

With the dominant presence of smartphones, the Internet, and social media, psychotherapists have been thrust into a rapidly changing age of business development and must proactively jump onto the fast-moving train. Most therapists did not major in business, and with all the study needed to become psychologists and psychotherapists, our business development skills have gotten short shrift. I will not profess to be an expert in this arena, but like many others, I have been thrown into the maze to learn as I go. I will share a few thoughts and ideas on this subject that have helped me—with the hope of getting you started.

Therapists enter the field because they are interested in psychological themes. Therapists like the interesting dynamics of the human condition—relationships, families, and other aspects of human success and failure. Often therapists have had their own traumas, life struggles, and conflicts that they are trying to resolve and likewise are interested in helping others achieve resolution.

The therapist personality profile is not similar to the typical business-oriented type who has strong interest and expertise in economics, profit and loss algorithms, and business strategies with clearly delineated target goals. We come into this profession with an analytic and relational viewpoint, usually with a liberal arts undergrad background and graduate studies in social work, psychology, or organizational development. We learn the history and development of various types of psychological approaches, become apprised of a multitude of research studies, obtain theoretical and clinical knowledge, complete our internships, pass our licensing exams, and are finally ready to start practicing.

The Reluctant Therapist

Let's begin with a typical therapist's attitude toward his private practice and career. Many therapists are in the field to "help others." This is a sincere motivation, yet often results in a self-effacing stance. There can be a subtle or not so subtle lack of healthy entitlement that results in an absence of a business agenda geared to professional success. The typical therapist may lack enterprising business acumen when it comes to his private practice. The self-effacing style manifests in concrete ways: reluctance to engage in practical activities to market his practice, network with other professionals, self-promote, and go on cold calls to meet possible referral sources.

Therapists tend to keep their patient load up by offering reduced fee schedules with too many patients in the low-fee category. They are reluctant to raise fees even when theirs are not aligned with the marketplace. Many therapists overwork because their fees are too reduced, and often they don't charge for phone calls, emails, or missed sessions. Most importantly, therapists have no formalized comprehensive policies and procedures that outline fees and charges and educate the patient on their policies while protecting themselves.

Therapists work all hours and overextend their availability to accommodate their patients rather than request that patients accommodate their chosen office hours. Therapists stretch out the workday rather than consolidate patients within certain hours or days because they fear losing patients. An exhausted, overworked therapist cannot do good work and models a lack of healthy self-regulation and a dismal lifestyle.

I am astounded when I meet clinicians and they express an exaggeratedly cautious attitude about charging what I would consider appropriate fees. After all the time devoted to study and resources spent at university and internships to become a professional, they consistently undervalue their worth. Therapists do not sufficiently realize that they are in business for themselves and need to create a business model that guarantees success: namely, earn sufficient income to feel a sense of abundance and ease of lifestyle. A successful therapy business means the therapist is earning sufficiently to support her lifestyle and feel no hardship funding her office or other expenses necessary for her business to thrive.

Granted, insurance companies pay insufficiently for sessions but in time clinicians can work with more private-pay patients or have other positions and creative enterprises to offset the limited reimbursements from insurance. Success and well-being are possible in this profession, but it takes organization, imagination, and industriousness to build a viable business.

The self-effacing attitudes and business naivete result in negligence regarding therapists' entire business operations. Billing procedures are inadequate or nonexistent as exemplified in the absence of a medical billing service to assist with monthly patient statements and insurance billing. Some therapists are set up to take credit cards or PayPal as payment options; others do not have those options because they lack the bandwidth to incorporate those vehicles. I have observed a lack of infrastructure regarding accounting, as many therapists do not hire a bookkeeper to help them organize and keep tidy accounts. The clinician, lost in his own paperwork, takes valuable time away from marketing efforts, seeing patients, and accruing sustaining billable hours or having adequate time for pleasure and relaxation.

Other professional assistance may be necessary to make the business run smoothly and efficiently, such as a personal assistant. Personal assistants take on multiple tasks that free the therapist to do what he does best. Of course, help must include a technology consultant, as most of us are not sufficiently tech knowledgeable and able to repair our systems and manage all the devices, upgrades, and problems inherent in the tech world. We need to ensure we are up and running with working Internet connectivity and email, text, printer, scanner, and fax capacities as well as Skype or HIPAA-compliant telehealth platforms—all set up and working efficiently on multiple devices.

Therapists can be pathological givers and have difficulty receiving, and that propensity leads to reluctance to have assistance—they don't feel they deserve it and are reticent to spend money on these types of services. I consider this a small-world attitude—one that keeps their business in a state of contraction because they won't expand to get help that could increase their resources and enhance their business. It is a revolving door that keeps the clinician from taking his business to the next level.

Define Your Approach

It is most important to clearly define and design your approach and services so you can take a coherent package to market. There are many excellent professional therapists in the competitive marketplace, so it is important to define and clarify your particular services. That delineation of your approach and services brings us back to a problematic point I made earlier—that there is a minimum of clinical training in graduate school. Unless you take extra postgraduate training from an institute of applied clinical theory and practice in a specific modality, you likely lack a coherent clinical approach. All licensed mental health professionals have continuing education requirements, and classes are offered in a class setting or online in every topic. These are interesting and useful yet can result in a potpourri of approaches that are tried on for a time and likely dropped in the wastebasket. Learning and mastering one clearly defined method is rare for the average clinician. That leads to eclectic approaches that at times leave the therapist without clear direction or an orientation that grounds her and therefore the patient.

As you go to market your services it is an excellent exercise to define your style and approach and formalize what it is you do. Think about your target audience, the people you hope to serve, and the problems they have. You understand their struggles; can you define those struggles and what you provide that can help? The individuals looking for help need to know that your approach is clear and you can guide them.

What do you offer that is different? Define your services, your method, and define it with pizzazz. What differentiates the way you work from other clinicians? What is your set of offered services? Are you an expert in family or couple therapy, divorcing families, and conflict resolution? Are you trained as a group leader and provide groups for a variety of subpopulations? Do you have a specialty in transgender issues or the LGBT population? Are you an artistic type with skills in guided imagery, art therapy, relaxation MP3s, or other expressive arts? Are you an excellent business coach that can offer services to executives and managers? Clarify your services.

Expand Your Creative Options

Part of a successful therapy business is expanding the creative options of a practice. So alongside one-on-one therapy there might be other modalities offered. I encourage professionals to embark on other modalities to create diversification. Some of these options might be all- or half-day workshops on a variety of themes. Many therapists have other interests and skills such as fine art, music, dance, or physical practices such as yoga or tai chi. These skills can become focal points along with therapeutic exercises for an all-day workshop or retreat. Creating workshops is interesting and gives individuals with whom you work additional venues of development. The therapist can lead an ongoing weekly group that provides an opportunity for patients to meet and develop their relational and communication skills.

I started two groups for some of my patients that have lasted 25 years and are still going strong. The groups practice relational skills of honest communication and directness, in a supportive, stable, and consistent context—and has helped all the participants over many years. A community is formed that supports the process of therapeutic growth and connection.

Utilize your individuality as a therapist and create your own workshops, groups, and events. If you like art, bring that modality in and create a workshop with that aspect as part of it. If you like to dance, include movement in a group or a workshop. There are many additional skill sets—guided imagery, art therapy, meditation and mindfulness, poetry writing—that can be included as part of the therapeutic process and enhance the therapist's career path.

Marketing Ideas

I suggest creating a brochure to help you formalize your services and approach. That can be your first coherent marketing material, along with business cards or other paper products in the form of mailers, flyers, and advertising postcards. As you work on these products you create your own *brand* with colors and a style that suits you. You feel equipped to take your show on the road and your approach and services are clearly presented and enticing. You can place these in your waiting room for patients to take and pass on to others.

There are a few other basics needed for your therapy practice to thrive. I am not including all the mandates from your board or your state and local governmental agencies but am addressing the business aspects of setting up shop. You will need a website that represents you and gives all the information needed for patients to find you. Make sure your site is optimized so it isn't lost at the very bottom of the list of all the therapists in your locale and in your area of expertise. This step can be easier once you have defined your approach and services and have created a brochure that defines the look and feel you want.

Then working with a web designer can help get you online with a desirable website and help with optimization. We are not experts in web development, and having an expert to help you build a website and another to assist you in an organized marketing campaign can take away pressure. Check out my website: OrgnonomicTherapy.com. My site has morphed over the years since I started my business.

Assistance saves you time so you do what you most enjoy and earn money doing it. Possibly your personal assistant might help you in day-to-day tasks and help you put together materials for a workshop or ongoing seminar or group. An assistant can help you set up a database so you can do online newsletters and blogs or send out information on your next event. A database compiled over years of practice is a helpful tool so that you keep track of all your patients and interested participants. Of course, you always need to ask permission to put them on your database. Anyone can unsubscribe if he chooses.

If you don't have someone to help you with marketing, then take online marketing seminars on the topic and learn the basics so you can implement a consistent marketing program. Allow time in your weekly schedule to think creatively and put marketing efforts in place.

Join your local professional organization, put up a profile, post on the listserve for members, and advertise your programs, and use it for referral posts if you have a patient you need to refer. Consider joining your state and national professional organizations and create professional profiles for each. Check out your local Chamber of Commerce and other business networking groups. There are online professional network groups like LinkedIn where you can post your profile.

There are many online therapist referral sites such as Psychology Today where you can list your professional profile. Remember to update and expand it regularly. You can set up a professional page on Facebook and an account on Twitter. Remember to watch your privacy settings if you have a personal page as therapists need to keep track of their personal online presence and guard against personal exposure. There are multiple social media sites if you want to attract a following.

Seek out other professionals and get to know them, such as physicians, nurses, other therapists, school counselors, teachers, and others in your community. Meet with them, bring your materials, and let them know what you do—become their go-to referral source.

Enjoy the business aspect of your practice as it is a creative avenue, and it sources interesting patients and participants and results in abundant resources to source your life. You need regular vacations to offset the committed aspects of our profession—we are booked hourly most days with little breathing room in between. Create ample resources for wonderful, restful, and interesting vacations. Consider the business aspect as part of your healthy activation and engagement in the world. You are taking care of yourself when you put yourself out and enhance your avenues for success.

Your Crib Sheet

- Model healthy self-regulation: Work comfortable hours, exercise, socialize, and take regularly scheduled vacations—have fun!
- Stay healthy by investing in ongoing personal therapy.
- Value yourself by charging accordingly and thrive.
- Organize your business so you are not a paper pusher. Incorporate a medical billing service, bookkeeper, technology consultant, marketing expert, and personal assistant.
- Establish an up-to-date infrastructure.
- Elegantly define your approach and services.
- Expand your options by creating multiple modalities.
- Market your method and modalities with pizzazz across multiple platforms, including but not limited to paper products, paid advertising, social media, professional networking, and lecture circuit.
- Set up an ongoing database of participants and contacts.
- Join your local association and online referral sources.
- Imagine, persist, and enjoy your efforts!

Part VI
Psyche to Soma

14 Mind Meets Body

From Character Analysis to Somatic Interventions

As mental health professionals, why not work with the body directly? Why not expand treatment beyond a strictly verbal analytic therapy model, as we increasingly realize the importance of body-mind components that factor into the etiology of physical disease, stress-related symptoms, and capacity to heal? I hope to engage you in these questions and provide answers. I am incredulous that the vast majority of analysts never engage the patient's body in the process, likely because somatic interventions are rarely taught in a methodical way that is congruent with theoretical principles of analysis. With verbal therapies, the mind and emotions are engaged but not the body, therefore the mind-body split continues. The alchemical image of the Ouroboros symbolizes coming full circle—Part VI, Psyche to Soma, brings the reader back to the beginning of the book, to Reich's conceptual material outlined in Chapters 1 and 2 that define the basics of Reich's innovative model of mind-body treatment. Orgonomy embraces health with a functional mind-body approach that helps patients access their naturally abundant free flowing energy, and couples it with capacity for lively contact and clarity of perception in an unarmored body. This approach is distinguished from other therapies by its energetic concept of functioning. When there is blockage in our mind and body, our capacity to function at our fullest is limited by both aspects. Our physicality is part and parcel of the health equation.

After 40 years in private practice, it is apparent to me that impressive and powerful mind-body alterations result from engaging the patient's body in the treatment.

> Greg, a 35-year-old man, came to therapy with a pale face and a wide-eyed frozen expression. He was challenged by chronic fearfulness, confusion, constant ruminative thinking with difficulties functioning in the realms of career and relationship. His body was thin and lacked suppleness and strength. Although likeable and intelligent, he was so frozen in fear that he felt inadequate and not up to the task of generating a successful life. Greg was a schizophrenic character type, and his body and mind

lacked cohesion and muscular strength. His eyes reflected frozenness, like a deer in-the-headlights, and he suffered from long-standing confusion accompanied by moodiness and crying jags. Alongside working with his character verbally, I initiated the biophysical work. As he settled onto the couch I asked him to breathe. His breath was shallow and his chest barely moved; there was some belly breathing with a subtle rise and fall. Encouraging him to breathe and sigh began to change how he related to breathing and created a slight expansion as he learned to breathe more fully and fluidly. That is a goal of Orgonomic therapy—to teach the patient to breathe more naturally over time. This allows an increase in energy as the body is oxygenated. I pressed on his chest as he exhaled to increase the range of motion in his chest and encouraged deeper breaths. With chronic fear accompanied by tension in all areas, the capacity to breathe is limited, as the chest, ribs, back, diaphragm, and belly are taut and inflexible. (See Figure 14.1 for a photo of bodywork with a patient.)

After encouraging expanded breathing, I focused my attention initially on his head tension, his frightened eyes, and the cervical tension that inhibited his vocal range. He had a pinched, tight throat that resulted in a soft-spoken, gravelly voice that sounded as if he was being strangled. I massaged his tight neck muscles vigorously and worked the SCM (sternocleidomastoid) muscles to loosen his throat. I asked him to make sounds as I worked his throat and encouraged his vocal expression through exercises. I deeply pressed on his cranium to loosen the holding and head tension that resulted in chronic headaches and constant ruminative thinking, resulting in a tight bolus of confusion. By releasing tension in his head, he could relax and his thinking slowed down in session. I helped Greg relax his frozen eyes with eye rolls, expanding

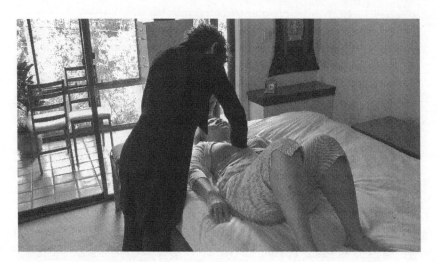

Figure 14.1 Bodywork Session with a Patient

the radius as he made steady eye circles while looking at a penlight or my finger. I encouraged him to have a loose jaw and soft lips so he could make sounds—a challenging request, but nonetheless he tried and made more and more sound over time. With the release of his cranium tension, more mobile eyes, release of his tight jaw and neck tension, and increased breath with a relaxed chest, he began to feel more alive in his body, less frozen, and therefore less scared. He was able to make sounds to express his fear. Sadness and rage surfaced. The more he felt and expressed, the more his body relaxed and began to cohere. We worked to loosen his diaphragm and relax his abdomen, and I encouraged vigorous kicking so he could feel stronger in his legs. Greg gained weight, and with his newfound enjoyment of working out he gained muscle mass and looked healthy for the first time.

He gained confidence as his body became a vehicle for breath and expression; he enjoyed pounding his arms and expressing anger with angry eyes. Greg could feel his power, and this manifested in a new career and a healthy relationship with a woman as he went forward without debilitating fear.

Our lifelong memories are housed in our body; our physical structure reflects our genetics and our historical experiences. Our bodies are templates carved out of life situations and events. Many aspects of our physical health in maturity are directly related to our early psychological history. There are numerous studies documenting the long-term physiological effects of stress in childhood. A study cited in *The New York Times* shows that early stress may be linked to hardening of the arteries in adulthood. Finnish researchers studied 12- to 18-year-olds across many social, emotional, economic, and stress measures within the family and again at ages 40 to 46, measuring coronary artery calcification. Controlling for other contributing causes, the research found that "the higher the childhood stress score, the greater the risk for coronary artery calcification" (Bakalar, 2016). Orgonomy addresses the historic stress embedded in all physical systems and creates a vehicle so that the material can be psychologically and biophysically metabolized and released.

With the Orgonomic biophysical treatment modality, the body is mobilized as a vehicle of expression for deeply held emotions. With strictly verbal work, the physical expression is contained and inhibited by a seated upright position that relies exclusively on cognitive and verbal communications—leaving the defenses more intact. Many patients have difficulty expressing feelings—they have never cried as adults even when they desperately wanted and needed to. Others were warned not to raise their voices or get angry, and that inhibition has had deleterious effects on their own ability to be assertive and communicate openly in relationships. When patients experience biophysical work on the couch and are given permission and instructions to express emotions new and old, they feel liberated. Their awareness of self and what has occurred in their lifetime grows from the inside out. They experience deep release and relief as their physical tension and contraction give way to energetic movement and expansion. As Reich states, the natural state of the organism is pulsation—expansion and contraction. The natural healthy pulsation is reinstated through consistent sessions of bodywork. As constriction, tension, and blockages are released through expression of real feeling coupled with physical movements, the body can let go and patients may experience pleasurable streamings (energetic waves from head to toe) and deep relaxation that become integrated into their nervous system.

Historically, our survival depended on developing a coping style that resulted in the least amount of adversity; the character structure embeds in the psyche and becomes the individualized defensive style of the patient. That same defensive structure is the organizing template for all bodily processes and felt physical experiences of the patient. "Body armor" is the way character armor is expressed in the body—impacting the respiratory, nervous, hormonal, immune, circulatory, organ, and reproductive systems and the flexibility or rigidity and strength of the musculoskeletal system. Body armor affects all elements of basic functioning—sexual responsiveness and performance, digestion, elimination, and sleep regulation—and results in our felt sense of health. Our body-mind is one, and we can create improvement by working directly with both parts. Unfortunately, the majority of mental health therapies do not approach this obvious relationship. Focusing just on talk therapy leaves half of the equation ignored.

When we intervene directly with the body we reinstate natural breathing, unwind and release bound muscular tensions, and undo chronic blocks to the free flow of energy within the system. Most importantly, we realign the autonomic nervous system (ANS) so the sympathetic part of the ANS (stimulating activities of fight, flight, or freeze responses) balances with the parasympathetic functions (what *Wikipedia* calls "rest-and-digest" and "feed and breed" relaxation responses; "Science," n.d.). By balancing the ANS, which regulates the body's unconscious responses, we can gradually lower chronic stress reactions, resulting in reduced inflammation and overall better health. The ANS is an example of expansive and contractive systems within the body. As we impact the ANS therapeutically, we reinstate a balanced pulsation between the two parts of the nervous system that directly impact the functioning of the entire body. We are changing a patient's approach to life at its root—how the patient exists within his body-mind.

Many patients suffer from a variety of symptoms that emanate from the lack of balanced expansion and contraction—pulsation in the body. They might feel edgy and irritable; suffer daily feelings of low energy, exhaustion, and fatigue; experience numbness, deadness, and lack of vitality; endure chronic pain in their gut with chronic bowel problems, or have pain in their joints, muscles, or head, and/or have endless back pain; have respiratory symptoms like asthma; and have chronic sleep problems. By balancing the ANS to allow for a natural pulsation, expansion, and contraction, the system can relax and unwind rather than sustain a state of contraction, tension, and hypervigilance—and many chronic symptoms naturally get better.

The application of this method is quite precise, with a detailed protocol and contraindications. It necessitates an organized study of medicine and functional medicine. I am not recommending incorporation of these techniques nor am I giving explicit instructions on how to do this method; I am not suggesting the therapist immediately add this technique to his tool kit. My goal is to introduce you to the method with the hope that you will want to learn more about how to apply it. This chapter is an overview that will stimulate your appetite to study and ultimately add this component to your practice. Understanding the theory and its delineation of segmental armoring gives you something to work with in verbal work and helps you diagnose character—as your capacity to observe and translate what you see about the patient's visible biophysical expression will elevate your skills of differential diagnoses of character structure.

If the patient still resides in his "old" body with its chronic conditioning, he still lives in an armored body—his growth potential is limited. When we help patients loosen their breath, unwind their bound-up systems, and increase their available energetic flow, new behavioral coping strategies can be created. Sexual health can be improved as the patient overcomes difficulties relationally and in sexual performance due to various psychological and biophysical limitations.

The therapeutic relationship has been built carefully through verbal exchange and that continues unabated. Biophysical work is an additional component of therapeutic activity utilized if and when appropriate to an individual's course of treatment. It necessitates some changes in the format of the session. For the biophysical part of the session, the patient moves from a chair opposite the therapist to a couch where he can stretch out on his back, with the therapist seated on the side or standing up in order to give the patient directions. The therapist offers help increasing breathing capacity and applies hands-on pressure to various places of armoring.

The patient is always encouraged to focus on her breathing and learns to breathe fully and more naturally. Breathing fully has significant impact on the patient's health and well-being. Patients with shallow breathing learn to habitually breath more fully and expand their ribcage in all directions to allow for more breath. I encourage the patient to be aware of her back body, breathing into her back ribs and spine, back of the head, neck, and legs. We tend to focus more on the front side of our body, and our backside can lose suppleness and resiliency through chronic sitting and lying down. Guide your patient to focus the breath internally—with subtlety—so he can visualize breathing into all of his tissues and cells and bring breath into the many places in his body normally ignored. The patient is encouraged to release feelings through physical expressions and sounds such as kicking, pounding her fists on the couch, reaching her arms in longing, squeezing or biting a towel as he yells with anger or excitement or makes sounds of frustration, screams in fear or rage, sobs or cries with grief and sorrow, and any other sounds that express pent-up inner feeling.

Patients feel enormous relief as they develop a new sense of freedom of expression and release long-held feelings as they recapture archaic memories. They experience a growing capacity to deeply relax afterward as their parasympathetic system robustly activates the relaxation response and they learn to give in. They become able to express their strength and power as well as give in to vulnerability. The energy flows throughout the body rather than remain blocked (trapped) in the head, chest, diaphragm, or abdomen, which prevents a flow (streaming) to the pelvis and limbs (Frisch, May 15, 2016, blog, "Psyche and Soma").

Application to Traditional Verbal Analysis

First, every patient is unique. Some patients are uncomfortable with the idea of bodywork and will never entertain this modality. That is a fine outcome for many patients, as through character analysis, defenses are broken down and some body armor dissolves naturally as character defenses and their accompanying physical manifestations are dissolved. Stresses are diminished and healthier lifestyle choices are instituted and patients feel better. Expressing important issues in verbal work has an all-encompassing life-affirming and biophysically healing effect as the patient shares his significant and privately held worries and feels supported in myriad ways by the therapist.

As you work with patients verbally, you must be cognizant of what is called "body language" and can utilize your observations, resulting in a type of somatic intervention. If you comment on the style of a female patient who slouches on your couch and disappears into the pillows, the patient can think about what her body language communicates and begin making alterations, including finding her backbone, breathing deeply to energize her system, and doing exercise outside of therapy that will help her get stronger, more assertive, and less collapsed.

If a patient communicates in a squeaky-voiced childish way with immature gestures or an overly smiling cheerful need-to-please manner, the therapist can note those qualities, and that feedback will encourage psychological and somatic changes. The patient's face can relax its constant smile, the tight throat can loosen, and she can relax her compulsive gesturing. A patient may twist her body up into a knot as she tightly crosses her legs and contracts herself into a straw-like form. She can learn to expand her body, loosen her legs, and breathe in a fuller fashion while discovering the roots of her contracted body posture. Notice body language and work with these aspects directly— breath, posture, gestures, pallor of skin, facial tension, eye contact, mouth and jaw holding. Notice and work with all visual clues such as personal grooming habits, the patient's body language, and appearance. Notice whether the face and body seem depressed, sullen, frozen, or anxiously hypervigilant. Notice if the patient repeatedly closes his eyes, avoiding contact with the world, or if his eyes are wide with a look of alarm. Ask the patient to move his eyes and relax them, or look at you and away from you so his expression does not freeze up.

In verbal analysis, the therapist can encourage deeper breathing and suggest ways of expression that encourage more expression of real feeling. Ask your patient to raise his vocal tone and express the feelings of anger rather than swallowing or choking back his expression with a subdued tone or a gravelly or squeaky voice reflecting a tight throat. You can demonstrate an angry response for the patient with a loud voice: "I hate when he talks to me that way; it pisses me off!" Then ask the patient to do his version with an angry, animated voice.

Help the patient give in to sobbing by asking her to make sounds as she cries rather than whimpering silently. Encourage a patient to make a sound of frustration and relax his mouth rather than squeeze his lips together so tightly that his jaw quivers with tension. Make home assignments like taking a run or walk when agitated, punching a pillow to allow pent-up energy to release; yelling in the car or the shower are also helpful suggestions. Yelling into a pillow at home can give relief to an overwrought patient. Encourage mobilizing the face by making faces that move every part—ask the patient to lift her forehead up and down, open his jaw wide and close it repeatedly until it loosens, and gently massage her cheeks. Show your patient how to do shoulder rolls and add it to his daily routine. Breathing with an audible sigh, stomping feet when walking if angry, and shadow boxing are ways that the patient can work with his body and add to the successful outcome of therapy. Ask your patients to buy foam rollers and other tools so they can roll out their tight muscles in the back, legs, neck, and shoulders using small balls and long and short rollers. This activity helps patients engage with their bodies and release tissue and musculoskeletal pain on their own. The tissues in the body hold exquisite tenderness and pain caused by the loss of elasticity in the tiny filaments and fibers. These more rigidified fibers build up toxins and fluids that result in increased sensitivity. Stretching, cardio exercise, yoga, strength training, rolling out, massage, and emotional expression can help ameliorate pain in tissues, muscles, and joints.

Encourage your patient to become aware of his breathing patterns, when he is holding his breath, and ask the patient to breathe more freely. Sometimes that is impossible as there is too much armoring in the chest and the ribs; the pectoral muscles of the thoracic are constricted, and the intercostal muscles between the ribs are too taut and don't allow for flexibility of the chest in response to the inhale and exhale.

Regular rigorous exercise encourages expanded breathing and blood blow, particularly to the brain. Weekly vigorous exercise creates aliveness in the body-mind. In fact, a study quoted in *The New York Times* states that if one takes a weeklong break from his cardio routine, blood flow to the brain becomes diminished. Blow flow to the brain aids our cognitive and emotional stability and creates new neurons and synapses and increased brain volume in areas related to higher-level thinking (Reynolds, 2016).

Suggest relaxation techniques. At bedtime allow the body to take up space, legs apart, arms apart, mouth slightly open, tummy relaxed with a felt sense of the breath expanding the abdomen as the chest relaxes with a light breath. The patient can put her warm hand on her belly to make contact. Suggest the patient visualize a comforting image such as a babbling brook or a gentle land-scape that gives her a sense of peace and comfort. Relaxation of the body-mind is hard to come by in our busy, digital world and it needs to be cultivated. The therapist can encourage ease and time without activity, gentle walks not for exercise, contemplative periods of silence to allow the nervous system to rest. This emphasis helps to reinstate the relaxation response necessary to health.

When to Start Biophysical Interventions

Many patients come to me because they want a mind-body approach. If a patient is open to including the biophysical component, bodywork can start once the relationship is firmly established. All the preliminary steps noted in prior chapters must be completed and firmly in place: an intact therapeutic frame, thorough history-taking, acting-out behaviors reduced to a minimum, basic trust established, and firm commitment to consistent sessions. Usually these accomplishments are completed by the middle to the end of the first stage of therapy. At this juncture biophysical work can be initiated.

Map of Body Armor

Orgnomic bodywork is a comprehensive system with a specific method. This organized approach pairs character analysis with bodywork, which distin-guishes it from other types of somatic work. Character types represent pat-terns of character armoring. Body armor is defined by areas of blockage in a sequential yet interdependent fashion from the head down to the lower limbs, described as segments. Character typology is correlated with various patterns of body armor or blockages. Each segment is worked independently yet some segments do not give way until others are freed. As the body is habituated to its chronic conditioning, sustained mobility is challenging, as the body natu-rally returns to its immobilized state.

The patient lies on his back on a flat elevated single or double mattress covered with a sheet, similar to the height of a massage table. He wears com-fortable, loose clothing—shorts and a T-shirt or yoga clothes. We ask the patient to bend his knees with the flat of his feet on the couch to facilitate an unrestricted pelvis. We ask the patient to breathe with his mouth open, not through his nose. We ask the patient to inhale deeply and exhale fully. As the patient breathes, he is asked to sigh with an audible exhale to keep his throat open with the sound.

Bodywork is initiated by encouraging an expanded natural breathing func-tion; in most patients the breathing function is inhibited. Breathing builds a charge of energy in the system that facilitates the work. As the patient breathes, the therapist notices places of constriction that block the free flow of energy. Applied pressure on the spastic muscles helps increase the contraction in the muscle until it can no longer hold and relaxes. With continued breathing and applied pressure on areas of armoring, the body begins to experience sensations that may stimulate feelings and memories. Armored segments reflect areas of constriction that originated in inhibited impulses. If a patient felt "weak" and "ashamed," if and when he cried, then he likely, early on, armored in the ocular segment causing chronic dryness in his eyes and tightly squeezed lids. His face would show signs of armoring in his frozen cheeks, tightly clenched jaw, and clinched throat. No sobs can get through that constricted maze. The therapist may communicate just the resonant sentence that might open up the patient's feelings, or the therapist may suggest an expressive exercise to help facilitate the progression of the session. The verbal work that started the session may provide fodder for what happens on the couch.

Imagine a map of a vertically upright individual with horizontal bands that define seven sections called segments from the top of the head to the feet (see Figure 14.2). The first is the *ocular segment* comprised of the eyes and eyelids, muscles surrounding the eyes, the forehead, and muscles at the base of the occipital region of the head including the brain. The second is the *oral segment* comprised of the mouth, chin, and jaw. The third is the *cervical segment* that includes the neck muscles and sternocleidomastoids. The chest and arms make up the fourth, the *thoracic segment*, including the intercostal muscles, chest, and its contents (heart and lungs); arms (all arm muscles); and hands. The fifth is the *diaphragmatic segment* including the stomach, solar

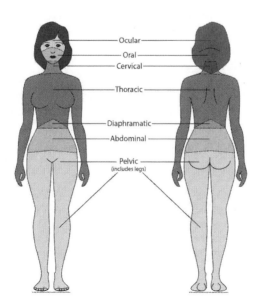

Figure 14.2 The Seven Segments of the Body

Source: Adapted from *Man in the Trap*, Elsworth F. Baker, MD, 1967.

plexus, pancreas, liver, gall bladder, kidneys, and muscles along the lower thoracic vertebrae. The sixth is the *abdominal segment*, which includes the large abdominal muscles and the muscles of the back and sides. The seventh and last segment is the *pelvic segment* comprised of all muscles of the pelvis, gluteal muscles, legs, and anus. This is our map generally defined. Predominant areas of armoring can be correlated to a specific character type. Let's discuss segmental armoring as it correlates to character types by looking at specific cases (Baker, 1967, 48–61). Please reference the diagram of the segments inspired by Elsworth Baker (Baker, 1967 42–43).

Segmental Armoring and Interventions According to Character Types

Ocular and Cervical Segment

Most patients, regardless of character type, have some ocular blocking. In the course of treatment attention must be paid to the patient's eyes to help clear ocular armoring. We learn early to close our eyes to harsh realities, squint when we feel fear or suspicion, avoid eye contact with a shifty expression when we are nervous, look down when we feel embarrassed or ashamed. These habitual patterns become chronically embedded, to some extent, in all patients and are improved upon as the patient becomes healthy.

Patients with significant eye (ocular) blocks often manifest a lack of direct eye contact usually described in a variety of ways—furtive eyes; a tendency to close their eyes; a filmy, glazed look; a distant expression; or eyes described as small and beady. Dominant eye blocks lead to symptoms expressive of distortion in viewpoint. Chronic fear, distrust, suspicion, and paranoia are a result of seeing reality through a distorted lens. Often this character type avoids others as others are seen as threatening. I am discussing a schizophrenic or a paranoid type described previously. As his major block is in his eyes, the head captures most of the energy, with the brain existing in a state of contraction with minimal expansive capacity. Energy does not flow with vitality to the rest of the body. Many schizophrenics have a diffuse, slack body type meaning there is not much muscle tone, yet there is a lack of bodily sensation due to severe armoring in the cranial area. When they are seated on your sofa, their bodies appear spread out, without coherence, and can appear saggy and limp as opposed to rigid and strongly put together. Other schizophrenics have a toned, cohered body type yet the body is rigid or numb due to too much energy locked in head and eyes. Their bodies may appear supple and robust but they have little perception of sensation.

> Asha, a 27-year-old woman, is from an immigrant East Indian family. I diagnosed her as a schizophrenic type who lives well below her potential functional capacity. She experienced high anxiety and pervasive fear most of her life. She had difficulty with launch phase markers, did not

leave home, never decided on a career path, had limited relationships with friends or lovers, and spent most of her time with family or alone when she wasn't working at a job that was below her capacity. Her dominant segment of armoring was her eyes and reflected her chronic fear and anxiety, suspiciousness, and paranoid interpretations of others. She came from a family that prized the importance of the family unit over independence. Asha's mom was paranoid and Asha learned to defer to her, rather than think for herself. Therapy was challenging, as she felt guilty whenever she was critical of her family. Yet she was filled with constant frustration at the limits they still placed on her. After working a year in strictly verbal work to encourage her separation and autonomy from the family, she moved out of the family home and began a more independent life. It is better to initiate bodywork when the circumstances are more conducive to arousal of deeper and more intense feelings and realizations. Had she still been living at home, she would have felt suffocated by the family style of enmeshment and would have been in constant conflict with her newly emerging feelings.

I began by encouraging her to breathe more robustly. Her breath was extremely shallow with barely a noticeable rise and fall of her chest when she was on her back. Next, I focused on her ocular segment—asking her to move her eyes in a circular fashion, reaching the full circumference of her eye, so she could stretch her eye muscles, which were quite constricted. I loosened the tight muscles at the base of her skull-occipital region, to release occipital tension and help loosen her eyes. I also directed her to shift her eyes quickly from side to side, corner to corner while asking her to feel her distrust aroused by that movement. I encouraged Asha to scream into a towel in fear after she did the eye-shifting exercise. Sometimes that exercise aroused anger as she experienced the depth of her distrust. The ocular exercises were helpful in clearing and mobilizing her eyes, thus helping her perceptive capacities. Paranoid distortions subsided as we worked with various emotional expressions in her eyes. I encouraged her to yell with fear, the dominant feeling for schizophrenic types. She would open her eyes wide, as directed, and scream with fear into a towel. Over time those expressions of fear relieved her chronic anxiety. I had her look directly at my eyes and express anger at me through her eyes with an angry mouth and pound and yell. At first this was difficult; she couldn't do it. It was disrespectful to look with angry eyes at someone she respected. With time Asha was able to look at me with a hateful expression and yell; she felt so free after that experience. Then she could yell with anger and frustration while pounding her fists as her eyes were now clear and could express her authentic feelings.

Schizophrenics have a dominant throat or cervical block and their vocal expressions are muted and sound gravelly and pinched due to their constricted throat and neck. When I pressed into the side muscles of her throat and neck, it was painful as the muscles were taut and tight. This is not massage but rather a technique that penetrates deeply into specific armored muscles to help release holding. Digging my knuckles into the SCM muscle helped loosen the chronic constriction and free her voice. Asha had never ever yelled—giving her permission and physical capacity to yell and shout with anger and frustration was a refreshing experience for her. This translated to more assertiveness in her life; she had her voice for the first time. As I worked the upper segments—eyes, cranium muscles, jaw, neck, and throat—she had much more energy as her upper armoring was loosened and the energy contracted in those areas was freed and could move down her body. We worked constantly on keeping her breath full, which also increased her energy level. She had been prone to chronic headaches due to the accumulated tension in the muscles surrounding her head; her headaches disappeared within the first months of bodywork. Through opening up her expressions, her body became less tense and more fluid. She was able to translate her new qualities into action; free to demand what she wanted, to express her needs with her family by speaking out and moving from a paranoid state to one of clear perception. She could feel more authentic feelings and those guided her to new career directions. She also felt yearnings for a relationship for the first time.

Oral Segment

Oral segment armoring is common in all character types: either oral repressed or oral unsatisfied. In cases of depression, the oral block is repressed. The chronic depressive type frequently presents with a tight thin-lipped mouth, as he holds back oral longing for love and nurturance and suffers from enduring sadness. Depressives are often in the role of a caretaker, doing for others what they so desperately want. The depressive loses his vital energy due to his depressive character acted out in self-sacrifice. He does not sustain the energetic stance of a phallic narcissistic type. The depressive condition is partially the result of an oral repressed block that doesn't let him take in resources—a closed rather than open mouth in all situations.

Depression is a stasis of energy movement in the organism; not enough resources of any kind come in or go out. Chronic depression, a debilitating condition, is circular, as the stasis energetically breeds more depression. That is why studies show the ameliorative effects of a regular exercise program along with therapy on depressive symptoms. We treat stubborn depressions effectively with Orgonomic techniques. Activating anger and rage that comes from significant deprivation is helpful as well as mobilizing and releasing sadness that is unexpressed yet experienced as depression. The patient's energetic capacities are mobilized with biophysical interventions.

Remember my patient Allen, the fiction writer, a chronic depressive. Biophysical work helped him unlock his anger, which usually seethed under the surface due to a large stack of stored resentments. He would give to others generously, cook for them, lend them money, and listen tirelessly to their problems while secretly harboring strong resentment expressed through his tight-jawed and snarly, disgusted contemptuous attitude about others. Loosening his oral segment—his cheeks, tight jaw, and lips—allowed him to express his snarling rage with an open mouth. Biting a towel helped relieve tension in his jaw and allowed for the expression of the primary biting impulse. I applied pressure to his lower jaw as he pressed his jaw up to my hand in resistance as I directed him to feel his defiance. This releases defiant feelings consciously.

Releasing angry expressions resulted in dissolution of oral armor, and his mouth could soften, open, and express his needy feelings rather than defending against vulnerability with a clenched jaw and tight lips. Softening his mouth allowed him to express hidden disappointment and feelings of despair that resulted in his chronically depressed state. We worked through his anger, rage, and past grief, and he was now receptive to engaging healthy others and established an intimate relationship founded on his new-found entitlement. Allen also felt inspired to write industriously and publish his novel. His collapsed chest was mobilized through deep penetration into his tight thoracic and back muscles, allowing him to breathe fully and sustain a higher energy level, thus combating depressive stasis.

Depressives breathe shallowly, which keeps their energy level low due to faulty oxygenation. Coupled with their habit of shallow breathing, which results in a contraction of their whole system, they hide within a small, unentitled presence and are invisible; the stunted breathing leads to their inner collapse. When the therapist loosens the chest and back muscles through deep penetration, the breath becomes freer and energizes the body-mind. With Allen, I directed him to kick his legs vigorously and express strong, aggressive sounds. This helped him expand his small self through movement, sound, and assertive expression; he enjoyed the aggressive movements. As chronic depressives habitually contain aggression and resist their grief, biophysical interventions help them. Their life-long state of contraction is remedied by the expansive work and gives them a new sense of self as vocal, energetic, and buoyant individuals that can take up space. This antidote to psychoactive pharmaceuticals can benefit many patients. Some patients definitely require the support of medications that can be very helpful for short durations—bodywork is another method that helps activate the system and reduce depressive symptoms. Reliance on pharmaceuticals can be a problematic. The medication cocktail may create confusion as to what is really going on.

The increased breathing function helps all patients. Throughout our lives we learn to hold our breath due to habitual tension and end up with a stiff immobile chest that doesn't give in to softness and vulnerability. Also our diminished breath lowers our energy level. Encouraging and facilitating healthy breathing capacity is a basic goal of this method. One of the first places we armor as babies, after the eyes, is the chest, resulting in a reduction in our capacity to breathe naturally.

Encourage your patients to breathe freely, in a relaxed manner, and enjoy breathing in all circumstances. Slow, relaxed breathing when stressed helps the body-mind be at ease and reduces the tendency to overreact and respond with habitual stress patterns that result in illness. Rapid breathing increases our fight, flight, and freeze responses that cause relentless release of stress hormones as the nervous system is signaled to respond with fear and alarm. When we slow our breathing down through deep breaths, we consciously create an internal sense of mastery over a variety of situations. Healthy breathing is a sign of health and contributes to our overall sense of well-being.

Oral unsatisfied types tend toward overeating, substance abuse, hoarding, and retail therapy—life is a constant endeavor to keep themselves filled. They smoke, talk obsessively, drink too much, gamble, and constantly consume anything and everything.

> Sasha, age 30, suffered with this syndrome and had fought her weight since childhood. She loved to eat and drink and at times she binged, usually at night after work, with chips and guacamole accompanied by a number of glasses of white wine. She was a successful director in a large corporation, but her oral compulsions were symptomatic of larger problems that included pervasive anxiety and insomnia. She would wake in the middle of the night and snack. She smiled incessantly, chattered nonstop, and used humor to hide her pain and self-consciousness about her body. She often felt inferior as well as guilty, as she described herself as "lazy" because she refused to exercise regularly. I diagnosed her a hysteric with an oral unsatisfied block. She was mentally healthy in many areas—self-activated, independent, energetic, capable of expressing a broad array of feelings— and was not plagued with self-hate. Her defensive "running" with food and alcohol and away from intimacy through her oral preoccupations cut into establishing a lasting primary relationship. Underneath her consumptive acting-out behaviors, she was intensely anxious. Her extra weight added a layer of body armor, insulating her from her difficult feelings.
>
> Bodywork helped connect her to how anxious she was. Sasha suffered severe profound historical losses—her father died of cancer when she was nine; her mom, soon after the death of her father, became engaged to man whom Sasha did not like. There was little acknowledgment of her loss and grieving was not allowed. She felt abandoned by her dad through death and abandoned by her mom, who became preoccupied with her new husband and his kids. She longed for her deceased father and suppressed that longing through habitual overeating.
>
> Through the bodywork she was able to experience the sources of her anxiety and grieve the loss of her father with deep sobbing and wailing.

She could express her anger through kicking and pounding after I worked diligently on her oral segment, penetrating her overworked jaw and loosening her chest. Her insomnia improved, and she stopped compensating for fatigue by eating sugary foods. She was able to regulate her diet in an effective manner, inserting good habits, healthy food, and less alcohol. By breaking down her body armor and releasing the stored tensions and repressed feelings, she became capable of self-regulating and realized a steady exercise regime made her feel better. Sasha wanted to exercise to sustain her sense of increased vitality and changing body image. The concept of self-regulation was at play; as the body-mind gets healthier it naturally self-regulates rather than feeling forced to comply with mandates imposed from the outside that frequently result in rebellion.

Thoracic Segment

The phallic narcissist, known for his defensive need to attack, control, and dominate, is armored predominantly in the chest and back, although he often has a tight, angular jaw as well. He can have taut thigh muscles and rigid, muscular legs. The phallic narcissist is often described as having a military chest, inflated, "puffed up," and rigid, lacking in softness and capacity to give in and express vulnerability.

Daniel, our British successful real estate developer—described under the phallic narcissist character type—benefited greatly from biophysical interventions. He typically held to his British stiff-upper-lip, reserved style, repressing all vulnerable feelings seen as weak and unattractive and carried on at all costs. He had little access to a range of feelings and exuded the man-in-charge personae—the man in the know.

Through aggressive penetration into his tense and bulky neck and bulging chest muscles, I directed him to yell with the pressure rather than endure without a sound. This was challenging, but eventually he allowed vocal expression. To loosen his chest, I pressed vigorously into his thoracic muscles with my palms, fists, and fingers as I loosened the muscle groups. I pressed down vigorously on the thoracic cavity as he exhaled, to increase the thoracic mobility and expand the breathing. As he inhaled I released the pressure and encouraged a deep, expanded breath in; as he exhaled I pressed down again on his chest to help him deflate it thoroughly. In this way, Daniel learned to expand his breathing, both his inhale and his exhale. Also, massaging his tight back muscles helped him breathe. I use my elbow to penetrate the area between the shoulder blades and my forearm to slide along his paraspinal muscles to release the holding; those interventions can be paired with yelling.

Along with compressed breathing, Daniel had a tight-lipped oral segment, so I loosened his jaw and lips so his mouth could part and open. Working his thick, stiff, "up-tight" neck loosened his attitude of controlling dominance. As he experienced the depth of his rigidity and tension, he was motivated both psychologically and physically to dismantle it. He had symptoms early on in treatment like exhaustion, digestive complaints, and chest pain. He sought medical attention from a cardiologist and his test results were uneventful. But his symptoms were a warning that his chronic state of stress, driven-ness, and compulsivity were risky behaviors. As his nervous system recalibrated with his dissolving armor, he naturally sought a different lifestyle and scheduled time for rest and relaxation.

Abdominal Segment

Patients with abdominal armoring often have serious digestive symptoms and complaints of irritable bowel syndrome such as constipation, diarrhea, gas, bloating, pain and heartburn, or esophageal reflux. As the gut is known medically as the second brain, it has pervasive emotional sensitivities from the many neuronal receptors that communicate emotional tension and respond accordingly.

Patients with gut and other pervasive symptoms may develop an obsession with restricted eating that becomes an eating disorder. The proposed distinct eating disorder (not yet in the *DSM-5* or ICD-10), orthorexia nervosa, is characterized by excessive preoccupation with eating certain foods and not eating others that are seen as deleterious. This obsessive, compulsive fixation on diet, meal planning, and restrictive eating dominates normal life and social activities. Dining out is restricted and laden with anxiety, and eating is stripped of social pleasure, joy, and spontaneity. Meals become obsessive rituals with limited food choices coupled with serious obsessive analysis of foods, allergies, analysis of gut bacteria, low FODMAP diets, and other esoteric meal plans.

(That said, gut flora or the microbiome of the gut may aggravate or have a role in susceptibility to various diseases. Awareness of this aspect of health and disease can contribute to healthy eating and is important to consider. A balanced condition of microbes, without some microbes growing abnormally, does help ensure a healthier gut. Our awareness of the value of fermented foods is increasing.)

I recommend directly confronting obsessional patterns and preoccupation with food restrictions rather than validating them or being passive with this content. Help your patient understand that this particular way of controlling her life and pleasurable activities is damaging and off-point. She is over-managing her eating habits as a way to cope with deep, underlying fears and anger that she is not facing directly. Like the somatic syndromes listed earlier, patients replace emotional insight and change with preoccupation with physical symptoms and become obsessed with manipulating their bodies—what goes in and what comes out.

> Allison, age 55, had a lifelong struggle with gut symptoms. She watches her diet to make sure she eats lightly, spacing out meals with careful selections—eliminating allergenic foods such as gluten and dairy products. But these

attempts have not changed her syndrome. She comes from a family where arguing dominated the family environment. Her mother was a relentless critic and was jealous of her daughter and sabotaged her daughter's efforts to become independent. Her father was kind but passive and dominated by his wife. Allison had an early eating disorder, anorexia, which she finally conquered in her late 20s, but her chronic gut tension remained. She lives in a chronic state of fear and alarm with a felt sense of urgency that consistently impacts her gut and floods it with stress hormones, while inhibiting the parasympathetic relaxation responses necessary for proper digestion and elimination. This pattern burdens the system with chronic constipation, bloating, gas, and pain. With thorough work on the upper segments we could proceed to working on her abdominal armoring. With light touch on the muscles of her belly, and consistent tummy massage, she could experience relaxation of the abdominal wall. Deep belly breathing helped to calm her "tummy nerves." I recommended she apply a heating pad at home at night to give her a sense of security and ease through the felt sensations of warmth. When we have a chronic "nervous stomach," we tend to house our anxiety in the gut. As Allison faced into the sources of her anxiety, she was able to soften her gut and feel the emotions psychologically rather than through digestive symptoms. When she felt growing ease with herself, her symptoms subsided.

Often the gut houses deep sadness and sorrow; allowing sobbing that emanates from the gut rather than the throat and chest helps the belly release its holding and resulting pain. Vigorous kicking helps the belly express aggressive emotions. Even though kicking is an approach to releasing the pelvic area, it is an exercise utilized throughout work on the upper segments. Kicking unlocks energy stuck in the head with compulsive rumination, helps clear the eyes of tension and the filmy quality that blocks vision, increases breathing, and allows the body as a whole to move, give in to verbal sounds, drop the control; in general, kicking has an overall beneficial effect.

Somatic Symptom Disorder/Somatization Syndrome

Patients with chronic pain and a multitude of roving symptoms frequent our practices and medical offices, frustrating physicians as they realize many of the symptoms are psychologically induced, but they do not have the time or expertise to resolve complicated psychological issues. Sometimes the patient cannot express conflicts in any other way except through bodily symptoms.

Cindy, age 31, a single woman with a master's degree in English literature, entered treatment with a myriad of symptoms. She had chronic headaches, severe PMS, allergies to gluten and dairy, digestive complaints, muscle aches, joint pain, fatigue, anxiety, difficulty concentrating, constant rumination, and sleep problems. She was lightly armored, meaning she did not carry bulky, spastic muscles. She was a slender build, with a flexible ease in her body from frequent yoga classes, yet suffered pain and discomfort with her various symptoms. Her history told a story of a bonded relationship with her father, a successful doctor; an anxious and depressed mother; and competitive brothers. For most of her life, Cindy had experienced severe anxiety and feelings of insecurity and inadequacy. She felt she did not measure up to her siblings, who had successful careers. She wasn't utilizing her master's degree and worked as a nanny. She had talent as a fiction writer but felt it was not a practical career path. Her physical symptoms were the way she expressed her conflicts; they manifested her fears in somatic form. Without bulky layers of armoring to absorb and bind her anxiety, it existed in a free-floating state and became anchored in her various symptoms. As we worked through her historical and current issues and the feelings they evoked, her symptoms declined. Through bodywork she changed from a pleaser to a more aggressive mover and shaker. She could express all her feelings vigorously and did not hide them in her body. She decided to pursue her writing and was enjoying that avenue immensely. She stopped trying to mirror and please her family and made decisions from her authentic self. She developed more confidence and did not need to create symptoms to express her feelings. We call her syndrome of multiple symptoms somatic symptom disorder (DSM-5)—bodily symptoms become the expression of psychological issues that are not conscious. The ICD-10 (International Statistical Classification of Diseases and Related Health Problems) includes hypochondriasis, persistent somatoform pain disorder, and other disorders in the syndrome labeled "somatization syndrome." This diagnosis highlights the multiple and frequently changing symptom picture, frequent contact with primary doctors and specialists, and no positive confirmation of a medical condition, and is associated with disruption of functional day-to-day activities in a variety of areas.

Hypochondriasis presents challenges as it is an expression of health anxiety, fear of illness, disease, and death. A red blemish on the face is construed as a possible case of life-threatening melanoma; the fear remains even with medical tests that disconfirm the assumption. A painful joint turns into rheumatoid arthritis in the patient's mind. The patient is plagued by a sense of impending doom from a medical disaster. Multiple fears may lead to a contracted life— not hiking out of fear of ticks, constant hand washing due to fear of germs, and food restrictions to ward off fear of future disease. Hypochondriasis can lead to paranoid ideation as it breeds a lack of trust in self or other. Controlling behaviors and an attitude of me-against-the-world becomes a way to cope with fear and dread.

Terry, age 55, had been consumed with fear all her life. Her family of origin was unstable; her parents married quite young, partied like teenagers, and neglected Terry and her sister. Terry always felt alone and would wander the city neighborhoods looking for a hospitable spot to land. One of the ways her fear manifested later in life was in hypochondriasis as a literal way to make her overriding fear into something real and tangible. She visited doctors multiple times a month, called the ER late at night, or called various hot lines to discuss her symptoms and hear a reassuring voice. She took note of any and all physical anomalies making sure she was not overlooking anything. Bodywork focused on her ocular block with expressions of fear and terror expressed over and over again. Once her fear diminished we could work on her hostility and turn it into effective, neutral aggression. She began to feel strength, courage, and capacity to assert resulting in a quieting of her fear even more. The expressions of aggression manifested in all her life choices and she stopped feeling as if a dreaded disease would overwhelm her. Terry was in charge of her own life and she could yell strongly to prove it. She strengthened her sense of self and became more assertive; her preoccupation with her health diminished further. She felt more in control of her life such that she did not feel that any random disease was going to strip her of her strength and mastery over her life circumstances.

Chronic pain is another way psychological symptoms manifest in the body. Painful sensations can occur throughout the body, from the tip of the head to the soles of the feet. A lifetime of unmet needs, abuse, neglect, and loss lodges its protest in raw pain. If there is no organic cause that can be deciphered through thorough testing, then one has to look psychologically at the symptom. I have seen pain crisscross the body—a way the body screams *help me*. There are emotional issues to be untangled and new habits created that help, too. I have seen severe chronic musculoskeletal and neuropathic pain, previously treated with opioid painkillers, resolve with regular exercise, therapy, and an absence of medications.

Patients who have had traumatic histories and exposure to chronic stress may have a heightened sensitivity to any inner perception of pain sensation. Working with the cognitive aspect is important so that catastrophic thinking is noted and minimized, as distorted assumptions contribute to subjective experiences of pain. Translating pain signals more neutrally helps, rather than identifying basic neurological signals as "serious and threatening pain." Fear engages the fight, flight, and freeze sympathetic nervous system response patterns and activates the hormone cortisol and other stress hormones known to increase pain sensations. Stress hormones have a negative impact on the immune system as well as the digestive and general nervous system, and increase subjective experiences of pain as they cause contraction (hypervigilance) rather than expansion (relaxation) within the body.

It is important for patients with these somatic syndromes to keep active with an exercise routine to thwart their overly protective tendencies that lead to chronic identification with being physically compromised or disabled. That faulty self-assessment results in a decline of healthy movement routines such as walking, hiking, or attending exercise classes. This attitude leads to further pain and symptoms exacerbated by stasis in the body-mind.

Work on body armor taps into a wealth of pain in the body and allows the embedded feelings to be expressed vocally. As the patient peers into the sensations of her pain, the expression can reveal itself directly rather than through the gauze of physical symptoms. Patients without chronic pain are astounded at the amount of pain they experience in their body when they make contact with their physicality. Yelling "help me" as a cry that was never voiced does wonders for pain.

The protocol for Orgnonomic biophysical intervention is to dissolve armor from the head down. It is best to clear the upper segments sufficiently before the therapist works the lower segments of diaphragm and pelvis. The diaphragmatic and pelvic segments house ample stores of energy, and if the ocular area is not clear and contactful, the patient may not be able to tolerate or integrate the intense energy from the lower segments in a healthy way. Frequently, I will loosen the diaphragm to allow for fuller breath. Many patients have quite a locked diaphragm that causes shallow breathing or abdominal pooching, as the lower abdomen bulges out rather than flattens and relaxes with the exhaled breath. Applying substantial pressure on the diaphragm can allow the muscle to give in and the breath to loosen. This muscle can store angry feelings that release when the tension begins to dissolve. But serious work on the diaphragm and pelvis should not begin until all upper segments are substantially freed up.

Pelvic Segment

As patients move toward health, the pelvic area can be opened up once the upper segments are mobilized; this usually occurs toward the end of the middle phase or end phases of treatment. With pelvic opening, sexual responsiveness increases. Reich discussed "orgastic potency" as a capacity in the healthy organism to surrender to sensations, acquire the capacity in the body to charge up with energy, and then discharge and release energy as the individual gives in and experiences loving sensations and feelings. This word does not define the simple capacity to ejaculate or orgasm but rather defines the larger capacities of responsiveness to lovemaking that result in surrender and gratitude to your partner as well as a complete release of body tension through slight convulsions of the body afterward. Developing this capacity is one goal of Orgonomy; that patients have healthy sexual functioning. If energy is obstructed in various segments, then free-flowing energy or streaming does not travel to the pelvic area to be released. Reich believed that chronic blockages that inhibit full sexual release cause many psychological and physical symptoms seen with our patients. Supporting the patient through dissolving stasis in the body will result in better sexual function and enhanced relationships and provide a healthy release valve for pent-up energy so it is not fueling other symptoms.

Many patients suffer from problems of sexual intimacy, and bodywork directly helps with these problems.

Pelvic armoring contributes to symptoms in the genital area: chronic urinary tract infections, yeast infections, genito-pelvic pain disorder, which can cause severe muscle spasms in the vagina. Men suffer from sexual dysfunction, inability to have or sustain an erection, premature ejaculation, and other sexual difficulties. Typical problems in sexual functioning are caused by armoring—as the armor blocks a free flow of energy to the genitals. Lifelong sex-negative attitudes inhibit a healthy, active sexual life.

There are many muscles in various states of tension and chronic contraction in the pelvic area: the buttock area, low back, and leg muscles can be palpated and spasms released. The patient can often immediately feel energy flowing down through the pelvis and into the legs. The sensation of streaming can initiate a gentle arcing movement in the pelvis, as the tension and rigidity in the pelvic area gives way to more mobility and a new sense of openness and vulnerability.

Trauma and Healing Touch

For patients who have had serious trauma by experiencing sexual abuse, violence, psychological abuse, or other traumatic incidents—bodywork should be carefully titrated. As trauma is often sealed off through mechanisms discussed in the e-resource section Progression of Therapy: Trauma, the therapist does not want to upset those mechanisms early on. As the eye work evolves, it helps break through dissociative defenses over time. This is delicate work, as the patient needs strength, confidence, and deep trust in order to unravel traumatic experiences; and that context arrives after years of therapy, years of verbal work, and slow sustained biophysical interventions.

The biophysical work gives access to all thoughts, feelings, and memories that filter up to consciousness in their own time. As the patient breathes, different feelings and thoughts emerge; some float by barely recognized, others remain in liminal consciousness and bring with them barely sensed sensations and emotions. Early feelings from the first years of life, even in utero sensations, are not cognitively stored in our memory banks, as we have not yet learned words and concepts that facilitate cognitive storage of those memories. With biophysical work, the patient accesses memories and feelings, through sensations and a felt intuitive sense but often without cognitive recollections. Through expression of a variety of feelings, sounds, and physical movements, the patient can sense an awareness from the recesses of her psyche coming to the surface and expressing itself in a way not determined by her conscious will but rather emerging with a life of its own. The patient is breaking through to the depth of feeling from preverbal as well as current time. Dissociated experiences may also be revealed in brief glimpses, sufficient to increase tolerance of the material. These experiences unlock sensitivities and give them clarity in present real time. Intuitively, recognitions come to the surface and questions are cleared up.

Kind, gentle touch can be therapeutic for most patients, and that contact evolves through the various stages of treatment. Initially the interventions are quite practical and directed to dissolving armor; in fact, the pressure can be painful on muscles in a state of chronic contraction. The therapist has to titrate the pressure so it is helpful and accomplishes the task but does not over-whelm the patient with uncomfortable sensations. Over the course of treat-ment, as the armor dissolves, the type of touch may change as the vigorous work is completed. Now the patient is working into softer feelings in the chest and heart area, in the belly and the pelvis; there may be feelings of longing, of deep need in the belly, the vulnerability of needs never met, and love that was desired but not found. The secure touch of a trusted therapist now becomes part of the healing. It is a wordless exchange, and the body feels enveloped by secure warmth. Patients may have never experienced safe, nurturing touch, and in and of itself, in the therapeutic context described, the touch is healing. It can be a gentle touch of a palm on the chest, two hands holding the head and applying slight pressure. The patient may cry intensely, and the therapist has a hand on the patient's back, or at the end of session, if appropriate, the therapist may gently rock the body with light touch or rock the patient's feet.

In strictly verbal therapies there is no access to the healing power of touch except for maybe a hug. The nonverbal communication that says it all and speaks directly to the nervous system allows the body-mind to relax and give in—finally. Many of us were deprived of nurturing, safe and secure touch, occurring within an emotional context of support and trust.

The biophysical work creates a deep bond between patient and therapist, as it exists in a context where defenses are confronted early on in treatment resulting in increased honesty and vulnerability as therapy proceeds. This type

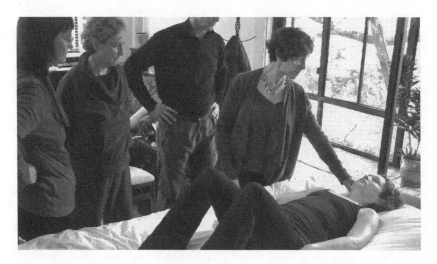

Figure 14.3 Training Group with Trainee Patient

of work creates an intimacy, but always within the therapeutic frame so it can be trusted. An intimacy, within the boundaries of treatment, allows a profound feeling of safety. The nonverbal aspect—touch in conjunction with the abiding presence of the therapist—allows the patient to navigate through extremely intense memories and feelings, making biophysical interventions extremely potent. The therapist's hands can communicate directly to the body, bypassing the patient's thinking or defensive structures to create a portal of change and healing (see Figure 14.3).

Orgonomic biophysical interventions are effective when the therapist has been trained systematically. Untrained clinicians should not venture into this area. I encourage students and professionals interested in somatic work to study my method and/or Reich's method at the American College of Orgonomy in New Jersey, or with Morton Herskowitz, DO, in Philadelphia, Pennsylvania, and learn how to skillfully apply this approach. For further information on body psychotherapy including peer-reviewed journal articles, evidence-based research, and other body-oriented psychotherapy articles, consult the American Associations for Body Psychotherapy (usabp.org) and the European Association of Body Psychotherapy (eabp.org).

15 Conclusion
Whole Therapist, Whole Patient

The career of a licensed therapist—whether psychologist, marriage and family therapist, licensed social worker, or counselor—as defined by various state legislatures, is a unique and challenging profession. One comes to it for a variety of reasons: the urgent need to heal thy self, to share the rewards of personal self-growth with others; a desire to help others and the community; a spiritual interest in transformative processes; and an academic interest in research within the vast field of mind, behavior, and mental health. Whatever originally brought you to this career may or may not still be relevant as you now sit in the chair of the therapist. You are face to face, on a daily basis, with a variety of individuals, with a multiversity of issues, looking to you to help them discover a route to a better place. There are times the route is embedded in a mist; you can't see where it is going, and the despair and hopelessness sits like dense fog between you and the patient. Other times, we are bathed in sunlight and the route is clearly demarcated in front of us; we have a road map guiding the way, and we will follow it through hill and dale. My intention for this guidebook has been to provide a road map to be used as a how-to reference for your clinical practice for new and mature therapists.

Understanding how to work with character and developing the skills to assess character types is the first reference point on your road map. You won't get lost if you are aware of the overarching dynamic of the patient—*how* the patient is, how she behaves in your office, how she acts toward you and functions in her life. Sift through her history to find the larger stones in the sand so you can line them up and corroborate your sense of her narrative arc—a summary of her life that forms a coherent narrative of her dynamics. Look at the options in the typology of character types I have delineated and find a corresponding type or combination for consideration. Then you will have a clear route on which to embark. You have figured out her character defenses, her basic type, and understand how she arrived there through sifting through critical historic details and lining them up. Your interventions will then be aligned with your assessment of her character, and you will know what to expect. You will clarify her repetitive defensive style and its repercussions in her life, and you limit her behavioral acting out so it doesn't block her progress. She will become aware when she is acting in maladaptive ways both in the therapy room as well as in her life. You have your bearings, and she will get hers as she gains increasing knowledge of how she obstructs a healthier life. She will come to understand the core dynamic of all her problems and all her symptoms.

The second reference point on your road map is setting a consistent, clear frame for the therapeutic relationship and sticking with it at all times. Therapies have a chance of success if the program is understood and laid out in a clear, organized fashion. The therapist explains the road map from the start, so when you begin climbing up steep grades with hair-raisingly narrow roads, no one panics. Yes, the terrain is scary but the route is clear. You have mapped it out from the beginning and held to it. The patient knows to follow all of your practice guidelines: attend all scheduled weekly sessions, don't cancel impulsively, be on time, commit to the process, pay bills in a timely fashion. The patient has been apprised of the tenacious nature of resistance and how it may manifest. The therapist does not compromise the frame and that keeps the therapist from acting out her own issues consciously or unconsciously. The route is demanding and one or the other may want to give up and bolt, but the frame holds the process together coherently so the necessary work can be completed.

The third reference point is the therapeutic relationship and understanding how to establish it, how to migrate through the maze of patient responses and therapist reactions. The combinations are exponential. The therapist learns how to assess herself and her reaction patterns frequently and in a thoughtful and insightful manner, often engaging the help of a supervisory mentor. She must maintain a clear attitude that allows her to adequately assess the patient's state. The relationship with the patient may be an enduring one that traverses spans of time. Throughout session after session multiplied by years, a steady continuity is established that ensures patient stability, offering a sense of safety and layered insight while helping to increase his courage, autonomy, and independence. Whether the duration is 1 year or 20 years, the patient develops the capacity for flexibility as he learns to move gracefully with the volatile currents and hold the course of his life intact. Patients that are therapists are in a form of personal training therapy that demands a high standard of insight for both patient and therapist.

The fourth reference point is maintaining the arc of the session. Each session counts—there are no throwaways. That means each session has an important job to do. Maintain consistency in the treatment by keeping your eye on what you are working on—what are the important themes in this patient's life to move forward and accomplish, what defenses need to be broken down, what acting-out behaviors need to be stopped, what are the healthy goals you are working on establishing. Stay on point. Don't get stuck in the weeds of extraneous or defensive material that results in session digression and the session running out of gas. Keep the edge, the tension; encourage the patient to work. Then therapy can move forward as each and every session makes an impact. That may sound like an unattainably high standard. It is not. If you think about the session and the patient before the session and have a clear sense of issues of importance for this patient, then when they unravel their material you will have a sense of how to intervene that keeps the patient moving consistently in a healthy direction. If the therapist feels she is going in circles with the patient, then she has lost the arc of sessions and the patient/therapist may be stuck. Get back on track with your supervisor and figure out where you went off the road.

I have discussed quite a few therapeutic basics and have delineated a variety of tools encased in an organized tool chest to make your tools easily accessible. The therapist can be prepared for challenging junctures and difficult patient interludes, and remember, these challenging times are not unusual but, in fact, are expected. The new therapist can see how a course of therapy may progress through various phases, how trauma can be resolved and how termination is handled. Please read Chapter 16, "Progression into Trauma," in the online resources provided by the publisher. This chapter covers all aspects of developmental trauma and how to deepen into grief and abandonment depression, and it provides a sensitive, organized treatment protocol for working with trauma. The chapter includes specifics of the termination phase.

The depth of dream analysis is presented with a bare but sufficient road map so you, as the therapist, can enter that rich and important realm of the patient's unconscious. You can travel the pathways of intuition and psychic awareness and find yourself in other dimensions—rich with imagery, synchronicities, and exciting mysterious connections. Discussing patient dreams is one of the most fulfilling aspects of this career for me, as the process creates a transcendent experience for both patient and therapist. Chapter 17, "Dream Analysis and Individuation," is in the online resources as well. It describes the potency of the unconscious, dream functions, Jungian archetypes, a transformational approach to treatment, and the importance of the individuation phase and provides a therapist's guide to dream analysis.

I hope I have piqued your interest in bringing psyche and soma together. The mind-body approach offers a further depth and thoroughness to the work. This brief introduction to Reich's mind-body theory could inspire you to train in this area. Within the verbal character analytic context consider using some of the tools I suggest, such as encouraging the patient to breathe deeply and in a more expanded fashion, develop a regular exercise and/or yoga program, utilize foam rollers to release pain from all nooks and crannies of the body, learn healthy self-regulation through integrating healthy behavioral habits, create a satisfying sex life, and suggest ways to be more flexible in mind and body. You can map out this type of plan that encourages the patient's connection to his body without specifically doing biophysical interventions on the couch.

Therapy is a business that has to be nurtured in order to create a lucrative lifestyle for the therapist. This aspect is often disregarded as other elements of the career demand time and emotion. Attending to the business ingredients that make your practice a success is an imperative for the therapist to feel positively about his career path and comfortable with sufficient resources. The therapist models healthy engagement, confidence, activation, and industriousness for patients. We are professionals in business and need to wear that hat with style.

I titled the book *Whole Therapist, Whole Patient* to emphasize the importance of wholeness within for both therapist and patient. As therapists, it is our ethical obligation to be mentally healthy and to not live in a hypocritical manner professing one thing and living another. We are obligated to do our own personal therapy. We are not perfect, but we have to make sincere efforts to do our own personal work continuously throughout our lives. Consistent, long-term personal therapy may be required depending on your own unique history and circumstances. The point is to feel whole and balanced within yourself so you can work effectively with patients without contaminating them. We all have moments when we lose our clarity and are captured in our own psychic confusion or distortions emanating from our patient's projections or unconscious relational webs. If we continue to work on ourselves in the many ways we have available, we can achieve and maintain our wholeness. In graduate school this is not sufficiently emphasized. The integrity of our profession relies on our individual responsibility to sustain healthy choices in our lives that ensure our wholeness, our mental stability, and our capacity to become authentic mentors for others.

As we strive for personal wholeness we can authentically help patients find theirs. Many patients, due to traumatic histories, are split in two or more parts and can be filled with self-hate and self-loathing, rarely sustaining a feeling of goodness and wholeness. We hear and watch as they jockey back and forth between feelings of inflated potency and collapsed defectiveness. We can see the road ahead of potential wholeness, but their psyches now reflect the mutilation of a cavernous split down the middle. We bear witness to this psychic fissure that defies establishment of a sense of wholeness within. Over years of treatment the crevasse begins to heal, woven together by delicate gossamer threads, sewn by the therapist and the patient. An experience of wholeness is hard-won and takes tenacious efforts by the therapist and the patient.

Toward the end of a therapeutic relationship, wholeness is apparent and experienced by both the patient and the therapist. It is a profoundly rewarding feeling experienced by both sides of the dyad. The relationship dynamic changes and there are two whole mature individuals in the room, with mutual respect and a feeling of equality within the relationship. Both cups are full of life and there is a sense of completeness. Therapy is at an end for that relationship, and the wholeness within both thrives.

Therapists have potential for a most rewarding career. This work has meaning; we are blessed to have purpose, as many careers are missing the soulfulness of true meaning—making a difference and contributing to the betterment of others and our planet. We do not live in a realm of superficiality, just in it for the sale or the buck or to survive financially. I do respect all the wonderful established businesses, start-ups, and entrepreneurs, as their diligence and creativity light up the world of business and finance. We are predisposed to a different set of interests, and if we succeed in our clinical practice we obtain both decent financial compensation and depth of meaning and purpose. For many therapists our careers can be our spiritual paths as there is a unification of career and spirituality. We live our purpose and our spiritual values. The spiritual challenge is to bring the values of excellent ethics, generosity, tolerance, compassion, fierceness, tenderness, and equanimity into the realm of our work.

We start with an arduously long educational journey and complete our undergraduate and graduate degrees while simultaneously working as interns in practicum sites and internship clinics. We sit for our exams after multiple years and after engaging in intensive study, and finally are licensed and set free to take a clinical position and/or start a private practice. At this point we need to seriously develop our clinical skills, as clinical expertise and acumen was not emphasized as we moved through our paces to complete our degrees and licensure. Yes, we are exposed to various theoreticians and types of approaches with a variety of supervisors, but we do not have time or guidance to develop true clinical skills and an organized approach. After licensure starts, it is time to study with mentors or enter a formal institute program and learn an approach that is compatible with your nature. This leg of the journey may require more years of study that affords certification in a specific clinical approach.

Most importantly: Find your style; find yourself and bring him or her into the room with the patient consistently. Be the person you want to be; find your authentic voice that is uniquely yours. Feel your own naturalness; feel your spontaneity with each patient; feel your comfort zone where you are authentically yourself. You can feel comfortable, at ease, naturally you. Laugh when you feel like it; tear up if tears well; if you feel quiet, allow your pensiveness. Don't contort yourself for the patient—allow your expansiveness, your aliveness, your contactfulness to be fully present in the room. Sustain and maintain your aliveness without compromise to the best of your ability each and every day. You are not there to follow an old script with your parent or sibling or teacher or spouse; you are a free, mature adult willing to be yourself without fear of loss and abandonment or a chronic need to please or accommodate. You are not in the room to be admired, adored, or loved. You are there to experience your compassion paired with available aggression, your ability to set limits and boundaries, to self-assert when necessary, and to cultivate your sleuth-like curiosity and abiding equanimity.

Stretch yourself and go beyond your limitations. Seek new input and incorporate new challenges. I sustained my excitement in my career because I kept stretching my limits. One opportunity I created was at San Quentin Prison where I stayed for 10 years as an independent contractor with my own nonprofit corporation. I also created additional contracts with the California State Department of Corrections. I developed programs at that time with my business partner Alan Emery, PhD, that tested my conceptual and clinical skills by serving inmates and officers with a variety of programs while training psychology interns. After that experience, I founded the Orgnonomic Institute and taught the innovative mind-body approach of Reich and along the way developed my own method that included audio teaching programs and an independent study program. The institute allowed my creativity to flourish as I combined ideas and created trainings. I studied with Nicolai Levashov, a Russian mental intention healer, for 10 years and that encouraged a serious study of medicine and anatomy as well as developed my non-touch healing capacities. I went on retreats with Thich Nhat Hanh, learning mindfulness, meditation, and community spirituality embraced in the Sangha. Many of his ideas infiltrated my practice as the practice of mindfulness personally affected me in a myriad of ways. I enjoyed giving five-day workshops at Esalen Institute in Big Sur for nine years, and that lovely retreat center afforded me an environment to try out creative ideas, exercises, and techniques. Doing workshops, retreats, leading groups, and seminars—all ways to stretch, expand, and try out different ways to work with participants as well as enjoying the pleasure of the experience.

Begin where you are and unfold your natural creativity. Each therapist has a unique style, a predisposition that can be expanded upon. Think of your work as a continual blank canvass to be filled with newly created paintings with interesting color combinations—in that way you never tire or become bored with your work and your life. Each of you embodies a unique history, a lineage, and cultural legacy with rich veins of experience to bring to your work. Create your narrative and apply it to the way you work. Appreciate how your uniqueness can be offered to the patient in your specific way.

As you mature as a therapist, continue to read, study, and enhance your skills. We are mandated to earn continuing education credits to sustain our licenses. That is a good thing as we can then expose ourselves to new ideas, to other inspiring clinicians, and stay fresh and alive in our practice. There are so many brilliant theoreticians, researchers, and clinicians who can inspire us throughout our lifetime of practice.

I never tire of learning and expanding my knowledge base—as a therapist there is always ongoing growth. Patients challenge you when you least expect it. If, for a moment, I get too complacent, I am assured an even more difficult challenge will present itself, and I will be knocked off my game. The abrupt jolt wakes me up. It is an ever-challenging career that forces us to be the best that we can be. I invite you to live this challenging career and enjoy it—every step of the way.

Bibliography

Abrahams, P., McMinn, R., Marks, S., and Hutchings, R. (1998). *McMinn's Color Atlas of Human Anatomy* (4th Edition). Maryland Heights: Mosby.

American Psychiatric Publishing. (2013). *Diagnostic and Statistical Manual of Mental Disorders* (5th Edition). Washington, DC: American Psychiatric Publishing.

Appel-Opper, J. (2010). Relational Living Body Psychotherapy: From Physical Resonances to Embodied Interventions and Experiments. *The USA Body Psychotherapy Journal*, Vol 9 (1), pp 51–56.

Bakalar, N. (2016). Childhood Stress Is Linked to Hardening of the Arteries. *The New York Times*.

Baker, E. (1967). *The Man in the Trap*. Princeton: The American College of Orgonomy Press.

Baker, E. (1982). Sexual Theories of Wilhelm Reich. *The Journal of Orgonomy*, Vol 20 (2), pp 175–194.

Blum, H. (2004, Spring). Separation-Individuation Theory and Attachment Theory. *Journal of the American Psychoanalytic Association*, Vol 52 (2), pp 535–553.

Bollas, C. (2015). A Conversation on the Edge of Human Perception. *The New York Times*. Retrieved from http://opinionator.blogs.nytimes.com/?s=schizophrenia.

Bowlby, J. (1973). *Attachment and Loss, Vol. II, Separation*. New York: Basic Books.

Carey, B. (2015). New Approach Advised to Treat Schizophrenia. *The New York Times*. Retrieved from www.nytimes.com/2015/10/20/health/talk-therapy-found-to-ease-schizophrenia.html?smid=fb-nytimes&smtyp=cur.

Dunne, C. (2000). *Carl Jung: Wounded Healer of the Soul*. New York: Parabola Books.

Edinger, E. (1991). *Anatomy of the Psyche: Alchemical Symbolism in Psychotherapy*. Chicago: Open Court Publishing.

Edinger, E. (1994). *The Mystery of the Coniunctio: Alchemical Image of Individuation (Studies in Jungian Psychology by Jungian Analysts)*. Toronto: Inner City Books.

Edinger, E. (1995). *The Mysterium Lectures: A Journey Through C.G. Jung's Mysterium Conjunctions (Studies in Jungian Psychology By Jungian Analysts)*. Toronto: Inner City Books.

Ehrensaft, D. (2016). *The Gender Creative Child*. New York: The Experiment.

Foley, G. and Hochman, J. (2006). *Mental Health in Early Intervention: Achieving Unity in Principles and Practices*. Baltimore: Brookes Publishing.

Freud, S. and Breuer, J. (2004). *Studies in Hysteria*. London: Penguin Books.

Friedman, R. A. (2015). How Doctors Helped Drive the Addiction Crisis. *The New York Times*. Retrieved from www.nytimes.com/2015/11/08/opinion/sunday/how-doctors-helped-drive-the-addiction-crisis.html.

Frisch, P. (1999). The Orgonomic Institute of Northern California. Retrieved from https://orgonomictherapy.com/blog.

Giovacchini, P. (Ed.) (1975). *Psychoanalysis of Character Disorders*. New York: Jason Aronson.

Goldman, L. and Schafer, A. (2011). *Goldman's Cecil Medicine* (24th Edition). Philadelphia: Elsevier Saunders.

Goroll, A. (Ed.) (2009). *Primary Care Medicine: Office Evaluation and Management of the Adult Patient* (6th Edition). Baltimore: Lippincott Williams and Wilkins.

Hall, J. (1983). *Jungian Dream Interpretation: A Handbook of Theory and Practice*. Toronto: Inner City Books.

Hall, J. (2010). *Guyton and Hall Textbook of Medical Physiology* (12th Edition). Philadelphia: Saunders.

Harkin, D. (2010). Part II—the Adolescent Brain: Clinical Applications. *The USA Body Psychotherapy Journal*, Vol 9 (1), pp 32–40.

Herskowitz, M. (1997). *Emotional Armoring: An Introduction to Psychiatric Orgone Therapy*. New Brunswick: Transaction Publishers, Rutgers State University.

Hillman, J. (1996). *The Soul's Code: In Search of Character and Calling*. New York: Grand Central Publishing.

Hoffman, J. (2016). Estimate of U.S. Transgender Population Doubles to 1.4 Million Adults. *The New York Times*.

Hortocollis, P. (1977). *Borderline Personality Disorders—the Concept, the Syndrome, the Patient*. New York: International Universities Press.

Jacobson, E. (1964). *The Self and the Object World*. New York: International Universities Press.

Jung, C. (1974). *Dreams*. Princeton: Princeton University Press.

Jung, C. (1980). *Psychology and Alchemy (The Collected Works of C.G. Jung, Vol. 12)*. Princeton: Princeton University Press.

Jung, C. (1993). *The Basic Writings of C.G. Jung*. New York: Random House, Inc.

Jung, C. (2014). *Collected Works of C.G. Jung, Volume 16*. Princeton: Princeton University Press.

Jung, C., von Franz, M. L., Henderson, J. L., Jacobi, J., and Jaffe, A. (1968). *Man and His Symbols*. New York: Random House (Dell Publishing).

Kaplan, A. and Schwartz, L. (2005). Body Pragmatic Case Studies of Body-Centered Psychotherapy. *The USA Body Psychotherapy Journal*, Vol 4 (2), pp 23–42.

Kernberg, O. (1975). *Borderline Conditions and Pathological Narcissism*. New York: Science House, pp 163–177.

Koemeda-Lutz, M., Kaschke, M., Revenstorf, D., Scherrmann, T., Weiss, H., and Soeder, U. (2005). Preliminary Results Concerning the Effectiveness of Body Psychotherapies in Outpatient Settings—a Multi-Center Study in Germany and Switzerland. *The USA Body Psychotherapy Journal*, Vol 4 (2), pp 10–22.

Kohut, H. (1980). *The Restoration of the Self*. New York: International Universities Press.

Konia, C. (1978). The Chronic Depressive Character. *Journal of Orgonomy*, Vol 12 (1), pp 64–74.

Lax, R., Bach, S., and Burland, J. (1980). *Rapprochement—the Critical Phase of Separation-Individuation*. New York: Aronson Press.

Levy Berg, A., Sandell, R., and Sandahl, C. (March 2009). Affect-Focused Body Psychotherapy in Patients with Generalized Anxiety Disorder: Evaluation of an Integrative Method. *Journal of Psychotherapy Integration*, Vol 19 (1), pp 67–85.

Lewin, K. (1997). *Resolving Social Conflicts and Field Theory in Social Science*. Washington, DC: American Psychological Association.

Longo, D., Fauci, A., Kasper, D., Hauser, S., Jameson, J., and Loscalzo, J. (2011). *Harrison's Principles of Internal Medicine* (18th Edition). New York: McGraw-Hill Professional.

Mack, J. (Ed.) (1975). *Borderline States*. New York: Grune and Stratton.

Mahler, M. (1968). *On Human Symbiosis and the Vicissitudes of Individuation*. New York: International Universities Press.

Mahler, M. (1972). On the First Three Subphases of the Separation-Individuation Process. *International Journal of Psychoanalysis*, Vol 53 (Pt 3), pp 333–338.

Mahler, M., Pine, F., and Bergman, A. (1973). *The Psychological Birth of the Human Infant*. New York: Basic Books.

Masterson, J. (1972). *Treatment of the Borderline Adolescent: A Developmental Approach*. New York: John Wiley and Sons, Inc.

Masterson, J. (1978). *Psychotherapy for the Borderline Adult: A Developmental Approach*. New York: Brunner/Mazel.

Masterson, J. (Ed.) (1978). *New Perspectives on Psychotherapy of the Borderline Adult*. New York: Brunner/Mazel.

Masterson, J. (1980). *Borderline Adolescent to Functional Adult: The Test of Time*. New York: Brunner/Mazel.

Masterson, J. (1981). *The Narcissistic and Borderline Disorders: An Integrated Developmental Approach*. New York: Brunner/Mazel.

Masterson, J. (1983). *Countertransference and Psychotherapeutic Techniques: Teaching Seminars on Psychotherapy of the Borderline Adult*. New York: Brunner/Mazel.

Masterson, J. (2015). *The Personality Disorders Through the Lens of Attachment Theory and the Neurobiological Development of the Self: A Clinical Integration*. Phoenix: Zeig, Tucker and Theisen, Inc.

Masterson, J. and Klein, R. (1989). *Psychotherapy of the Disorders of the Self: The Masterson Approach*. New York: Brunner/Routledge.

Masterson, J. and Klein, R. (Eds.) (1995). *Disorders of the Self, New Therapeutic Horizons: The Masterson Approach*. New York: Brunner/Mazel, Inc.

Masterson, J. and Klein, R. (Eds.) (2004). *A Therapist's Guide to the Personality Disorders: The Masterson Approach. A Handbook and Workbook*. Phoenix, AZ: Zeig, Tucker and Theisen, Inc.

May, J. (2005). The Outcome of Body Psychotherapy Research. *The USA Body Psychotherapy Journal*, Vol 4 (2), pp 93–115.

McDevitt, J. and Settlage, C. F. (1971). *Separation-Individuation*. New York: International Universities Press.

Monsen, K. and Monsen, J. (2000). Chronic Pain and Psychodynamic Body Therapy: A Controlled Outcome Study. *Psychotherapy: Theory, Research, Practice, Training*, Vol 37 (3), pp 257–269.

Netter, F. (2010). *Atlas of Human Anatomy* (5th Edition). Philadelphia: Elsevier Saunders.

Raknes, O. (2002). Wilhem Reich and Orgonomy. *Journal of Orgonomy*, Spring/Summer, pp 9–10.

Raknes, O. (2004). *Wilhelm Reich and Orgonomy: The Brilliant Psychiatrist and His Revolutionary Theory of Life Energy*. Princeton: The American College of Orgonomy Press.

Reich, W. (1925). The Role of Genitality in the Therapy of Neuroses. *Orgonomic Medicine*, Vol 2 (1).

Reich, W. (1960). *Wilhelm Reich Selected Writings: An Introduction to Orgonomy*. New York: Farrar, Straus and Giroux.

Reich, W. (1972). *Character Analysis*. New York: Simon and Schuster Touchstone.

Reich, W. (1973). *The Function of the Orgasm*. New York: Farrar, Straus and Giroux.

Reynolds, G. (2016). Brain Benefits of Exercise Diminish After Short Rest. *The New York Times*.

Rhoades, R. (Ed.) (2009). *Medical Physiology: Principles for Clinical Medicine* (3rd Edition). Baltimore: Wolter Kluwer, Lippincott Williams and Wilkins.

Rhoades, R. and Blaker, W. (2003). *Human Physiology* (4th Edition). Pacific Grove: Brooks/Cole.

Röhricht, F., Papadopoulos, N., and Priebe, S. (2013). An Exploratory Randomized Controlled Trial of Body Psychotherapy for Patients with Chronic Depression. *Journal of Affective Disorders*, Vol 151, pp 85–91.

Schore, A. (1994). *Affect Regulation and the Origin of Self: The Neurobiology of Emotional Development*. Hillsdale, NJ: Lawrence Erlbaum Associates.

Schore, A. (2006). Right Brain Attachment Dynamics: An Essential Mechanism of Psychotherapy. *The California Pscyhologist*, Vol 39, pp 6–8.

Science: An Elementary Teacher's Guide/The Human Body: Brain and Nervous System. (n.d.) *Wikipedia*. Retrieved from https://en.wikibooks.org/wiki/Science:_An_Elementary_Teacher%E2%80%99s_Guide/The_Human_Body:_Brain_and_Nervous_System.

Sexual Orientation. (n.d.) *Wikipedia*. Retrieved from https://en.wikipedia.org/wiki/Sexual_orientation.

Short, B. (2015). Ownership of Mind: Separation in the Countertransference, in: Masterson, J., *The Personality Disorders Through the Lens of Attachment Theory and the Neurobiological Development of the Self: A Clinical Integration* (pp 88–104). Phoenix: Zeig, Tucker and Theisen, Inc.

Silberman, S. (2016). Overselling ADHD: A New Book Exposes Big Pharma's Role. *The New York Times*.

Spitz, R. (1965). *The First Year of Life (A Psychoanalytic Study of Normal and Deviant Development of Object Relations)*. New York: International Universities Press.

Stedman, T. L. (2011). *Stedman's Medical Dictionary for the Health Professions and Nursing, Illustrated* (7th Standard Edition). Baltimore: Lippincott Williams and Wilkins.

von Franz, M. (1998). *On Dreams and Death*. Chicago: Open Court Publishing.

White, K. (2001). A Study of Ethical and Clinical Implications for the Appropriate Use of Touch in Psychotherapy. *The USA Body Psychotherapy Journal*, Vol 1 (1), pp 8–15.

Wilhem Reich Infant Trust. (1957). Retrieved from www.wilhelmreichtrust.org/.

Winnicott, D. (1965). *The Maturational Processes and the Facilitating Environment*. New York: International.

Index

 Taylor & Francis eBooks

Helping you to choose the right eBooks for your Library

Add Routledge titles to your library's digital collection today. Taylor and Francis ebooks contains over 50,000 titles in the Humanities, Social Sciences, Behavioural Sciences, Built Environment and Law.

Choose from a range of subject packages or create your own!

Benefits for you

>> Free MARC records
>> COUNTER-compliant usage statistics
>> Flexible purchase and pricing options
>> All titles DRM-free.

REQUEST YOUR **FREE** INSTITUTIONAL TRIAL TODAY

Free Trials Available
We offer free trials to qualifying academic, corporate and government customers.

Benefits for your user

>> Off-site, anytime access via Athens or referring URL
>> Print or copy pages or chapters
>> Full content search
>> Bookmark, highlight and annotate text
>> Access to thousands of pages of quality research at the click of a button.

eCollections – Choose from over 30 subject eCollections, including:

Archaeology	Language Learning
Architecture	Law
Asian Studies	Literature
Business & Management	Media & Communication
Classical Studies	Middle East Studies
Construction	Music
Creative & Media Arts	Philosophy
Criminology & Criminal Justice	Planning
Economics	Politics
Education	Psychology & Mental Health
Energy	Religion
Engineering	Security
English Language & Linguistics	Social Work
Environment & Sustainability	Sociology
Geography	Sport
Health Studies	Theatre & Performance
History	Tourism, Hospitality & Events

For more information, pricing enquiries or to order a free trial, please contact your local sales team: www.tandfebooks.com/page/sales

 Routledge
Taylor & Francis Group

The home of
Routledge books

www.tandfebooks.com

Made in the USA
Middletown, DE
06 March 2020